DEVIL IN THE DARK

JAMES HERBERT

DEVIL IN THE DARK

CRAIG CABELL

metro

Published by Metro Publishing Ltd,
3, Bramber Court, 2 Bramber Road,
London W14 9PB, England

First published in hardback in 2003

ISBN 1 843580 59 4

British Library Cataloguing-in-Publication Data:

A catalogue record for this book is available from the British Library.

Design by ENVY

Printed in Great Britain by CPD Wales

1 3 5 7 9 10 8 6 4 2

Papers used by Metro Publishing are natural, recyclable products made from
wood grown in sustainable forests. The manufacturing processes conform to the
environmental regulations of the country of origin.

Every attempt has been made to contact the relevant copyright-holders, but some
were unobtainable. We would be grateful if the appropriate people could contact us.

To Mum and Dad –
for the light and shade

CONTENTS

Acknowledgements iv

Author's Note xi

Introduction by Ingrid Pitt xv

Prologue The Blood is the Life xix

PART ONE HERBERT'S DOMAIN

Chapter One Shadows of the Past 3

Chapter Two Grimly Fiendish 19

Chapter Three Children in Danger 31

PART TWO A CHAMBER OF HORRORS

Chapter Four A Dream of Rats 43

Chapter Five A Foggy Day in Hell 55

Chapter Six More Than a Survivor 65

Chapter Seven A Fluke, or Sheer Hard Work? 73

Chapter Eight Supernatural Power 79

Chapter Nine The Spear of Longinus 83

Chapter Ten A Formidable Lair 93

Chapter Eleven A New Career in a New Town 99

Chapter Twelve Devil in the Dark 101

Chapter Thirteen Loving the Jonah 109

Chapter Fourteen An Unhallowed Shrine 115

Chapter Fifteen Vermin's Domain 123

Chapter Sixteen Moon Influence 131

Chapter Seventeen	A Dream Home?	137
Chapter Eighteen	Secrets of the Sepulchre	143
Chapter Nineteen	To Be Haunted	153
Chapter Twenty	In Search of Ghouls	161
Chapter Twenty-One	Portents of Doom	167
Chapter Twenty-Two	Deep in the Chiltern Hills	173
Chapter Twenty-Three	Non-Fiction	179
Chapter Twenty-Four	A Year of Living Dangerously	181
Chapter Twenty-Five	Time to Meet the Others	185
Chapter Twenty-Six	Once …	191
Chapter Twenty-Seven	Once … Again	195
Chapter Twenty-Eight	Nobody True	199
	Conclusion	203
PART THREE	THE LEGACY	
	A Walk in the Fog with James Herbert	209
	Heaven by James Herbert	215
	Extinct by James Herbert	219
	Cora's Needs by James Herbert	227
	James Herbert at the Movies	233
	James Herbert UK Collector's Guide	239
	Copyright Notices and Photo Credits	261
	Further Reading	263

ACKNOWLEDGEMENTS

Many people have helped me to write this book, in ways both large and small, from collating research material to organising interviews. I would like to thank the following: Robert Winder (for my first Herbert article), Tony Mulliken and Steven Williams (Midas Public Relations), Melvyn Bragg and his colleagues at the South Bank Show, Bill Williams, Peter James, Ingrid Pitt, John Connolly, Bernard Cornwell, Campbell Armstrong, Clive Barker, Ian Miller, Alice Cooper, Stephen Jones, Simon Clark, Stephen Laws, Nick Sayers, David Barlow, Graham Thomas, Helen Ellis, Chris Underwood, Alan Hunter, Eamon Exley, Kathy Clegg, John O' Sullivan, Richard Ball, Brian Aldrich; Bill Mason, Avril, Sue, Samantha and Allan (at Nav Sec), Andrew Chrysostomou, Andy Hall, Louise Cowlin, Tracey Allen, Amanda Harris, Kate Wright-Morris, Roland Philipps, Martin Neild, Kerry Hood, Lucy Dickson, Sheena Walshaw, Sarah Keen at Chivers Press, David Mellin at Magna Print Books, Reg Nagle, the Searchers (Video Film Search Specialists), Davy's of London (for quality French wines), and Crispin Jackson at Book and Magazine Collector for many Herbert questions and opportunities. Also, thanks to John Blake, Michelle Signore and Adam Parfitt.

I would also like to thank the unsung heroes: my wife Anita, my two children Samantha and Nathan, my parents Shirley and Colin, and not forgetting Mavis and Ian Dow, Tom and Alice, David and Berny Bush.

I would also like to acknowledge and thank the late proprietor of Legend Books. Not only did she uncover some essential and rare promotional material for me, but she was also one of the kindest and sincerest people I have ever worked with.

Many thanks also go to Gay Baldwin, for a chance to experience some Isle of Wight synchronicity while on the Algernon Blackwood trail. Believe it or not, it helped. And thanks also to a host of 1970s rock stars for some excellent musical accompaniment while I proofed this book.

Finally, eternal thanks to James Herbert and his lovely wife, Eileen, for their time, friendship, and the lifts to and from the train station.

Sincerely, many thanks to all.

CC, London, April 2003

AUTHOR'S NOTE

"'Jim is it, rather than James?"
Poggs said. "Good. Very stuffy name, James,
I've always thought." '
(PORTENT)

James Herbert is an enigma; to his fans and critics alike. Rarely does he give interviews nowadays and his public appearances are even more uncommon.

To the people who know him, Herbert is either a 'lovely chap' or a 'complete nightmare'. The latter statement came from a publicity manager who found Herbert extremely difficult on a book tour. Herbert responds, 'I don't suffer fools gladly. In everybody's life story, they are the hero. So if they are made to feel inadequate or a little stupid, then who's the hero? Not me. I'm the bastard. And of course, I've upset a lot of people because I just try to get things as right as possible.'

I can only speak personally about James Herbert. Having met him many times – for business and pleasure – and of course having worked with him on this book, I can say he has been extremely supportive and never difficult.

Herbert has been criticised for being reticent on many matters concerning his life and work. My only comment on that is: when serious work started on this book, a series of frank and in-depth interviews followed. We spoke deeply about areas of his life where there was still much hurt. For example, his court case over copyright infringement with 'occultist' Trevor Ravenscroft. When I told Herbert that it was important to detail this part of his life, he agreed and we went through the whole thing from start to finish. He also took time off from writing his own novels to give me more interview time – and even went to the length of writing notes so that no stone was left unturned.

Why did he do this? For a simple reason: to get the facts right, as he told me, 'You're writing a book and you've got to be given the opportunity to do your research.'

Herbert took my book as seriously as his own. 'The one thing I value about myself is my integrity,' he said. 'And the one thing that upsets me is when it is questioned... I've spent my time working hard to get where I am. I've never really found anybody to help me in my work.'

So Herbert was keen that I got my facts right, and if I did criticise him in any way, he wanted to make his point of view clear. However, I asked myself what Herbert meant by, 'I've never really found anybody to help me in my work.' Is Herbert a loner? Socially, no, he isn't, but as a writer? Maybe. And if professionally he is a loner (as the great science fiction author Robert Heinlein said of all writers), then perspective must be given to the statement: Herbert is protective about his stories. He writes alone and keeps his stories to himself, until it is time to release them.

I first met James Herbert over a dozen years ago, but when a reporter and a writer meet up on various promotional tours and launches, communicate by letter, and exchange the odd phone call or greetings card, a friendship evolves. Indeed, I now have the dubious pleasure of calling him 'Jim'. I say dubious because every time I say 'Jim' I think of Mr Spock addressing Captain Kirk. But that's okay, because my friend Jim is not the James Herbert you find on the shelves of bookshops.

There are two sides to James Herbert – Jim and James – and this book is an exploration of both: the man and the author. And as I have found both to be equally entertaining men, full of fascinating stories and possessing a wry sense of humour, it is fitting to pay tribute in such a way.

All forms of biography are an attempt to present previously unreleased or unappreciated facts about their chosen personality, but only through an authorised work can a true picture – away from pure speculation – be achieved.

Herbert once said to me, 'What I really hate is when people get the wrong idea about me, or tell untruths. I can take any criticism about me as long as it's valid. But when people invent things, that really makes me angry. Because it's not me at all.'

It must be understood that Herbert doesn't agree with some of my opinions in this book, but he has had to let them stand because some of the points raised are valid. In some cases he has re-qualified his position but he has not requested any cuts because such cleansing would have an adverse effect on the whole point of the book. In short, he has his say and I have mine.

Nobody is always right, and as Herbert correctly states, 'In everybody's life story, they are the hero.' So here is James Herbert's life story.

With 50 million copies of his books sold throughout the world, his 20th novel now in paperback, and his 30th anniversary as a best-selling novelist fast approaching, there is further reason to look at the life and career of Britain's best-loved horror writer, and shed some light on the enigma – or should we say the very private man – that is James Herbert.

1

The Rats.

Prologue:

The old house had been empty for more than a year. It stood, detached and faded, away from the road, screened by foliage gone wild. No one went there, nobody showed much interest anymore. A few windows had been shattered by neighbourhood kids, but even they ~~soon~~ lost interest when nothing more than silence responded to the crash of broken glass. In fact, the only interest ever been shown by ~~others~~ people was, the day they took the old woman away.

They knew she'd been living alone since her husband had died, never went out, and was only rarely seen peering from behind lace curtains. She never parted the curtains, just gazed through them, so only a hazy, form could be seen by anyone interested enough to look. Her groceries were delivered every week and left on the back step. Powdered milk was included ~~with~~ them. The local grocer said the old woman's bank paid her bills regularly every three months with never any queries as to the contents of his delivery. ~~This~~ Which ~~suited~~ pleased him. ~~At first~~ He'd been given a list at the beginning for a regular order, but ~~now~~ if he forgot to include a pound of butter or

*next to a disused canal,

mat nael

spectral

INTRODUCTION

BY INGRID PITT

James Herbert is a monster! But cuddly with it. A possible view of purgatory would be manacled to James and made to co-operate on writing a book. I can imagine the scene. A huge, grotesque Satan, straight out of Herbert's fervid imagination. A hell with burning books and distorted, liquid-screen computers reaching out blooded, claw-like hands. Jimmy sits coolly waiting for exactly the right amount of tension to build and then, with a few magical sweeps of his pen, he .... But my handcuffed hand stops him from adding a cunning twist to the plot. I try to co-operate but it is beyond me.

He is not happy with my lack of control and makes no attempt to hide his displeasure. I get annoyed and try to grab the solitary felt-tipped pen that Satan has provided. We struggle silently for possession. The Devil roars with laughter and throws a few more books on the fire. More claw-like hands erupt from the blood-filled screens. Herbert shrugs me off and brings calm to the chaotic scene. And that's just the title sorted.

Where most writers would make an emergency U-turn when they hit an immovable block, he just accelerates the pace and proves that nothing is impassible. My first introduction to the Herbert magic occurred in the 1980s. I was asked to write a screenplay based on his novel, *The Dark*. No problem. At least until I had read the book. The opening was one of the most dramatic I had ever read. Okay, so I've led a sheltered life and Edgar Allan Poe is dead. But how do you convey the essence of a room full of maniacs copulating as they commit bizarre forms of hari kiri? What do you do when the lead character gets killed off about a third of the way through and you are presented with another lead – who also gets it after a couple of chapters? I struggled womanfully but the fact that the screenplay never lit up the silver screen tells its own story.

Several Herbert books have made it to the screen. None of them have been particularly successful. Which is surprising when you have to acknowledge that what makes Jimmy's books so dynamic is the graphic way he describes the scenery and the action. In an easy, confident style he draws you into the location so that every move that is made, every plot reference, is covered. In his 'alternative history', '48, set, believe it or not, in 1948, there is a scene when the hero enters The Savoy in the Strand, London. It is several years after Hitler, who, in a last suicidal throw, has released a doomsday bomb. Few have survived and most of those who have are beginning to suffer the effects of the devastating weapon. The reader is led through the once magnificent rooms, peopled now by only the desiccated remains of guests who will never be asked to settle their bill. It's a wonderful scene – especially if you have ever actually walked through the hotel as it is now. Later, when the hero is cornered in a house in the East End of London and manages to escape over the rooftops, he doesn't do it alone. You are there with him, terrified that the pursuers will be waiting around every corner or behind each rusting vehicle.

One of the most harrowing scenes I have ever read comes near the beginning of *Others*. The leading character, a disabled detective on day-leave from Hell, Nick Dismas, is one night attacked and brutally assaulted on Brighton beach, where he goes for a breath of sea air.

The encounter is told in the first person. No nuance of the dramatic and frightening situation is missed. The group of punks starts with verbal abuse, which rapidly builds to physical abuse. Robbed of his money and dignity, and semi-conscious after a ferocious and explicit kicking, Dismas is left on the shingle. Only then is it revealed that the members of the gang were girls.

I suppose writing is like acting – the more you do, the better you get. Except in Herbert's case he seems to have sprung from the womb talented. What other author can claim a Genesis from The Rats and still be far from an Exodus 30 years later with *Once...* – a story about fairies? During that time he has developed some attitudes, which have hardened over the years. I was talking to a former editor responsible for knocking Jimmy's manuscripts into shape. She told me that he hates to have a word changed and that trying to get anything altered is like climbing a cloud. But, she added, sometimes she does tweak the copy a little and he doesn't catch on. Just as she said that, Jimmy sidled up. 'You think I don't know that?' he said with what I think is called an expansive grin. He walked jauntily off, leaving a very red-faced editor. Jimmy still finds the act of putting pen to paper, and letting the story take over, an exciting reason for getting up in the morning. When I visited him recently he took me to his study, swore me to secrecy and then showed me the first line of his next book. I was flattered and his excitement was catching.

Away from his strict writing regimen Jimmy is a good friend and entertaining companion. He is very self-aware. If he does make a transgression from the social straight and narrow, he is painfully mindful of what he has done. It mightn't make him a better person but it does make him a fellow sufferer. He is acutely conscious of where he came from and frequently explores the east London parish of his youth in his books. But he has no trouble accepting the status that success brings with it. Music is something he is passionate about and one day we are going to form a duet – Jimmy on guitar and me on the omnichord. We will be a sensation. We're going to call the duo Monsters Unleashed.

The Blood
is the Life

"'… but I had eyes for one thing alone. It was the
porcelain miniature of a young man in a smartly curled
bag-wig, and bore the initials 'J.H.'" '
(THE TOMB, H P LOVECRAFT)

'*Adventures come to the adventurous, and mysterious
things fall in the way of those who, with wonder and
imagination are on the watch for them; but the majority of
people go past the doors that are half ajar, thinking them
closed, and fail to notice the faint stirrings of the great
curtain that hangs ever in the form of appearances between
them and the world of causes behind.*'

(*The Insanity of Jones*, Algernon Blackwood)

His dream pulled him back to a past reality. A dark shadow that
troubled his subconscious.

From behind a small netless window, a dull yellow light flickers.
Its glow a soft, gentle seduction, coaxing him closer.

He moves forward. His footsteps silent.

He feels no anxiety, not until he draws nearer to the window
and there – strangely – he holds back, as if refuting the inevitable.
No boy of six should ever bear witness to such sights, but the
natural flow of life doesn't enforce such moral laws.

The man stands to one side, watching himself – a child once more – staring through the window.

The dream was always the same, never different. The horror would never leave him.

Tears begin to cascade down the boy's quivering cheeks as the wretched scene unfolds its full horror: his parents lying slaughtered on their bed. Blood from their naked bodies soaking and dripping from the soiled white sheets.

Fear – horror – is a lonely, personal experience. A jumbo jet plummeting from a midsummer sky, crashing into an empty field, holds hundreds of individual deaths. The unselfish – mainly parents – will think of the children who will count among the dead. And isn't the death of a child so much more horrific than anything else?

However, fear doesn't have to be so extreme or so final. Fear can be standing outside a deserted railway station in the middle of the night waiting for a loved one to arrive.

Everybody experiences fear, even enjoys it, for it is the horror movie you watch in the dead of night, or the chilling book you read on a crowded commuter train.

Everybody loves to be scared, to experience the thrill of a fantasy world, because it is only that – fantasy. You can always put the book down, turn off the TV or video if it becomes too much, but it rarely does.

Fear is a fundamental part of growing up, experiencing life, becoming stronger, obtaining individuality. If you are pampered and sheltered from horror – fantastic or real – you will grow up with an introverted, naive way of looking at the world. But the very fact that you are still reading this proves my point: you are interested in fear, the life's blood of the horror genre, the ghost of a terrible memory that creases your brow as you sleep through the dark and lonely hours before dawn.

So the horror of reality is echoed in the horror of speculative fiction. There have been many practitioners of the horror genre but not many make it their life's work. Not even Stephen King has devoted much of his latter work to the genre that made him famous. However, some writers remain loyal to the horror genre and, by the constant process of speculating, probing and above all researching the intricacies of the genre, they move on to new pastures within the genre.

> *'She could not see anything at all in the blackness. She could only hear his gurgling chokes. And that was enough.'*
> *(The Dark)*

James Herbert's writing has evolved over the years. He has moved away from the cut-and-thrust novels that made him famous to focus on a more subtle, emotional way of scaring his audience. For example, in Others, when he describes the terrible, humiliating attack of disabled Nick Dismas he gives a great deal of compassion and depth of feeling to the scene, so much so, it is difficult not to feel sympathy for Dismas. The injustice hits you between the eyes, giving an extra injection of real-life horror: '... I heard them calling me names, snarling their hatred ... and I absorbed it, let the pain and name-calling sink into my system ... and then I allowed it – blows and words – to deaden me. That was the only way I could make it tolerable.'

As the scene unfolds, we are appalled by the abuse. We are aware, as sensitive adults, that such discrimination happens in present-day society, and by being humiliated by senseless acts of violence – albeit in a fictional setting – we feel shame, but also something more, respect. Our hero survives his torture – both physical and mental – and this elates us. The strength of the human spirit, that in-born need to survive, comes through and we are totally on his side.

Most novels offer a message or a moral undertone. If we want to acknowledge it, that is our own prerogative, as James Herbert enthuses, 'You pay your money and you take what you want.'

Horror or morality tale, it's up to the reader to decide. But what I find most interesting is how an author's life influences their novels, to different degrees. It is true that Herbert has been influenced by the things he experiences in everyday life, but there is an awful lot that comes from his past – his childhood. So let us explore the man behind the novels and see who James Herbert really is …

'If I turn my head I can see the knife he used on me. Its blade is rich with my own blood. Isn't it funny, Lord? If I could use it against myself, I could hurry along my death.'

(Sepulchre)

PART ONE

HERBERT'S DOMAIN

CHAPTER ONE

SHADOWS OF THE PAST

'THESE GHOSTS OF THE PAST – FORGOTTEN IN THE
TUMULT OF THE MORE RECENT MEMORIES – THRONGED ROUND
ME, TOOK MY HAND IN THEIRS, AND, EVER WHISPERING OF
WHAT I HAD LONG FORGOT...'
(THE HOUSE OF THE PAST, ALGERNON BLACKWOOD)

It was an April day in 1871 when Robert Louis Stevenson walked along the beach at Cramond with his father, Thomas. Louis explained to him that he had no desire to complete his engineering studies at Edinburgh University and follow the family profession of lighthouse engineer. He told his father that he wanted to become a writer.

On 8 April 1943 – the 72nd anniversary of this historic literary event – a boy was born in London's Hackney Hospital. As the Luftwaffe dropped their bombs overhead, James Herbert was born into this world. A man who would, by his 35th year, give up his job in advertising – the profession he studied for at Hornsey College of Art – to become a full-time writer.

Very few writers start their days with the intention of making such an anti-social job their eventual profession. Sir Arthur Conan Doyle only started writing his fiction during quiet periods in his medical practice. H G Wells only began to write his fiction after trying his hand at shopkeeping and teaching. So, if it weren't for these separate events, we would be lacking the characters of

Sherlock Holmes and Dr Watson, and novels such as *The Time Machine*, *War of the Worlds*, and Herbert's favourite novel, *The History of Mr Polly*.

Strange how so many different literary lives can be pulled together. Another thing all these writers have in common is their deep fascination for the macabre. Stevenson's *Strange Case of Dr Jekyll and Mr Hyde* is a good example. First released in January 1886, the theatrical production was still shocking audiences two years later, when Jack the Ripper worked his diabolical trade on the very streets where James Herbert grew up. And it was stories like this, intermixed with the unique character of London's East End, that fuelled Herbert's imagination, as he recalls, 'Very old, almost Dickensian streets, with gaslights – cobblestones. I still remember that. There was an alleyway (Old Castle Alley), down which Jack the Ripper allegedly fled when he spliced one of his victims. The street was so full of atmosphere.'

Herbert's parents, Kitty and 'Herby', were street traders during the years overshadowed by the Second World War, owning a fruit stall in Bethnal Green Road. His first home was a flat in a Guinness Trust building. 'My earliest memory is being in our little front room, which my mother only opened when we had people around,' he recollects. 'I was shown a pair of binoculars. They were put up to my face and I saw this huge nose. I couldn't make it out at the time. I didn't know what it was. It was only later I knew that it was a magnified nose.'

Obviously, the intrigue made an indelible impression on Herbert's young mind. However, he does remember other things, as he goes on to explain. 'I must have been four years old, outside the Guinness Trust building, and I had a fight with a kid. I went to punch him but missed and hit the wall instead. I grazed all my knuckles but I won the fight. Around the same time, I was playing outside and caught my foot in an empty tin can and I couldn't get my foot out. So I went clumping around all afternoon until my dad got home and worked it off.'

Herbert wasn't an accident-prone child but he did get locked in the Lord Mayor's car once, as he recounts. 'It was about the same time again, the Lord Mayor came round to see the new flats in the area and me and my friends were playing beside his Rolls Royce. I got into the car and the door closed and I couldn't get out. I remember sitting there in a little sailor boys overcoat until the Lord Mayor came out with all his dignitaries and found me sitting in the car [laughs] and told me off.'

In the late 1940s, Herbert's family moved from the Guinness Trust building to a shop in Hackney Road. Shortly afterwards they moved again, to a house behind Petticoat Lane in Whitechapel. Behind this house – 26 Tyne Street – were stables where other market traders kept their stalls. It was also alive with rats, much to young Herbert's terror. 'I was scared of giant rats. There were gutted houses around us, all full of them.'

However, it wasn't just rats that held gothic appeal, as he admits. 'We had cats in our neighbourhood that used to cry in the night like tortured babies... our own cat came home through the window one day while we were having lunch, with an enormous rat in his mouth. I'll never forget that.'

James Herbert was seven years old when the family moved to Tyne Street. The condemned building was due for clearance, and Herbert's parents thought that they could acquire a nice new council flat by moving there. Sadly, that wasn't the case and they spent the next 12 years there.

'Nothing influenced me more than that house,' says Herbert. Indeed, the place left an impression of horror on him that has lasted into adulthood.

What didn't help matters was the fact that he spent a lot of time there alone. His elder brothers would be out with friends and his parents would be either working or often having a post-work drink in the local pub.

In a revealing interview for *Hello!* magazine in 1994, Herbert spoke about his parents' relationship and how it affected him and his brothers. 'It wasn't a happy marriage. I was the youngest of three brothers [Peter was the eldest, and then John]. We learned to become very unemotional ... I don't know if this sort of experience is character forming or not. It can make you very cold ... It made me very introverted and my world became what was going on in my mind ... I spent a lot of time ... reading and drawing.'

Kitty Herbert is keen to enforce this statement. 'Jim was always in a world of his own, always reading and drawing. He was very talented at art and taught himself to play the guitar. He used to sit on the stairs practising.'

Herbert's father was a typical East End working man, often prone to drinking and brawling. 'He abused his body throughout his life,' says Herbert. 'He never changed. My mother had a very hard life. She had to put up with my father's drinking and gambling. As a father and husband he left a lot to be desired.' However, Herbert is keen to state that his father never hit him or his brothers and, up to his father's death, Herbert still used to see him occasionally.

It can be argued that Herbert had an underprivileged childhood but he disagrees. 'You don't notice such things when you're a kid. Everybody around you is in the same boat, some much worse off.'

Herbert's first school was Our Lady of Assumption in Bethnal Green, the local Catholic school. It was here that the first signs of the budding writer-to-be manifested themselves. During break time he would make up stories to entertain the other children, who would even pay him for the privilege. Strangely enough, other horror writers started working their trade in a similar way: Dennis Wheatley would conduct midnight feasts at boarding school, telling his fellow students stories of pirates and headless horseman, long before writing his own fiction.

Although not that well off, Herbert's formative years had their fair share of treats. His brothers, Peter and John, used to take him to the cinema. By sneaking in through the back door and hiding under the seats, they could watch all the old black and white horror movies, starring names such as Bela Lugosi and Boris Karloff. 'I saw the X-rated movie version of *The Monkey's Paw*

6

when I was six,' says Herbert. 'I also saw *The Old Dark House*, another creepy movie.'

Peter Herbert, who has never left his East End roots, admitted when brother Jim appeared on the TV show *This is Your Life* (broadcast on 12 April 1995), 'I think I'm the instigator of all this horror stuff.' And he could be right. However, to add an extra thrill to the trip home from the cinema, it was brother John who would take a short cut, leading his younger brother through an old bombed-out churchyard. At dusk, or sometimes late evening, they walked along a winding dirt track. With overgrown foliage and leaves whispering the secrets of the long-since dead, they glimpsed the smashed tombs and sepulchres of what was once a grand burial ground. They weren't scared, they loved the thrill, as Herbert fondly recalls: 'I had some great times as a kid, and the thrill of walking through that churchyard was one of them.'

It was here that Herbert first started to learn to appreciate the importance of diverse locations – a recurring theme in his novels. For example, the peaceful burial ground of the bombed out churchyard, in comparison with the loud and busy Whitechapel Road – diverse locations only separated by a crumbling wall – gave him a sense of wonder and perspective (coincidentally, this location is used in Herbert's first novel, *The Rats*). So much horror could be festering in a peaceful location, but a short way away, along a busy London street, there was normality. Sanity.

One of Herbert's favourite pastimes as a kid was reading comic books. His brother, Peter, stepped in to provide an extra thrill here, picking up full-colour comics from a local American army base. These were lavishly illustrated US comics, not like their poor British counterparts, as Herbert explained in his Foreword to Alan Moore's *Swamp Thing*: '...I was reared on comic books. Before the age of ten I'd had the rare privilege in England of reading all those early DC and ECs: *Tales From the Crypt, Frankenstein, Batman* ... American comics, full colour ... suffice to say, the art of comics was my joy.' Peter used to hide his comic collection under the floorboards outside his bedroom, and younger brother Jim would take them out and read them.

As far as British comics were concerned, Peter admits, 'We used to buy and "borrow" a few from the local markets.'

It was through these British comics that Herbert was introduced to the character of Casey Ruggles, a hard and tough cowboy. 'Casey Ruggles was an American newspaper adult strip story, which only appeared in comic book form in England.' Whilst visiting Herbert in 2003, he showed me his collection of Casey Ruggles comics. We went through the strip stories, Herbert explaining his admiration for the artist, the space he gave small cartoons and the detail to his figure drawings. Some of the themes of the later Ruggles stories included rape and incest, but the strips were also loaded with a fair proportion of dry humour as well.

It wasn't just the character of Casey Ruggles that fascinated the young Jim Herbert, but the style of good, comic-book artwork: 'It was here while imitating the illustrations in the comics (all of which had to be 'unlearned' at art college) that my imagination really took off.' And the joy of art has been one of his greatest passions ever since.

Many writers use the imagery of their youth to fuel the writing of adulthood. Even the great Charles Dickens did so in *David Copperfield*. It's as though the early life influence never dies and the writer searches his soul for either a final exorcism, or a chance to relive pleasant moments. So what does Herbert want to do, exorcise or relive?

In his book, *James Herbert's Dark Places*, which looks at locations and legends used in his novels, he answers this question: 'It's London I return to time and again ... the reason for that is partly because I know it so well, and partly because in my researches I'm still discovering new and different facets, many of which could provide story plotlines for years to come.'

Herbert has a fondness for his youth. He can look back and cherry-pick memories then blend them into his fiction. London was the adventure playground of his youth – bombsites and huge open spaces that are now crammed with lavish office blocks, as he recalls: 'The Tower of London was my playground when I was a kid, so were the bombsites around St Paul's.

'When I was very young, I had a push scooter and I used to scoot all the way around Whitechapel and Petticoat Lane. And at Sunday lunchtime all the market stalls along Petticoat Lane were packed away and it just emptied. Water lorries would come in and wash the streets. In no time at all, it was a ghost town and I used to race through there, through the city where, in those days, because it was empty, you could hear echoes. I used to scoot up to St Paul's and Moorgate, where it was all empty, all flattened, all bombsites with gutted houses. And that was my adventure playground.'

This very experience is included in his novel, *The Jonah*. 'The higher they went, the worse became the stench from the old house … He wanted to turn around and go back down, to leave the house, get away from the bombsite. He didn't like it here anymore, didn't like the game they were playing. Billy was scared.'

Herbert, like most kids growing up in the 1940s and 1950s, was attracted to the danger of gutted buildings and bombsites. Here, along with his friends, he could re-fight the Alamo, the Second World War, or even become Flash Gordon thwarting Ming the Merciless – the list was endless. And having explored such sites first-hand, he could use the lasting, vivid imagery in novels such as *Domain*, which details the fictional state of London after a nuclear explosion: '… the Old War Office, the Ministry of Defence … all were gone … He briefly wondered if all the works of art in the National Gallery … had been destroyed beneath the deluge. What significance did they have in the present world, anyway?'

Some of the descriptions in *Domain* are so striking that most Herbert fans rate it as one of his very best books. In fact the images are so believably weird it's almost as though the devastation has been witnessed first-hand, as Herbert's long-term friend Tony Mulliken, of Midas Public Relations, comments. 'Jim has that uncanny knack of making the incredible seem real. It's a tremendous skill.' The best example of Herbert's ability to do this is in *Domain*, where he describes some of the most famous sights of London after the holocaust: '... the Houses of Parliament and Westminster Abbey, at the end of the road he faced, had been totally destroyed. Peculiarly, the lower section of the tower housing Big Ben was still erect, sheered off at a hundred or so feet; the top section containing the clockface protruded from the river like a tilted, rock island...'

The creation of a scene like this really stems from Herbert's childhood: once devastation has been witnessed, it is not easily forgotten. Also, while playing on bombsites Herbert couldn't help but marvel at the incompetence of the Luftwaffe; a great many of its raids were centred around bombing historic buildings, but how they managed to miss St Paul's Cathedral, while flattening the surrounding area, is beyond belief. It took Herbert's holocaust in *Domain* to partly fulfil the Nazi dream.

Herbert freely admits that he loves to wallow in nostalgia, and that explains why he is so fond of his novel *'48*. Set in the London of his youth, there is an extra zest and passion in the novel that hasn't been present in his work since *Domain*, a book written over ten years previously. *'48* works on the premise: what would have happened if the Nazis had unleashed biological weapons on Britain toward the end of the Second World War? The book is set on the very streets where Herbert grew up. In fact the characters even go to his own childhood home – 26 Tyne Street.

Herbert has constantly written about the impact of his youth, but he still shuns his past: 'I've always been a Londoner. That's what is deeply ingrained into me. But I hate all this East End boy done good stuff, because there's a kind of boastfulness about it. Hitler used to boast about being a painter and decorator when he was the Führer, and I don't do that. I've never practised genocide either!'

Regardless of his modesty in such matters, Herbert does speak openly about his youth, allowing us to explore the reality of his life in juxtaposition to the fantasy world he creates in his novels. 'I have very strong memories of my childhood,' he says. 'Generally very bad things.

'Not so long ago, I went to the Royal London Hospital, a vast place, which I wrote about in '48. I remember going there when I was about ten years old, visiting my mother who was quite ill at the time. I didn't have the money for the bus fare, so I walked from Aldgate to Whitechapel. And when I got to the entrance, there was a porter's cabin, and in there was this man smoking a cigarette, talking to one of his cronies. I went up to him and asked where I could find Mrs Herbert. He looked at me like I was a piece of dirt, looked at his mate, then sneered and said, "How should I fucking know." He then kicked me out. And that memory came back to me when I last visited the hospital. I've always hated thoughtless arrogance since.'

A more disturbing story concerning a hospital was related to him when he was young and became the backbone to his novel, *Others*.

'A story was told to me by a very elderly lady. And she told me how, years ago, she worked in a children's hospital. On her first night in the job, she found herself on the top floor outside this ward marked STRICTLY PRIVATE – KEEP OUT. This lady – being quite curious – went inside, and she found all these hideous babies, kids with stunted limbs. All kind of grotesques – and I hate using that word – but these were kids that either their mothers had rejected at birth, or they were so hideous, the doctors had told the mother, "Sorry, your baby has died." And all these babies are in this ward being kept alive. Now, this lady went back to the ward several nights later with some sweets and she continued to do this – always in the dead of night. In the end, when she walked in, they were all holding out their arms saying, "Mama, mama," and that story was so poignant, it stayed with me all those years.'

So stories like this give Herbert the premise of a novel, but what happens next? How does he transform the idea into a best-selling horror novel? He goes on to explain his train of thought.

'Afterwards I thought, well what happened to all those babies, because we never see them? Hospitals in London do have their own black museums, with specimens, jars of embryos, things that are not open to public gaze. Now, a couple of years ago, I found some pretty hard evidence that these people lived into their middle ages... The elephant man isn't a new scenario. These cases exist and what with genetic engineering, many other things do too. But why don't we see them? Why should these "others" be kept locked away from society?'

After completing *Others*, Herbert still couldn't quite exorcise himself from the book and the effect the research had on him: 'I should have taken it further, not as a work of fiction, but through my research and interviews in the newspapers. Suffice to say, there is an awful lot of truth behind the fiction in *Others*.'

Although James Herbert's East End upbringing plays a strong role in his books, there is an isolated incident from his youth that holds equal power. And it has nothing to do with London.

At the turn of the 1950s a charity organisation called the Country Holiday Fund was set up. Its aim was to send deprived inner-city kids to the countryside to live with foster parents and share their homes and lifestyle for a week or two.

At about the age of seven, Herbert was sent to Rayleigh in Essex, then Beccles in Norfolk. He hated the experience but loved running around fields and woods, hiking along deserted railway tracks. But one particular image has stayed with him to this day.

If it was the Country Holiday Fund's aim to introduce so-called 'underprivileged' children to farmyard animals and beauty spots, it also inadvertently introduced them to something else: the cruelty of the countryside.

One evening, the people with whom Herbert was staying took him to a hillside overlooking a field of corn. A crowd had gathered and Herbert noticed that many of the men assembled there had dogs with them, or were carrying long sticks, cricket bats and other club-like weapons.

As the farmer cut the corn in ever-decreasing circles, the people overlooking the spectacle became more excited. They knew that the rabbits trapped inside the diminishing corn circle would soon make a break for it and when they did, the blood sport would begin. Herbert was about to witness a rabbit cull.

Inevitably the rabbits broke free. The crowd cheered and the dogs were unleashed. The rabbits didn't stand a chance. They were savagely torn to pieces by the dogs, or had their skulls clubbed in by the cruel men.

Although he would later grow up to appreciate the ways of the countryside, Herbert couldn't help but wonder why the farmer and all the other people assembled enjoyed the killing so much.

It was incidents like this, experienced at a very early age, which showed him the dark side of the human personality. Indeed the natural horror of the countryside, such as poaching, is a strong theme in novels such as *The Ghosts of Sleath*.

Psychological terror is personal in Herbert's novels. The characters are almost forced into a moment of isolation, distanced from their friends and allies. This has occurred time and again in his books, such as *Others*. 'I'd returned to the empty, vandalised house ... The mirror on the dingy wall opposite had broken into myriad pieces ... I saw reflected there my own fearsome self mirrored a thousand times or more, my imperfections multiplied ... after a while I began to weep.'

Others is one of Herbert's most important novels because it highlights another world within our own society: that of the handicapped. The main character, Nick Dismas, is physically handicapped. He is ostracised by society because of this, even though he is a successful business man (he owns his own private investigations company). But as we witness in the above quote, when alone in a dark and eerie place, he – our hero – feels vulnerable, allowing his own suppressed self-doubt to creep into his conscious mind, thus provoking the final pay-off: insecurity, guilt, self-loathing. But then again, evil is always stronger in the dark and, the devil's favourite game is to watch the uninitiated squirm.

Oddly enough, horror writer H P Lovecraft tackled a similar theme of self-hatred in his short story, *The Outsider*. A man breaks loose from an old castle but doesn't remember how long he has been there. He hardly remembers his youth but knows that it was a long time ago. During the intervening years he has read much. He is intelligent, a scholar, but he is lonely and longs for companionship. So he decides to leave his castle, climb a perilously high turret and step out into the world. His will is strong and he succeeds in his quest.

He travels through the night, eventually arriving at a place he feels is familiar. There is a party going on inside. He enters and all hell breaks loose. People run around screaming. He looks around for the answer to their plight and staring at him is a horrific figure of a man. A husk of corruption and decay.

He outstretches a hand to touch the creature but only succeeds in touching the glass surface of a mirror. It is here that he realises what he is and, more painfully, how other people view him. He can now only walk abroad at night and live in isolation – an outsider.

Horror fiction, if well written, can expose the corruption in society and the isolation certain people feel within it through no fault of their own – Frankenstein's monster, for example. When Nick Dismas is horrified at his own reflection in the mirror, we are repulsed by his personal rejection, as if it is only us who have the right of repulsion. Then we think again, and guilt overcomes our conditioning; we no longer search for the perfection in life, we accept equality, and in a beautifully written scene, we find Nick Dismas does too: '... it was Alma-Tadema's painting of women bathers in a Pompeiian bathhouse, and it wasn't just the incredible feel for texture and surfaces that got to me – no, it was also the understanding the artist had for the human form, its grace, its vulnerability. Its perfection.'

Characters in isolation. Empty houses. The dark. Are all these the horrific germination of Herbert's childhood memories? Yes, as he qualifies in *Dark Places* when discussing his childhood home: 'Now I spent many nights alone in the house ... more often than not the house would suddenly be plunged into utter darkness – the light meter ... seemed to need constant replenishing at night ... If I was lucky I'd find a box of matches to light my way down to the cellar. Yes, of all the places, the electricity meter was down in the cellar ... I still wince at the memory.'

Herbert confirms these fears: 'I was scared of the creepy house I lived in. The walls were wooden partitions – and it creaked. Like the street itself, the place was so full of atmosphere.'

Imagine: a young lad living in an eerie house, in a small gas-lit street with a deeply macabre history. He is alone, drawing, painting – using his imagination. Suddenly the house is plunged into darkness and he has to go to the cellar to replenish the light of reality. In the meantime, in the total darkness, the boy's imagination is running riot, already fuelled by his drawing and painting. He hears a creaking.

Although his rational mind tells him that it is only the wooden walls, his imagination teases him that it may be someone – *something* – in the room with him. And a child's imagination is a very vivid thing.

'Imagination feeds off memories,' Herbert tells us in *Dark Places* and reminiscence of 26 Tyne Street has given him more than one sleepless night.

In *Moon* Herbert conjures up Jack the Ripper-type imagery to describe the mutilation of a female victim: 'At last she was dead ... Cold drizzle spattered the window... protesting against the cruelty inside ... A bag in the corner of the dingy room was snapped open ... the gleam of metal instruments was only slightly dulled by the poor light.' The rain on the window pane and the suggestion of a Victorian doctor's bag filled with butchers knives evoke the facts and legends of the most horrific Ripper murder: that of Mary Kelly, the prostitute slaughtered in a tiny room in Miller's Court.

The terrible scene-of-the-crime photographs come to mind: a

body so badly mutilated by the Ripper that your eyes are sadistically held by the image until you manage to reassemble the lumps of flesh into the human body they once were.

Although it can be argued that the body in *Moon* isn't torn to pieces, major organs are skilfully removed and the resulting comparison is a strong one, especially in the way the torso is cut open. 'I wasn't thinking of Jack the Ripper at the time,' says Herbert. 'But I must admit, the first draft of that piece was much more explicit, and I had to tone it down a little because even I thought I was going too far.' But when asked if he does enjoy writing such graphic scenes, he replies, 'Of course I do!'

Moon is set on the island of Guernsey. But for Herbert the story isn't big enough, and consequently not as satisfying for him as some of his other novels. There are no major catastrophes in *Moon* but perhaps that is part of its success. The horror comes solely from the extreme central character – the psychotic killer. A creature that delights in terrorising women and children, a creature that could exist in your own neighbourhood. A Norman Bates-type of figure but shrouded in much more mystery (for a large part of the novel, the reader has no clue as to the killer's identity – another Ripper-type image): '"*Is that blood? It's in my eyes ... please don't do that ... it's hurting ... it's cutting ... it's going ... too deep ...*" '

In *The Jonah* Herbert explores other areas of East End folklore. 'It had taken the law years to pin something on those murderous villains the Kray brothers. They were on trial now, guilty beyond doubt, but would they hang for their gangland killings? Not bloody likely! Scum like that couldn't be erased anymore.'

This quote caused serious repercussions for Herbert: 'I was warned by the Krays. Somebody I know still lives in Bethnal Green, and he said, "You shouldn't have said that about the Krays because they read your books." I find my books are very popular in prisons, in the Armed Forces – the police force. They do the rounds. So he warned me, he said, "What's Reggie going to think when he reads that?" And I said, "It's only the policeman in the book saying that, it's not me, don't blame me." '

Herbert didn't take the threat too seriously, as he mentions London's criminal underworld again in *The Ghosts of Sleath*: '... drive straight past and keep going until he was out of the village, beyond the hills, back to the grubby city where lunatics and thugs were the only threat.'

The Krays were more than ten years older than Herbert but they came from the same East End streets filled with character and atmosphere, as Charlie Kray (the twins' elder brother) told me in April 1995. 'When the twins were young, they were very good boxers. They lived boxing and, they were so good, everyone wanted to fight them. And as time went on, bad things started to happen.'

Coincidentally, the Krays experienced similar imagery growing up as Herbert did, as Ronnie would later explain in the twins' joint autobiography, *Our Story*. 'God the drama of it all, the colour, the sheer fucking excitement. I loved it. We kids used to play on the bomb sites and dumps, staging our own wars.'

The Krays grew up in the East End during the 1930s and 1940s but there was little difference between their time and Herbert's. The clearing of buildings and rubble, along with the redevelopment of large areas of the city and its suburbs, was something that would take a good few decades to sort out after the Second World War.

So London's East End boasted its fair share of diverse characters, from Jack the Ripper to the Kray brothers. People talked – gossiped – and grandparents told children tall stories. James Herbert was one of those children, both imaginative and impressionable, as his mother Kitty reveals. 'I was always telling Jimmy stories.'

Scenes of depravation, oppression and violence were a major part of every day life in the years surrounding the Second World War. It is no wonder that the children of the war-torn East End grew up strong in character but hiding their own distinctly individual dark sides. James Herbert brought his out through his artwork and, later, his novels. Diversely, comedy writer Johnny Speight would see the humour in the East End and express it through his character Alf Garnett. Diversely again, Ronnie Kray expressed his dark side through the illness of a paranoid schizophrenic, the divided self masterfully written about in Robert Louis Stevenson's thriller, *Strange Case of Dr Jekyll and Mr Hyde:* '"Between these two I now had to choose. My two natures had memory in common, but all other facilities were most unequally shared between them."'

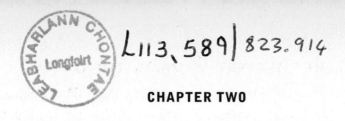
CHAPTER TWO

GRIMLY FIENDISH

As Oscar Wilde observed in his Preface to *The Picture of Dorian Gray*: 'To reveal art and conceal the artist is art's aim.'

Throughout his career as a novelist, James Herbert has strived to achieve this, giving the impression that he is a morbid man of the macabre rather than an ordinary guy with a keen sense of humour.

However, in his formative years Herbert had no desire to become a writer – he was totally absorbed in his passion for art. Herbert grew up with strong images from his childhood and first exposed this influence through his artwork. In later years he would throw all this information and experience into the industrial mixer of his imagination, creating images and characters with a lifetime of joy and sorrow in their likeness. Then he would put these characters and locations in his novels.

Before he embarked on his literary career, he had to find the logical conclusion to his work as an artist, a career that he hadn't even started yet.

Herbert passed his 11+ in 1954 and entered St Aloysius College in Highgate, north London. It was a highly disciplined grammar school, run by Catholic priests who had decided to take some students from more underprivileged areas of London, including the East End. 'I got caned for talking out of turn, not doing my homework, coming into school late, all sorts of things,' Herbert recalls. Although he didn't enjoy his time there too much, he does admit to finding encouragement from one of his teachers, Mr Blake. 'There was this rough character who took particular interest in me, mainly because I was the only one good at art in my year. He made me feel good about what I was doing.'

Interestingly enough, fellow horror writer Clive Barker also found encouragement in one of his art teachers – Alan Plant – and pursued art and amateur dramatics before writing novels. Like the young James Herbert, who worked in his small, empty house, Barker also enjoyed solitude to carry out his creative projects, as he told Melvyn Bragg on LWT's *South Bank Show* (10 April 1994): '[As a child] I lived in very conventional, rather reassuring circumstances, but feeling that my imagination was pushing me into areas of darkness, anxiety and unease... [My room] was the place where I wrote, it was the place where I drew, it was the place where I imagined. I was very secretive. I've always been fairly secretive. I needed to feel as though what I was doing almost had the feel of a dark, perhaps slightly forbidden, process.'

There is always a risk of over-analysing the genesis of a horror writer, as though, more than any other writer, the reader must be reassured of the reasons for them writing such terrible stories. 'People look at me and think I'm going to be a bit sinister, but I don't think I am,' Herbert says. 'Yes, I am James Herbert, this man who can dredge up all these terrible things, but I'm also Jim Herbert, the man who likes a nice quiet drink in the bar.'

When he appeared on Gloria Hunniford's BBC afternoon talk show in 1996, Herbert qualified this further: 'Everybody has a recess in their mind. You, me, everybody. We all have this ability to dream up horrific acts of violence. Some people can follow a direct path to it, others can't.'

It can be argued that the recess Herbert speaks of is the same one that leads to his childhood memories. They do appear to complement each other.

It was while at St Aloysius College that Herbert first started to pursue his interest in music. His greatest influence at the time was Buddy Holly, and he had learned to play rhythm guitar, later going on to sing and play at his school dance.

Again, it was elder brother Peter that got him hooked on music in the first place, as Herbert recalls. 'Peter used to go to the same boys' club in Vallance Road (East End of London) as the Kray brothers. And one day he pinched the radiogram from there. He brought it back on a wheelbarrow. It was a huge machine. The arm was so heavy and had a big tin needle. It also had a loud, thumping base, which used to rock the whole street. Our street was very narrow, almost like a funnel, and people used to come from miles around to see what all the noise was.'

Herbert played guitar at more than one college gig, but he had no delusions of grandeur: 'I played rhythm guitar because I liked to sing. And when I was at college, we did this gig which went okay, but the following week another band played there and made us look really sick: The Rolling Stones. They were just starting out at the time.' (Indeed other would-be super groups played at Herbert's college, including Syd Barrett's Pink Floyd.)

In later life, Herbert has found music to be a great companion. 'Sometimes, because it is horror that I write, I need to have an occasional break. I generally have a guitar beside my desk, and I play a few songs when things get a bit heavy. The process is almost like a therapy to me.'

"I chorded an E and the sound was rich and beautifully full, mellow but with that touch of hardness which could be softened or exaggerated depending on how the strings were struck. I did a few progressions, a few intricate runs... filling the room and my ears and my mind with music..." '

(*The Magic Cottage*)

One of Herbert's most well-loved novels is *The Magic Cottage*. The book is about a couple who find their ideal home – their Shangri-La – which enhances the magic they find in their respective careers, as well as their love for each other. Although hard and testing times challenge their relationship, there's a real sense of warmth and good humour about *The Magic Cottage*, which rarely appears in Herbert's novels – not even *Fluke*, another relatively light book.

As *The Magic Cottage* deals with dream homes and dream relationships, it also shows Herbert's own personal hobbies taken to their ultimate conclusion; almost as though the book fulfils some of his personal dreams. Mike, the leading man, is a session musician, while Midge, his gorgeous 'pixie-looking' girlfriend, is an artist. Both characters clearly show two of Herbert's talents, which, coupled with Herbert's love of the countryside, makes *The Magic Cottage* one of his most personal and revealing books.

Herbert has mixed with musicians both professional and amateur (American horror writer Stephen King, for example, also plays guitar), so it's not surprising how well researched the musical scenes are in *The Magic Cottage*: '"The attic room ... was the intended location for my own simple recording studio. I squatted on one of my own amps and considered the problems ... I didn't want every tape I made during the day to have a bird chorus. Fibreglass panels alternated with equal amounts of battening for bounce-back should overcome that particular problem, and two layers of plasterboard would also be needed for the ceiling." '

Although music was one of Herbert's passions, he didn't go on to music school, preferring instead to pursue art. He was 16 when he went to Hornsey College of Art in Highgate, and the future looked clear. He would study graphic design, print and photography.

The more laid-back attitude of art school came as a breath of fresh air to him, so much so, he nearly got kicked out. 'I started the first term quite late, missing the first two weeks. I never recovered that time, because I missed learning about the initial fundamentals of design. So for the whole of my first year at art school I was behind. And because of this I was unhappy and started to muck about and enjoy myself. Come the end of the first year, they threatened to kick me out, and that really made me buckle down. They moved me to another class and after that, I began to enjoy the work more.'

To support himself while at college, Herbert took various jobs during the summer holidays. These were as diverse as dish-washing to filling in National Health cards for the Civil Service. Like any other student, Herbert needed money and his thoughts began to turn toward a career of some kind. He had decided on graphic design, because it was a trade with a regular income. The life of a frustrated, penniless artist was not for him: 'Because of my background, I knew what it was like to have no money.' This is not to say that Herbert had a problem with fellow students because of his status. In fact, he relished the fact that he was mixing with various types of people, as he wrote in the promotional brochure to his novel, *Haunted*. 'The good thing was that I was moving through a broad spectrum of people, still living among East Enders but mixing with old college friends and the art school crowd. It opened up my eyes and mind.'

During his art school days, his imagination 'leaned towards the macabre', as he explains in *Dark Places*: 'I spent one day a week, along with my fellow students, sketching outdoors ... But the most popular place with me was where there was an abundance of death: Highgate Cemetery, London.'

It was here that Herbert could remind himself of those late-night treks back from the cinema with his brother, John, but this time draw and paint the images he saw with both his eyes and his vivid imagination, as he describes in *Dark Places*: ' ... it was there that the imagination ... could run riot... Victorian excesses could still be appreciated, the mutilated angels and stained crosses could still be wondered at ... I'd imagine movement in the soil, the muffled beating of a heart from a body long since rotted ... the raspy whisper of a voice not used to conversing with the living.'

So at the turn of the 1960s, while working toward his National Diploma, the future horror writer within James Herbert was already working his trade, looking for dark, depraved images that lived beneath the veneer of every day life, and the art school crowd opened his eyes and mind.

For his National Diploma of Design thesis, Herbert drew scenes of Petticoat Lane in London's East End. These were illustrations of market traders and customers who, although outwardly smiling, all seemed to be hiding a deep sadness behind their well-weathered features. When these illustrations are viewed alongside Herbert's line drawing 'Famine' (an illustration of an emaciated African peasant staring sadly down into an empty bowl), a sudden depressing sense of want dominates the overall theme. So quite early on, Herbert's imagination thrived on the dark side of life.

> *'In some kind of fantastic and frightening way, I became part of Midge's picture, living and breathing in it... I was hallucinating and I was totally aware that I was doing so... the clouds moved, and there were birds lazily arcing in the sky. It was alive and it existed. But it was only paint!'*
>
> (*The Magic Cottage*)

After graduating, Herbert found it extremely difficult to get work. He spent a year lugging his folder around various agencies and no one seemed interested. 'I slept a lot of the time,' Herbert told me. 'But I also had good friends who were not averse to buying me a pint or two. I also worked on my art in between trawling around London advertising agencies (I still lived at home, so I was fed).'

However, Herbert had to find work eventually, so an art school friend stepped in to help. 'I wasn't having much success. But I had a good friend by the name of Dennis Barker, and he was so much better than I was. He was a brilliant designer and, consequently, left school before I and most of my other friends did.'

Dennis Barker had been a friend of Herbert's throughout his college days. At one time they even had their own (nonprofessional) band – Jason and the Argonaut. However, Dennis would turn up trumps now, as Herbert explains. 'Dennis had two job interviews. He got the first one and called me up to see if I wanted to go to the other. Now, because Dennis had more experience than me at graphic design, I went along to the interview as Dennis Barker and I got the job. It then took me six months in the job to establish myself and admit who I really was. As it turned out, it wasn't a problem and I spent the next three years there.'

Herbert's first job was in a little studio agency at the back of Chancery Lane. The studio was in a loft and included Herbert and three others. 'I used to do a lot of paste-up work. Everything was done on the cheap. However, I learned as much there in six months as I did in four years at art school.'

After serving his apprenticeship, he applied for a job at Charles Barker advertising agency. Herbert was making £12 a week in his current job but told his potential future employer that he wanted £16 a week. He was eventually taken on at £14 10s a week as a typographer. His experience for the job really came from what he had learned at art school, plus a little of what knowledge he had acquired with his previous employer.

He found that the agency's work had been mainly for banks, such as Barclays, Midlands and Lloyds. 'There was a lot of work to do,' he says, 'but some people at the agency were not pulling their weight. I just wanted to get the work done. And that worked in my favour, because I was getting all my work done and finding that I had time to spare, so I got involved in design. I went into where they kept all the job sheets and took out all the good ones and then sat down, designed the ad and handed it in. I quickly found that the clients liked what I did – so did the accounts handlers – and then they started coming to me direct.'

Herbert was soon offered the job of Art Director, a role he was quick to accept. He was 23, the year 1966.

It was around this time that the agency started to go through some changes, opting for more consumer advertising. However, Herbert was going through his own personal changes: he had been seriously dating a girl, Eileen, who he had met in 1963. On 26 August 1967 they got married, at St Anne's, in Vauxhall, but the ceremony wasn't without incident, as Eileen explained when Herbert appeared on *This is Your Life*: 'Because it was a Catholic wedding, we had to take our vows again with the registrar, and she said, "Please step this way Mr and Mrs Herberts," and we said, "It's Herbert actually." And we found that somebody had written the wrong name down. Fortunately, the priest had a quiet word with the registrar and after some argument the name was corrected.'

Yet that wasn't the beginning of the wedding day shocks, Herbert added. 'The wedding nearly never took place at all. When we got to the church, we found that somebody had tried to burn it down the week before. I'm sure it was Eileen's mother!'

As his home life started to settle down, his career began to take off. By the age of 26, he had moved up from Art Director to Group Head/Associate Director, and over the next nine years, up to 1978 when he would become a full-time writer, he travelled the world. He recollects some of his experiences from that time. 'When I was in advertising, doing some work for Barclays Bank, we had to go around the world, taking photos of business centres, places like Hong Kong and Singapore, showing how these countries were suddenly growing up.

'I went to Singapore with this photographer by the name of Elliot Erwitt, a great New York photographer with Magnum. We had heard that anyone with long hair would have to have it cut before being allowed into the country.

'My hair wasn't over-long, but when we got to the airport they refused to let me through until I had it cut. I said, "No way, I'm not having it cut," and there was Elliot, very laconic and laid back, with a big cigar, and he's watching with a wry smile on his face. Then the airport staff brought the machine guns around, and I said, "What's all this about? All over a haircut?" And this guy said, "If you're staying, you've got to have your hair cut." So I said, "I'm on business here. I'm leaving tomorrow, so I'm not going to have my hair cut just to stay overnight." And this went on for ages. They even got the airline PR lady involved and she came down and started arguing with me: "Let them take a little bit off," and I said, "No way. They are not going to do it." And it got very ugly. In the end they let me through but they kept my passport overnight saying, "If you don't collect it tomorrow we'll come looking for you." And I just said, "Yeah, yeah," I was young, I didn't care. And that's when I heard about John Lennon. He went through the same thing, but our man of the people – the rebel – had his hair cut.'

Despite all this, Herbert had a good night out: 'We went to a nightclub, even though there was a curfew on. At 11 o'clock, everybody was running around for taxis and we finally got one, getting back to the hotel just in time. Imagine me out on curfew with long hair, you know? They'd chop me. I actually asked, "What do they do if they catch you out after curfew?" And the taxi driver said, "Latrines. They make you clean the latrines." Clean the toilets, I thought, oh yeah, I can see me doing that.'

Another memorable trip for Herbert was a visit to New York. 'Harold Robbins sent me his stretch limo, also his press secretary. And I remember going through New York on a Sunday afternoon, going past this art museum with all these teenagers outside and they saw this car go past with tinted windows. And there I was with jeans and T-shirt lounging in the back and they all came around looking in. I had a pair of dark glasses, so I slipped them on, then they really thought I was somebody and started knocking on the window. And that was my introduction to New York. I was on a high ... I went to a restaurant in Little Italy and as we walked in, I saw all these guys sitting at tables against the wall and, in the middle of them, was a little blond guy – Andy Warhol. And these were all his cronies around him.

'Years ago, in my yobbo days, I had this thing I used to do when coming out of a club, which was going up to a perfect stranger and saying, "Oh how you doing, haven't seen you in ages," and the guy would be, "Oh yeah," and try to place me, but I'd walk off and leave them there for the rest of the night thinking, "Who was that guy?" So, I've come into the restaurant, and there's Andy Warhol and all his crew against the wall and I've gone up to him, "Andy, how are you mate? No, no, don't get up, I'll talk to you later, I'm busy now," and walked off. All night he's looking over – even sent me over a bottle of Champagne. It was the ultimate yobbo trick. I never felt guilty about it. Well, I may do a bit now!'

At the same time, Herbert remembers walking along Madison Avenue at about 10:30 in the morning. 'This guy appeared further down the street. Very tall, very elegant. He had beige cord jeans on, a lovely white shirt and a beige waistcoat. Very erect. Very tall. And I'm just there in jeans and a leather jacket and I thought, I know this guy, and I'm eyeballing him and he's eyeballing me. I walked about ten yards past him and I thought, James Coburn. And this was in his heyday. And I've turned around to have another look and he's turned around and having another look at me. I don't know who the hell he thought I was!'

Herbert enjoys reminiscing about his advertising days, but what sort of person was he during that time?

Both Cyril Vickers and Tim Rathbone worked with him at Charles Barker, and they both admit to Herbert being 'terribly difficult to work with'. However, they also go on to say that 'he dragged the old mammoth of the company into the 20th century,' so he must have been doing something right.

To further illustrate the point and use an example from James Herbert the novelist rather than James Herbert the art director, let us consider the design and publication of his graphic novel, *The City*, and really see how difficult he is to work with.

Because of Herbert's training at art school and success within advertising, he knows how he wants his finished books to look. Since the hardback release of *Fluke*, he has designed many of his novels' covers, steering the artists who illustrate the jackets into his own mindset.

This is not to say that Herbert is unsympathetic to an artist's needs, but in the case of *The City* there was a situation where an artist, Ian Miller, had to lead the story with his artwork. Herbert had made his intentions clear from the start, providing a detailed storyboard in advance as a guideline: 'I didn't want to write another full-length novel about the rats,' he says. 'But when a publisher asked me to do a graphic novel, I thought, well, that's ideal. It was really good sitting down and doing the storyboards. The hard part came later on, when I had to go through every frame, make corrections, then it became a bit of a chore... There were a couple of things where I thought he had gone over the top with some of the mutant rats and action, and I had to hold it back. Make it a logical step forwards from the novels.'

Ian Miller didn't really believe he was dealt a fair hand by Herbert. He found him 'difficult' to work with, probably because Herbert was very specific about what he wanted and didn't let Miller explore the various ideas as freely as he would have liked. Herbert acknowledges this fact, and his reasons for holding Miller back: 'Maybe if we did more graphic novels we could have included some of the ideas but it was going too far for this first one. On the whole, I was so pleased with his end result. Ian's a brilliant artist ... In a way, it was the first time somebody came along and put something in front of me and I said, "Yeah, that's it." He actually took what I thought was a good idea and made it brilliant with his artwork ...'

During the publicity tour of *The City*, I conducted one of the few interviews with Ian Miller. I told him that Herbert was very impressed with his artwork but Miller was surprised. Not that Miller had a huge ego to massage, but he did want some kind of feedback from Herbert rather than a string of amendments and one, quite strong, disagreement, as Herbert explains. 'The only dispute we had was with one of the panels. I didn't think it had the right impact, and this was the part where we find that the wife has copulated with a mutated rat and we see the resulting baby. Ian had drawn it very small and I wanted it very large, so when you turned the page it was there in your face. The irony was that I was trying to tone down everything else!'

To be fair, both original and revised panel have their own qualities: Herbert achieves his shocking page-turner (almost exactly how he drew it in his original proof), but Miller's original panel has a deeply depressing, almost hypnotic, quality. In conclusion, it would be fair to say that Herbert has a strong idea of how he wants his books to look; but this is nothing new, as he had the same ideology in his advertising days and exercised it daily.

If this type of thing makes Herbert difficult, or creatively stifling, it must be accepted that he has his own high standards, so much so that his fans can clearly see his style in every aspect of his latest novel – from writing style, book jacket design and promotion.

Even after 30 years as a novelist, James Herbert is still an art director at heart. In fact he justifies his writing style (handwriting all his first drafts) with his passion for art: 'I like to draw the words on the page.' It's almost as though the novelist James Herbert came about by accident.

CHAPTER THREE

CHILDREN IN DANGER

'THE BOY SITS UP, RUBS MOISTURE FROM AROUND
HIS EYES (FOR HE HAS WEPT WHILE SLEEPING). HE GAZES AT
THE DIM SHAPE OF THE BEDROOM DOOR AND IS AFRAID.
AFRAID... AND FASCINATED.'
(HAUNTED)

Children can be cruel, especially to their siblings. It's a theme that runs throughout Herbert's novels, along with another: children in danger.

The first part of this book has essentially focused on Herbert's youth, and how its many influences shaped the novels of his adult life. It is now fitting that we explore the children in his books, to see if he has any special kinship with his young characters.

In *The Rats* a baby is torn to pieces by a mutant rat in a truly horrific scene, which Herbert regrets ever writing: 'I've tried to avoid it since.' There is a senselessness about the scene that has never reoccurred in his novels. Of course, children are terrified, and sometimes killed, in his books but there are dignified ways of doing this, as Herbert concedes: '*Shrine* involved a girl, but I made you dislike her. There was a creature inside her, so you were relieved to see her go in the end. Maybe that makes me predictable, I don't know. I don't want to exploit children. I don't want kids getting slashed and eaten by rats, or anything like that.'

So Herbert feels that he was exploiting children by killing the baby in *The Rats*. But the point is, he went further than anybody else had done at that time as far as out-and-out horror was concerned. Where does he draw the line? He explains: 'I know kids do get terrified in my books, but I didn't want to extend that, have them chased by monsters and somebody slashing their throats. It's done too much in the movies nowadays, and books. I don't want to follow that pattern, because I'm very protective of kids.'

We could over-analyse this and say that Herbert is protecting his childhood self, the boy in the blacked-out house in Tyne Street, searching the basement by candlelight, but we would be wrong.

When writing *The Rats* in 1973 Herbert was just starting his own family, and over the coming years he would raise three daughters, Kerry, Emma and Casey. He sheltered them from the cruel imagery he was creating in his books, even though, when at school, their father's latest novel would be passed around among friends as they searched for the naughty bits.

With increasing family obligations and serious book deals, Herbert started to evolve as a writer. His books were still very cut and thrust, but he didn't want to cheapen them with bland, over-exposed prose (although he would be accused of such).

'I always set out to write quality stories,' he says, but adds that, for him, writing is a nine-to-five job and he can not get into the persona of the horror writer. 'I'm very grounded. And that's a good thing about my background. It made me very stable as a person. And now I can go off on these flights of imagination and come back to earth. I get repetitive dreams where I can fly. But I cannot go straight up into the sky. I always come back to earth, and for years I wondered about that... What kind of monster would I be if I believed totally in flights of fantasy?'

In Herbert's second book, *The Fog*, he deals with children in a more sensitive way than in *The Rats*, starting from the very first chapter.

The second page of the book introduces us to two young children (brother and sister) buying sweets in their local village shop. They will soon disappear down a huge canyon in the road – the result of an earthquake – nevertheless during their brief appearance together Herbert clearly shows a greater sensitivity in his writing and, ostensibly, greater compassion for his characters.

For Freddy Graves, his young life is over, though his passing is mercifully quick – no suffering, no additional pain or torture. The boy's sister, Clara, is saved by John Holman, the book's hero, and although she is greatly distressed while teetering on the edge of a bottomless abyss, she is thankfully unconscious when pulled out of the canyon, thus minimising her suffering.

Additionally, Herbert's ability to create a rapport between the children and the reader is well engineered. Although you have only just been introduced to them, you don't wish them to come to any harm. During Holman's quest to rescue Clara, the description is almost meticulous in its detail – you can feel the child's fear, her exasperated breathing – and this clearly shows Herbert's greatest skill: bringing character and reader together to experience horror. But because the reader is on the outside looking in, the horror – fear – is transformed into excitement and entertainment.

Herbert believes that one of the greatest practitioners of the horror/thriller novel is Stephen King. Something, in truth, I find difficult to accept. King may be one of the world's biggest-selling writers, but he hasn't tackled any lasting themes of horror in his most recent books. It can be argued that the tragedy of a pregnant woman being killed at the outset of *Bag of Bones* is horror enough, but that doesn't disguise the fact that King has changed over the years.

However, Herbert and King do have something in common: they share the same moral code – they are protective of children.

In *The Shining* a young boy has been physically abused by his alcoholic father. Although time passes and the father kicks the bottle, the boy still distrusts his father. The story unfolds further: there is an unsaid tension in the family, not necessarily between father and son, but between husband and wife.

When the family move into the wilderness to the Overlook

Hotel, during the closed season, the solitude forced on them only compounds the father's own sense of isolation within the family circle. With the over-loading boiler in the hotel basement acting as a metaphor for the father's eruption into psychotic violence, we have an absolute horror novel that acts as a moral story in the real world and as sadistically satisfying in the horror genre.

James Herbert has previously placed *The Shining* in his list of top ten all-time favourite novels, saying of it: 'A deceptively simple plot ... Steve King's work never fails to impress.' (*By Horror Haunted*)

What Herbert enjoys greatly about the novel is the shining itself, and how the boy, Danny Torrance, harbours its powers, eventually saving both himself and his mother from the mad clutches of his demented father. Again, we see how fiction works in juxtaposition to reality – the fantasy of the shining against the backdrop of domestic violence.

Perhaps the ultimate expression of children in danger, for Stephen King, is *Pet Sematary*, a book that explores the curse of growing up and learning that all things – both pets and humans – must die. To paraphrase Woody Allen in his movie, *Sleeper*, 'The two most important things in life are sex and death' – two things we protect our children against longer than the reality behind the tooth fairy and Santa Claus.

Stephen King has gone on record as saying that *Pet Sematary* was 'too horrific to be published'. Probably what King meant by this statement is that *Pet Sematary* bursts the bubble of youth, not only through the filtering of life's realities into young minds but through the reverse side of the coin also: exploring the vulnerability of youth and how easily it can be taken away. A young child is tragically killed quite early on in the novel, and it is my personal belief that King didn't want the book to be released because it acted as a bad vibe. Having a young family himself at the time, he obviously didn't want to tempt fate and have every parent's nightmare come true.

Children, or symbols of them, have appeared on many of James Herbert's book jackets over the years. For example, a child's rag doll (*The Fog*), a child's broken porcelain doll (*The Survivor*), a young Catholic girl (*Shrine*), an unborn baby and its grotesque twin (*The Jonah*).

Children are vulnerable in Herbert's novels. Their innocence protects them for so long, but then corruption surfaces and the children fall into danger, generally because they have something their wicked elders crave. Quite often, they have psychic abilities – as in *The Jonah, Moon, Portent, Others, Once...* Children are magical in their innocence, providing the perfect opposite to the evil that adults perpetrate in Herbert's novels.

'In the hands – in the minds – of the innocents lay mankind's destiny, and only their champions could deliver them from the physical malevolence that conspired against them.'

(*Portent*)

Portent is a novel that truly expresses Herbert's feelings about the world. Although it concerns ecological issues, such as global warming (consequently showcasing the huge catastrophe Herbert is famous for), it is also optimistic. It highlights the fact that children really are the future of the world, and that they will learn by their forefathers' mistakes. This message, in its most succinct way, is summed up by Chief Seattle's Testimony, a real-life American Indian's testimony, a segment of which concludes the book: '"Teach your children ... Whatever befalls the earth befalls the sons of the earth. Man did not weave the web of life, he is merely a strand of it. Whatever he does to the web, he does to himself." '

Herbert was given a copy of Chief Seattle's Testimony long before writing *Portent* and always planned to use the wisdom. Seattle's words strike a chord within us all; everybody seeks reassurance for the future, not just individually but for future generations.

To a certain degree, Herbert casts a pessimistic eye over the world, especially in books like *The Fog* and *Domain*, but he does have a lighter, more philosophical side, as we witness in *Fluke*, *The Magic Cottage*, *Portent*, and *Once...*

The protection of the family unit has in itself been a strong theme in Herbert's books, from the close father–daughter bond in *The Dark* (Jacob and Jessica Kulek) to love's young dream in *The Magic Cottage* (Mike and Midge). However, if we go as far back as *The Fog*, we can observe one of the strongest and most relevant vignettes in the book. A man, McLellan, wakes up one morning and pulls open the curtains. The cruel, yellow-tinged fog is everywhere. And with that, he knows, comes madness and death: 'His eyes were heavy from unshed tears. He knew it was *the* fog.' But McLellan is not crying for himself. He turns round and gazes at his wife still asleep in bed. Then his thoughts turn to his children in the adjacent bedroom, and that's what truly upsets him: 'How long would it take for the poison to work on their minds, to make them insane? What would it do to him? Would he be the one to take the lives of his own family? He struck out at the air blindly. There must be a way to protect them.'

Unfortunately, it is too late for McLellan to evacuate the house and make a quick getaway – the madness would get him and his family before they reached safety. However, he can give them a fighting chance to live: he takes his daughter's toy blackboard from her room and chalks on it a plea for help. He places it outside the front door, then goes to the bathroom cabinet. He takes out a bottle of sleeping pills and wakes up his children, gives each a high dosage, then puts them back to bed. Next is his wife. At first she weeps and refuses to co-operate, but eventually logic prevails and she acquiesces. Finally McLellan takes eight tablets himself: 'He climbed back into the warm bed and drew his weeping wife to him. They lay there, waiting for sleep to come.'

Herbert has been accused of the most malicious acts of violence in *The Fog* but the vignettes of great courage and compassion are often overlooked. In the above scene, McLellan could be Herbert himself, protecting his own family from the atrocities of an ecological disaster perpetrated by government stupidity.

A writer is always influenced by the world around him. At the time of writing *The Fog* Herbert had a young family, and the plight of children and families is present throughout the book. Also, while writing the book, Herbert had a mini-crisis with his eldest daughter, Kerry, as she herself admitted on *This is Your Life*: 'He had a study at the end of the hall, and I wandered along one day. This was before I went to school and was able to read and write... He writes everything by hand, with a Pentel pen and a jumbo pad. So I went into his study and wrote over three or four hundred pages that he had already written. He had to rewrite the lot.' Herbert concluded the story by joking, 'Her version was better.'

When Herbert and I were discussing various stories and rumours about his writing career, I mentioned that some people believed he didn't write some of his novels himself – that he had a ghostwriter – or that some of the anecdotes he comes up with during interview were completely made up. As we had just been through the 'Fog scribble' story, he demanded that I view the manuscript and satisfy myself that the story was indeed true. Of course it was. He then demanded that I view all his original manuscripts to see that they were indeed written by him. And of course they were.

At roughly the same time as Herbert's *Fog* incident, fellow writer Stephen King was experiencing a similar problem on the other side of the Atlantic, as he explained in his documentary, *Shining in the Dark*: 'I came home one day. Joe, my eldest boy, who was three or four, had done all these cartoons with crayon drawings on this manuscript I had been working on. And it was all this sweet stuff like "Hello daddy"... Suns and big tall guys, like kids draw, with daddy-long-legs. And I thought, little son of a bitch, I could kill him... look at this stuff. And that became the basis of *The Shining*.'

Oddly enough, children do seem to have the upper hand over

adults in Herbert's fiction, especially if they are the dead female sibling taking revenge on their now adult brother. This theme was first tackled in *The Jonah*: 'She protected him because he was her life-force; without him there was nothing but dark eternity for her. She loved and despised his loves. No one would share him with her… No friends. No women. No one.'

Kelso's dead sister relies on him totally for her energy, but instead of being submissive, she is the dominating personality, despising any other female influence over her brother.

The Jonah is a stark, melancholy novel. The book opens with a baby abandoned in a ladies' toilet in the 1950s. The child is barely a few hours old and covered in slime and fluid. But there is something attached to it, something it desperately tries to kick away… a dead twin.

Although *The Jonah* is one of Herbert's most diverse novels, he is not terribly fond of it: 'The two books that I don't hold in very high regard – but still like – are *Moon* and *The Jonah*. Now I have people who write to me and say that *The Jonah* is one of their favourites, so you can never tell, it's all subjective. But to me, they are lesser works. I don't know why, because I put the best effort possible into them.'

When pushed further on this matter, he explains: 'They weren't big enough. I'm known for a certain type of book, and neither *Moon* nor *The Jonah* really went far enough. They should have been bigger.'

Here I disagree with Herbert. It is precisely because the two novels don't conform to the wide-screen action of his other books that they work.

The Jonah was a departure at the time, as it provided a theme Herbert would reuse in *Haunted*: the wicked dead sister. There's also a lot of subtlety within the book. Gone are the extreme acts of violence, with only the suggestion of corruption and decay, as depicted in the scene where Nick Kelso feels his dead sister nearby: '… he whirled around. No one there, but he could smell that faint, familiar aroma. Familiar because it had come before, sometimes in dreams, sometimes when he was awake... He had been a child when the strange smell had first come to him...'

Similar imagery is evoked in Algernon Blackwood's *Tales of the Uncanny and Supernatural*, in the short story *The House of the Past*. A dream pulls a man back to his previous lives, attempting to awaken memories that will allow dead loved ones to finally rest in peace. His dormant memories are reawakened by ancient perfumes – 'the scented presence of lost memories'.

The Jonah skilfully builds to its logical climax: Kelso facing the physical manifestation of his dead sister, a creature filled with jealousy and self-pity. It must be said that the book showcases one of Herbert's most emotional climaxes, mainly through the reader's own close association with the main characters and the expectation of a finale that releases Kelso from his life-long curse.

The character interaction is particularly powerful in *The Jonah*, bordering on the meticulous. It also has a strong hold over *Haunted* in as much as it is a completely self-contained novel. David Ash, the hero of *Haunted*, does not actually confront his dead sister, even though she is the true perpetrator of his hauntings throughout. Ash's horror continues into the book's follow-on (not sequel), *The Ghosts of Sleath*, but even then, he fails to have a final showdown with his sister.

However, *Haunted* does contain similar strains of the 'corrupt female sibling' theme that appears in *The Jonah*, in the character Christina Mariell (a girl who plays harsh games with her brothers and takes sadistic pleasure in taunting David Ash). Although Christina sexually submits to Ash, it is only a means of making his horror more complete. If Charles Dickens wrote for a more liberated 20th century audience, he could have placed Pip and the ever-taunting Estella in the same relationship in *Great Expectations*. It could have provided the perfect entertainment for the wretched Miss Havisham, who wanted men to go through life as emotionally scarred as she.

Readers would be forgiven for thinking that Herbert hates little girls, as they do seem to be the evil influence in his novels, albeit indirectly in some cases. However, that would be far from the truth, as he reveals, 'All children are great, although I do prefer girls. Don't forget, I have two older brothers, and they bullied me like mad when I was young.'

Some of Herbert's most poignant moments concern the death of children. The honest affection and emotional-overload depicted in a child's funeral in the opening chapter of *The Ghosts of Sleath* or David Ash gazing down at his dead sister in her open coffin at the start of *Haunted* are clear examples.

'Children being something other than what they are fascinates me,' says Herbert. 'Not necessarily evil, but just the fact that you walk in the room and the son you've just buried is sitting there.' This is exactly what happens in *The Ghosts of Sleath*. It is not the sadness and vulnerability evoked by the scene that makes it work, but the build-up to the expectation of the haunting. Fans know it's a James Herbert novel and the most dedicated will know that a child's funeral is only a new beginning, because somehow, children in danger – even beyond physical danger – are the innocent. They will always flourish, maybe not in this life but in the next.

Herbert tells his audience that no matter how strongly humankind bonds with the devil, through lust and greed, children – the true innocents – will always be protected. Despite nuclear disasters (and far worse), the children of Herbert's fiction show that good always transcends evil – by pure innocence alone.

'You must teach your children that the ground beneath their feet is the ashes of our grandfathers. So that they will respect the land, tell your children that the earth is rich with the lives of our kin.'

(Chief Seattle's Testimony, 1854)

PART TWO

A CHAMBER
OF HORRORS

CHAPTER FOUR

A Dream
of Rats

'A SOLDIER WAS BITTEN BY A RAT HE'D ASSUMED TO BE DEAD
BECAUSE OF ITS PRONE POSITION. HE SHOT IT AND REPORTED
TO THE HOSPITAL WHERE HE EXPECTED TO DIE.'

(THE RATS)

It was late one Friday evening in 1972 when James Herbert stepped through his front door exhausted from his week's toil. He collapsed into his favourite armchair and began to watch the late-night horror movie. It was a classic – Bela Lugosi's *Dracula,* directed by Tod Browning. Ever since he was a kid, Herbert has loved the old Universal monster pictures. Not just *Dracula,* but *The Mummy, Frankenstein, The Creature from the Black Lagoon* and *The Wolfman.* With their creepy sets and fabulous clichés, these films have left an indelible stamp on his heart: 'Even a man who is pure in heart and says his prayers at night, may become a wolf when the wolfbane blooms and the autumn moon is bright.'

Although Herbert was Group Head/Associate Director at Charles Barker, he felt his work was becoming a little too easy – the challenge had gone. He needed something else to focus on, something not directly linked to his work.

Little did he realise that the film he was watching would provide the spark of inspiration he craved. The movie unfolded its wonderful imagery: the count descending an enormous flight of stone steps, candelabra in hand … Three seductively ghoulish vampire brides gliding across the study floor toward the prone figure of Mr Renfield, only to be theatrically brushed aside by the dreaded count.

The film is drenched in wonderful imagery. Even contemporary film director Francis Ford Coppola used similar interior castle scenes in his poorly titled *Bram Stoker's Dracula*. But back in the early 1970s, James Herbert would take his own influence from the movie; it was the part where the poor demented Renfield (played by Dwight Fry) has a dream of rats: 'Renfield: … A red mist spread over the lawn, coming on like a flame of fire … I could see that there were thousands of rats, with their eyes blazing red, like his, only smaller. Then he held up his hand and they all stopped … Rats, rats, rats. Thousands, millions of them. All blood red.'

Absorbed in the movie and secretly searching for a new artistic challenge, Herbert tied in Renfield's fever dream with his own childhood memories. He was all too familiar with rats. Gutted houses full of them. Sharp teeth, piercing eyes. He could appreciate the horror of Renfield's dream – millions of rats, rats as big as dogs. He could tell a story about these detestable rodents.

> *'Bloody hell, he thought, it was rats. Thousands of them. He'd looked out his window, he remembered, it was night time, and there below him were thousands of rats, all perfectly still, just staring up at him in the moonlight. Thousands of wicked-looking eyes. Then they surged forward, crashing through the front door, scurrying up the stairs.'*
>
> (*The Rats*)

Herbert's story would instantly take on a theme of horror. An intense, graphic horror that, Herbert believes, was never truly achieved before, not in an accessible way that is. 'I was the first person to do it that way,' says Herbert. 'I don't know why I picked horror. I could have picked comedy, but horror movies interested me as a kid, and it seemed very natural to write *The Rats* in that genre.' The initial idea was as simple as that. Herbert began to write. 'The old house had been empty for more than a year. It stood detached and faded, next to a disused canal, away from the road, screened by foliage gone wild. No one went there, nobody showed much interest anymore.'

So opens Herbert's first novel, one that critics still love to hate. From the very first chapter, which concerns gay love and brutal murder, the novel hardly lets up on shocking vignettes.

At the time, Herbert didn't realise that what he was writing would change the face of publishing, but then how could he? It was just an exercise, something to fill in his spare time. He didn't even know if what he had written was fit for public consumption, as he stated on *This is Your Life*. 'It seemed like a good idea at the time, I was as naive as that.'

Dissatisfied with this answer, I asked Herbert to elaborate on his comment. 'I didn't mean to be glib,' he says. 'One night I went to the cinema and a friend of mine lived opposite the cinema. When we came out, I was still hyped up and didn't want to go home, so I said, "Lets go and see Dante and have a drink with him." So we knocked on his door and his wife opened it and I marched in. As I passed their dining room, I saw Dante, who I had been to college with, writing. And I said, "What's this?" And he didn't want anybody to know that he was writing a book. And I laughed, but then it just occurred to me the following day that writing a book seemed like a good idea. I thought, why not?'

So Herbert's old friend Dante takes the credit for Herbert's career as a novelist? Not quite, as Herbert elaborates. 'I think I was destined to do it really. All the copywriters at the agency had their manuscripts in their desk drawers, particularly one, who wanted to write the next *Godfather*.' Herbert was surrounded by aspiring writers.

For Herbert to write a book on top of a demanding day job seems a daunting task, but as he explains, 'I just had so much energy in those days. At 26 I wasn't getting much of a challenge.

Well, perhaps it wasn't even that. The job was a challenge, it was just synchronicity: four or five things happened at the same time and I was just full of energy, full of ideas – it could have been sheer vanity.'

Herbert doesn't genuinely know, or want to know, what made him pick up a pen and start writing a novel – after all, why would you want to over-analyse the mixture of ingredients that put you on the road to fame and fortune? What is interesting is the passion and energy harnessed by Herbert, not only to write a novel – without a commission – but to complete it within a year.

The Rats was written at great pace but also with great accuracy – the first hand-written page receiving only a couple of amendments. The whole book was written in longhand by Herbert at evenings and weekends, then typed by his wife, Eileen, then sent out to six different publishers after only nine months.

To me, this is no shock. It is often overstated how much of an author goes into a first novel, but this is indeed true of Herbert and *The Rats*. The memory of the family cat bringing a rat through the kitchen window one Sunday lunchtime is in the book (Chapter One), as is a childhood neighbour's own horror story: 'Another time, one of the neighbours had claimed she was chased down the street by a rat. Her husband had come out with a poker and had run after it, but it had disappeared into one of the bombed houses.'

The Rats includes descriptions that are very personal to Herbert. Sometimes small but revealing fragments, such as, '… the East End had no mystery for him. He remembered when he was at art school, telling some student friends about where he lived. "How colourful", one girl had exclaimed. Colourful! Well, that was one way of describing it.'

When asked about the above quote, Herbert comments, 'You notice that there is a little bit of resentment in there? That's because that kind of thing just used to annoy me. I knew my circumstances (at art school), because compared to some of the people I was mixing with, I had a hard life. To them, my upbringing was "colourful". And to pigeonhole it as "colourful" is so wrong. It's a misconception. To mask all the danger and viciousness that was there (in the East End of London) as "colourful" is patronising and wrong.'

The Rats is full of social commentary. Especially the state of suburban London after the quick fixes imposed by the government to ease overcrowding in certain areas: 'He remembered the anger he'd felt at the time a new "ultra-modern" flat had collapsed when by some miracle only nine people had been killed. His resentment had been directed not only at the architects who had designed the "block" construction, but at the council who had approved its design.'

The Rats succeeds because Herbert had done his research well – his whole childhood – which fell from his pen at a rate of knots. There was so much to write about, because there was so much injustice within society. That is why *The Rats* was completed and sent out to publishers so quickly. Herbert had to get the book, its ideas (his memories) and meanings out of his system, consciously or otherwise.

'I started writing about a year after I got married,' says Herbert. 'Because I already had a good job, Eileen thought I was mad.' (This is not to say that Eileen had a problem with her husband's hobby, as it then was. Indeed since the very first novel, she has typed all of Herbert's manuscripts and believes that he hasn't received the praise he deserves for his achievements.)

But write Herbert did, keeping his hobby behind closed doors, not letting anybody know about the story he was creating (a philosophy Herbert still holds today – he is always secretive with new ideas – unfinished novels).

On the whole *The Rats* received an unfavourable reaction when it was first released. Certain critics hated it. For some, the horror was far too graphic (wasn't that the point, to push the barriers of the horror genre?); for others, the political message appeared too left wing and Herbert's style was too raw. It was easy to knock Herbert's first novel, as he is prepared to acknowledge. 'I took the blame for a lot of trashy horror stories that came after *The Rats* in the 1970s.'

In the opinion of some reviewers, *The Rats* wasn't literature; nor was it an example of good writing. But the novel was not pandering to the conservative tastes of the reviewer. Indeed, fellow writer Peter James said of *The Rats*, 'I think Jim reinvented the horror genre and brought it into the modern world. He set a benchmark with his writing that many writers subsequently have tried, without success, to emulate.'

Herbert has been keen to state over the years that *The Rats* offered more than graphic horror. Like '48, written almost 25 years later, *The Rats* has an extra dimension to its prose. It has a depth, an awareness, a style that would win over some of the harshest critics – the public themselves – because it is streetwise, giving it mass-market appeal. It is raw – the rawest we will ever witness Herbert – but that's part of the message. Although the book can be taken as straightforward horror entertainment, it also works quite successfully on a moral level, exposing the dirt and grime of Britain's capital city to the world, as the text suggests: 'Whether the shame and the disgrace in the eyes of the world would ever be erased was another matter.'

The moral undertone doesn't just lie in the subtext; it is picked up consciously throughout by the reader. This is James Herbert as an angry young man. Herbert has never been shy to say what he thinks about London. 'I didn't want to bring up my daughters in London, because it's a terrible city now. It's collapsing in on itself. It's become a very nasty city.'

The Rats was James Herbert beginning to exorcise London, his hometown, from his system. In Chapter Eight, Harris (the main character) and his girlfriend spend some time in the countryside and the corrupting influence of the commercial world on rural life is evident on every page, though this would only be appreciated some time after *The Rats* was first released.

As a novel, *The Rats* was a product of the late '70s society it was born into. Influential TV films such as *Made in Britain,* written by David Leland, gave a startling portrayal of the country's disaffected youth at that time. Angry adolescents, soon to be followers of punk rock groups like The Sex Pistols would slap the book down in front of their elders and say, 'This will tell you what we are rebelling against.' Britain was full of angry people – there were riots, strikes, power cuts – and the government was to blame. *The Rats* was perceived to back up this ideology. 'There had been a public outcry, the usual campaigns from the press to clean up London. Angry debates on the television by politicians and councillors, and even a statement from the Prime Minister. Large areas of the dockland were sealed off ... '

The book's main character is an art teacher, a real-life hero in Herbert's eyes. And Harris wins over his class of streetwise kids with the same level of charm as Herbert wins over his many readers. He deliberately tried to harness a level of perception that gives the impression he knows more about the unseen events in life than he'll ever disclose.

The Rats is an exciting book, and this excitement is stimulated by the fact that the disease the vermin carry with them is fatal to humans. One tiny nip – enough to break the skin – is sufficient to pass the virus on to its victims and kill them, which adds an extra thrill to any scene where a rat confronts a likeable human character. People don't just have to avoid being killed, they have to avoid a mere scratch too.

In a way, the virus emanates the Great Plague – the real-life outbreak of bubonic plague in England in 1665-6, which was thwarted only by the Great Fire of London, but not before huge mass graves were crammed with diseased bodies like some horrific Nazi Final Solution.

At the beginning of *The Shining*, Stephen King quotes a long passage from Edgar Allan Poe's *The Masque of the Red Death* to show the human body's susceptibility to disease, madness, and ostensibly death. *The Masque of the Red Death* is a reminder that, despite enormous wealth, the rich must go the way of all flesh. And once the graveyard gates have been opened, speculation on the hereafter becomes prevalent: 'And Darkness and Decay and the Red Death held illimitable dominion over all.' (*The Masque of the Red Death*, Edgar Allan Poe)

Blood disease had been a popular theme long before *Dracula*. Even Shakespeare favoured death through elixir and poison. Over the years, the theme of poison – a favourite gambit of Agatha Christie – has been overtaken by the threat of drug abuse and chemical weapons, but the outcome is invariably the same: a painful death.

Herbert would later return to the theme of blood disease in '48. 'Blood – bad blood, diseased, coagulated blood – burst from his nostrils liked laced poison, and his hold on me relaxed.' In the novel's parallel world, Hitler unleashes the blood death on Britain. Only a tiny minority, with a rare blood group – AB Negative – are unaffected by the disease. Indeed, '48 gave a whole new meaning to the word vampire: a creature – a man in this case – who will stop at nothing to drain the blood of the one uninfected by the disease (in order to inject it into his own veins and save his own life).

Death is an unknown, because nobody comes back from the ashes of the funeral pyre and tells us what is on the other side. It is this factor that keeps the horror/fantasy genre valid, as rock star Alice Cooper once told me, 'Alice Cooper is still valid because he deals with issues that will never go away. People will find a cure for cancer, as they will find a cure for Aids. But death?'

Does the human spirit survive death? Are we reunited with loved ones in a better place? Are there really such places as heaven and hell?

If we are to believe the Old Testament, the Devil is indeed lord of the earth, so disease and horror should be commonplace to us. As Dennis Wheatley wrote in his occult non-fiction work, *The Devil and All His Works*. 'It is recorded that Satan took

Christ up into a high place, showed him all the kingdoms of the world, and said, "All this will I give unto thee if thou wilt bow down and worship thee", and it was made plain that it was Satan's to give.'

The balance between fantastical horror and real-life horror is what all good horror writers should strive to achieve. Some of the greatest horror novels in the last decade of the 20th century had their feet firmly planted in reality: Stephen Laws' much-underestimated social statement, *Macabre*; Philip Trewlinard's comments on childhood corruption and religious cult in *The Pastor*; and Simon Clark's ecological disaster gone rampant, *King Blood*, to name a few. But it was *The Rats*, with its level of justified horror, that paved the way for such novels in the 1970s.

The Rats was the right product at the right time, and today its place in the history of the horror genre is secured. It pushed the genre toward a more graphic style, and like most writers, Herbert forged that style out of personal experience, conjuring up images and influences from his youth and blending them with his own social commentary. Strangely, Stephen King started out in the same way. *Carrie* was released shortly after *The Rats* and in its own way it stripped down areas of society, exposing the corruption that festered there. Carrie herself was based on two different girls King grew up with, both of whom would die in their early twenties.

The corruption Stephen King exposed through *Carrie* was really the lack of acceptance humans have for each other, especially for those who are for some reason less fortunate. King witnessed all these things as a schoolteacher and thrashed them out in what is still one of his most well-written and famous novels. But has *The Rats* stood the test of time? For me, no. Herbert has written better books since, in style and content – even featuring rats. Nevertheless, it allows a glimpse of the angry young James Herbert and the influence he had at the time cannot be overlooked.

'... in Stepney ... Old bomb-sites had been neglected since the war; houses that were condemned for years still remained standing; garbage from markets and rubbish dumps were never cleared soon enough. All breeding places for filth ...'

(*The Rats*)

Herbert was pleasantly surprised when publishers New English Library (NEL) offered him a contract and an advance of £150 for *The Rats*, and he duly signed the contract on 16 May 1973. The book was published the following year and quickly became a runaway success (the first print run of 100,000 paperback copies sold out during the first three weeks of publication). The James Herbert roller coaster of horror had begun, but he had had to say two heart-felt prayers beforehand, as he reveals: 'When Emma was one year old, she nearly died. I was just in the process of sending *The Rats* manuscript to six different publishers. Being a Catholic, I'd said a prayer that I'd be lucky with this, my first novel, and that a publisher would accept the book (to this day, I always say a prayer just before I start a new story and when it's finished).

'At that terrible time I asked God to forget my original request and spare Emma instead. Well, both prayers were answered, and I've never forgotten.'

Herbert still had his nine-to-five job to think about. *The Rats* hadn't made him rich. Britain was under a labour government and the tax was crippling, so he couldn't get too carried away with his new-found fame.

The success of *The Rats* affected his work colleagues in two ways: there were those who were genuinely pleased for him and those who resented him. But why? 'I was a different person in those days,' he says. 'Sometimes quite difficult to work with.'

However, one lunchtime Herbert returned to work to find that a party had been thrown in his honour and a toy rat was presented to him with a bunch of grapes (sour grapes) from the copywriters

– those people with unfinished or rejected manuscripts in their desk drawers.

Although the party was morale boosting, Herbert still remained unsettled. Now dawned the winter of his discontent. Between the winter of 1974 and the beginning of 1978 – shortly before the release of *The Spear*, his fifth novel – he would wind down his lucrative career in advertising and move to the countryside to concentrate on his new life as a professional writer. In the interim, Herbert gave himself a lot of heartache and frustration. He had built up a good reputation in advertising, but because he was going through the motions of a huge career move, he made his passing very difficult for everyone. 'In truth, I wanted to be sacked, but no one would do it,' he explains. 'I wanted to be taken off the pay roll, but nobody would do it. And that was because I was good at my job, even though my heart wasn't in it anymore.'

This unrest didn't kick in for a couple of years after *The Rats* because Herbert wasn't convinced he could write another book. However, his publishers were determined to make him try.

CHAPTER FIVE

A Foggy Day in Hell

E ven before *The Rats* was published, Herbert was approached
for a second novel by NEL. 'I had written *The Rats* and the
publisher said, "Well let's see all your other rejected manuscripts."
And I told him that there weren't any. So he asked me if he could pay
me to write another book, and I said, "No you can't. I've got a great
job in advertising. I love what I'm doing, and I really don't know if
I've got it in me to write another book. This is very new to me." '

So Herbert wasn't instantly overcome by his ability to get
himself published. However, when the book started to sell – and
very well too – he wanted out of advertising.

Before *The Rats* was released, the publishers were keen to
secure Herbert's loyalty with a contract for another novel. 'They
tried to get me drunk, but it was one of their staff who was drunk
on the floor, not me. I just went away to see what I could come up
with next. Even then, it wasn't just about the money.'

For a while Herbert was the literary equivalent of a one-hit
wonder pop star. It was back to the job of advertising, and the
laborious but heated debates.

However, it was in one of those heated meetings that Herbert got the idea for *The Fog*. 'It was my creative director who inspired *The Fog*. Actually, he was a brilliant presenter. He used to present campaigns to clients and he was just wonderful at it. However, he could go on and on, and one day I was just totally bored. And when I'm bored, my mind begins to wander off into its own world. Now he was pacing up and down the room and I thought, what if he just went up to the window, opened it and jumped out. Wouldn't that wake everyone up! And then I thought, hey that's not a bad idea. What if everybody in London, in all those offices ... What if all the windows started opening and people started jumping out? What a visual idea. I came out of that room thinking of the next book. Never mind the campaign I was meant to be working on – I had to think of a reason for this mass hysteria. Would all these people simply go mad? Well, if so, what would make them go mad? Chemical gas?'

> '*Spiers opened the window; Holman was still too puzzled to move. Spiers opened the window and turned again to look at the surprised young man, his eyes for a second almost losing their blankness... Then he turned back to the window, climbed on the sill, and before Holman could make a move towards him, jumped out.*'
>
> (*The Fog*)

Herbert instantly tied in his 'gas' theme with his colourful East End childhood memories of thick fog: 'I remember the London smogs vividly. You could hardly see your hand in front of your face. It had an eerie yellow tinge to it. It also had a yellow tinge from the streetlights overhead as well. And I used to walk through it, my face and nose covered with a scarf.'

Once Herbert had formed his idea for *The Fog*, he had to find the time to write it: 'After the initial idea, I started writing *The Fog* at weekends. Thank God I had so much energy in those days. That's how it got written.'

When he had completed the novel and sent it to his publisher, the response was overwhelming. However, as he wrote in his 1988 Foreword to the hardback reissue of the book: '*The Fog* made me a lot of enemies.'

Anyone who makes an impact by breaking convention is going to make enemies. Unfortunately jealousy has been prevalent in the art world, and of course society at large, throughout history. In the short life of the film industry, perhaps this has always been true too. Orson Welles had his movies torn to shreds by a studio that despised his talent. Such is the way of the world, as the late Spike Milligan once told me: 'The human race can be so predictable.'

Herbert has had his fair share of criticism and praise, and has developed his own way of dealing with this: 'I just write. That's what I do. I'm not into the glamour of it, that is the reason why I do few interviews. And for every three bad reviews, I get seven or eight good ones. So if you can't stand the heat, get out of the kitchen.'

Despite ignoring criticism and burying himself in the work, Herbert does get annoyed at 'unconstructive critics'. 'The thing I don't understand is that there are people out there who attack you with so much venom for no reason whatsoever. I guess I make three huge mistakes. One, I'm a best-selling author and make a huge amount of money writing books. Two, I write horror, which is neither a respected nor a respectable genre in this country (though in America it is acclaimed). Three, I'm an East End lad. Michael Caine has said that certain people can't stand it if you're cockney and intelligent. And that's where the class war is still alive.'

Having said that, Herbert did set out to upset people with *The Fog*, as he admits. 'I wanted to see how far I could go. I wanted to go way over the top.'

If *The Rats* was the equivalent to a Bruce Willis *Die Hard* movie (in its relatively simple plot and tremendous pace), then *The Fog* was *The Poseidon Adventure* (a different type of disaster movie).

The death toll in *The Fog* steadily increases throughout the book, and the reader is constantly shocked by the mounting body count – both accidental and premeditated. Interestingly enough, Herbert's fog anticipated the potential of large-scale chemical and biological terrorism – the paranoia of the millennium. Indeed he mentions establishments such as Porton Down and military intelligence cover-ups. Terror – horror – in *The Fog* worked on many levels and truly established James Herbert as a young writer with great promise. However, he still hadn't won over some of his more conservative critics. They didn't like extreme violence, but not all of the killings were extreme.

When *The Fog* was originally published, the explicitness of the deaths did challenge convention – the general public was not used to this sort of unrelenting horror. For example, there is a chapter that concerns a girl, Mavis Evers, who stands on a beach in Bournemouth contemplating suicide. She is just an innocent teenager, lead astray by her childhood friend, Ronnie, who talks her into becoming a lesbian. For Mavis, her relationship with Ronnie isn't just a casual thing – she falls in love with her. However, the ultimate irony is that Ronnie meets a man and leaves Mavis.

Let's forget the entity of the fog itself for a moment and look more deeply at what makes the book work. In Mavis Evers's chapter we learn about her life, and because of this we form an emotional attachment to her character. We feel sorry for her. We don't want anything to happen to her – and there lies a very important literary trick, as thriller writer John Connolly explains: 'A writer must get into the emotions of the characters. With Agatha Christie you don't get to know the victims first, and how can you feel any sympathy or tension in that type of environment.'

Herbert has his own way of explaining this concept: 'I got fed up with cowboys and Indians movies – people being killed willy-nilly. So my idea was to let the reader find out a little bit about the characters first, because it is human life we are taking away here.'

Herbert uses a great deal of emotion in *The Fog*, despite the cold acts of violence. In the case of Mavis Evers, we don't want her to take her own life. We want her to think again – let rational thought prevail. Indeed, it is only because of Mavis's friend/lover that she is gay in the first place. She has just been led astray.

Then we learn that on her way to the beach, Mavis had to stop her car, not to ponder her pending suicide but because of the thickness of the fog surrounding her. Suddenly we understand why she is contemplating suicide. As a consequence, we almost concur to the fact that she is going to die. But Herbert doesn't just let her wade into the sea and drown; he looks at the bigger picture. And this is an example of where he goes further than anybody else:

'The people of the town were marching in a solid wall out to sea, making no sound, staring towards the horizon as though something was beckoning them. Their faces were white, trance-like, barely human. And there were children among them, some walked alone, on their own, seeming to belong to no one...'

The important point about this chapter is Herbert's ability to make death an individual, lonely, experience, despite the many characters involved. He identifies people within the crowd in order to create a further emotional attachment to the reader.

He describes an old woman being trampled to death by the advancing assembly, closely followed by Mavis Evers's own individual death as she inadvertently achieves her pledge of suicide: 'Her eyes were open as the last bubble of air escaped from her lips. The terror had gone. There was no pain. There was no recollection of her life, no memories to taunt her in her dying... Nothingness. Free of emotion and free of coldness. She was dead.'

Throughout the above scene, Herbert teases the reader with a speculative and very personal vision of death. We feel compassion for Mavis Evers, as if death itself provided the escape she really needed: she really loves Ronnie, and her belief that her ex-lover would reject the love of a man in favour of what they once had is unfortunately a forlorn hope. In short, death saves her from further hurt.

There is a morbid sense of relief by way of conclusion to Mavis's chapter, a depth that *The Rats* didn't come near to achieving, which clearly shows a progression in the development of Herbert's characters.

The Rats would spawn bigger and better sequels, while *The Fog* would provide a template for Herbert's future extravaganza novels – huge catastrophes such as those depicted in *The Dark* and *Domain*. But unlike the latter novels, *The Fog* allows us some pause for thought because of the build up to the individual deaths, with its almost priest-like attitude, as Herbert confirms: 'Life is a staging ground for something else, and I'm a firm believer that there's a better place you go to afterwards ... I'm a Catholic, not a very good one, but nevertheless I am one.'

Throughout Herbert's novels, the clergy get a bumpy ride, losing and regaining their faith, finding their own individual path to corruption, as we witness in *The Fog*: 'They sat and looked up at him when he climbed the steps to the pulpit, anxious to be confronted by his words in their time of sadness... Then the Reverend Martin Hurdle, Vicar of St Augustine's for eighteen years, lifted his cassock, undid his trousers, took out his penis, and urinated over his congregation.'

Unlike a lot of people affected by the fog, the vicar doesn't turn into a homicidal maniac and start butchering his congregation. His madness is subtle, personal – not unlike that of Mavis Evers. Even so, real-life priests have taken Herbert to task over the content of his books, to which Herbert responds. 'I've explained to priests that every book I've written is almost a morality play. You can see the good against the evil in every one. And I said to one priest that if I was in a room of young teenagers, I could convince them to walk the right path more easily than they could. I think the kids would believe me because I'm not too good myself – I'm a bit rough and ready. I write about dangerous things, while priests wear a uniform, and kids know what to expect from them. So from me I think kids listen more. That's my excuse, anyway.'

Herbert may crack an ironic joke, but some priests have actually tried to stop the sale of his books: 'A priest went into my local village bookstore and he insisted that they take all my books out of the window because he felt they were a corruptive influence on the community. Now this is a priest who has now been defrocked because of his alleged affairs. So the hypocrisy of that really got to me. There was this priest bad-mouthing my books, and also bad-mouthing me to friends of mine, saying, "Oh that Herbert, he's a horrible man." Whereupon a friend of mine replied, "You don't know him. Actually he's a good bloke." And the priest just said, "Oh no, he can't be." The judgement was there. And then he said he had never read the books anyway! Suffice to say, the Church and I don't always see eye to eye.'

'Chief Superintendent Wreford laughed at the rantings of his wife... for earlier that morning he had climbed the stairs from the kitchen holding a kettle full of boiling water in one hand. He had stood over his wife and poured the contents of the kettle into her upturned, open mouth. Her snoring had always sickened him.'

There is a semblance of black humour in the above quote, perhaps even more so when we find that the policeman has tied his wife up in bed sheets and locked her in the wardrobe. Herbert takes a lot of care when creating scenes of extreme violence, his choice of words – the details of the scene – gently unfolding every inch of horror. And because of this, we believe that somebody could pour a kettle of boiling water down somebody's throat (perhaps what is more disturbing is that the scene was based on a true incident known only to Herbert).

The Fog details so many different atrocities, from the small – the Reverend Hurdle urinating over his congregation – to the extreme – Wreford pouring a kettle of boiling water down his wife's throat while she sleeps.

When all these vignettes are placed together, as the direct result of one man-made disaster, an incredible amount of horror is placed in the reader's imagination. Each individual story bleeds into the next, and the most graphic are always the most horrific, such as a school teacher's vasectomy: 'Hodges released the throbbing member and slowly raised the shears, so that it was between the two sharp blades... The boys watched in silence as the two blades snapped together and the scream echoed around the gymnasium.'

It is Herbert's pen that makes us squirm; that and perhaps his slightly warped sense of humour. But when presenting us with the most horrific scene in *The Ghosts of Sleath*, he gives us no humour at all: 'The school bus drew up... Small, interested faces pressed against the glass as the carpenter began to plane away the skin and bone from Danny Marsh's face.'

Fantastical violence is more heart-rending if there is an element of reality attached to it. For example, it's not beyond the realms of possibility for a carpenter to go mad and shave off somebody's face; and even wronged women have performed do-it-yourself vasectomies on promiscuous spouses. And if we put all these terrible things together in a modern-day but fictional setting, a reader suddenly believes that ghosts do haunt quaint English villages and that a yellow-tinged fog does drive people insane.

'... by the time I crossed Hanover Square the mist had thickened and taken on a yellow tinge... There was a time when I enjoyed walking in the fog in the West End of London.'

(*In The Fog*, Dennis Wheatley)

The Fog, like *The Rats*, is based on Herbert's childhood imagery but it isn't the only similarity between his first two novels. If there were no graphic acts of violence within them, they would surely have fitted nicely into the science fiction genre, being not dissimilar in style to John Wyndham's *Day of the Triffids* and Nigel Kneale's *The Quatermass Experiment*. In fact, Herbert's first two novels are evocative of 1950s science fiction, sharing a central male-female team battling against a common enemy in order to restore normality and calm. Movies such as the original *Invasion of the Body Snatchers* and *The Day the Earth Caught Fire* spring to mind.

Both *The Rats* and *The Fog* take aspects of Herbert's budding deserted London theme, mixed with two of his most vivid childhood memories, as their story. If we add the movies and books that influenced Herbert while growing up – such as sci-fi writer Robert Heinlein's legendary *Starship Troopers* and *Stranger in a Strange Land* – we see where Herbert's imagination truly resides. The horror just gives his work that individual stamp, thus making the story richer in texture and substance.

The Rats and *The Fog* are not overfed with plot, but that doesn't matter; their shock and, on the face of it, entertainment value, are not compromised because of this. Both novels are wide-screen action movies.

In his foreword to the new edition of *The Fog*, Herbert admits that the book is a graphically horrific tale 'of murder, madness and mayhem'. While this statement is quite true, there is also a depth to the novel that many Herbert imitators have failed to emanate.

The Fog is one of Herbert's most important achievements for two reasons. First, it documents a time in the 1970s when Britain demanded more horrific entertainment (witness movies such as *Get Carter*, *The Exorcist* and *A Clockwork Orange* – all released around that time). Second, Herbert introduces some major themes that he would revisit and tackle differently in the future – such as deserted London, distrust in the government, a central male-female team not connected to any military or official agency but which nevertheless assists them in a positive way and, most importantly, every man against the system.

If *The Rats* made Herbert famous, it was *The Fog* that made him revered. He had done enough to set the horror genre evolving into a more graphic and nasty beast. This would not endear him to many mainstream critics – in fact it would alienate him forever afterwards, regardless of his growth and diversity over the years – but he didn't care about critics. However, the next novel would be radically different, in both style and content, and it would take nearly two years to write.

CHAPTER SIX

MORE THAN A SURVIVOR

While writing *The Survivor*, Herbert was still enjoying his career in advertising, travelling the world, and building a happy home for his wife, Eileen and two children, Kerry and Emma. The idea of giving up his day job was still a little way off in the future, but he was taking the novels very seriously. Because both *The Rats* and *The Fog* were very successful, Herbert decided to change tact slightly, making *The Survivor* his first true departure in terms of pace and style. He had received some important factual research from his job, as he relates, 'I got a lot of my research from books. But I did sit with a pilot during my advertising days and I gave a copy of the manuscript to him, to check the factual aspects of the story. He tied it to the back of his motorbike, drove off and lost it. He was devastated and spent ages retracing his steps, trying to find it. Thank God I had made copies.'

However, despite being a change in style, *The Survivor* still incorporated one of the main ingredients of the then archetypal James Herbert novel: a disaster-movie-type event, in this case, an airline disaster. Herbert didn't want to write a novel reminiscent of *Airport*, so he brought in a whole new angle: the supernatural.

Herbert's imagination was attracted to the unseen, which made *The Survivor* a speculative type of story, where the dead passengers and crew of an air disaster haunt the only survivor – the co-pilot, David Keller.

With each novel, Herbert was gathering more skills as a writer, and *The Survivor* would prove to be his coming-of-age book. He didn't feel the need to shock in every chapter; he would let a story build up and allow the characters to form steadier relationships.

The Survivor is set in Eton, taking Herbert away from the direct influence of London to concentrate on a more rural and gentle setting. There is the occasional *Fog*-type of horror, such as the chapter where we find Emily Platt slowly poisoning her husband. But acts of extreme horror are played down in favour of a more realistic, everyday horror in what is essentially a supernatural thriller.

In a way, *The Survivor* proved to be a throwback to classic British stories of the uncanny and supernatural, such as those written by Rosemary Timperley, Algernon Blackwood and F Marion Crawford. Herbert is happy to accept these comparisons for one simple reason: he hasn't read these authors. 'I don't know if it's a bad thing that I haven't read enough horror, because when do I know that I'm repeating something that has already been done? Or is it a good thing that other writers haven't influenced me? As long as I'm not accused of ripping people off, I don't mind.' Although Herbert contradicts my comment, it still stands, because it must be remembered that horror – terror – is an age-old human feeling and there is something so typically British about Herbert's horror fiction that clearly comes across.

The Survivor is a rather dark novel, devoid of excessive, out-and-out horror. It is bleak and barren. If the location had been moved from Eton to Dartmoor, it wouldn't have added any more gothic charm. In one paragraph Herbert kills off three hundred people in an aeroplane crash, but then spends the rest of the book exploring why the disaster happened. He evokes a whodunit kind of aspect, which naturally pulls off its own surprise pay-off.

It is also a story about procedure, the mechanics of finding out why an air crash occurred in the first place. Indeed Herbert's thorough research could have made the book a good thriller, but he didn't want to conform to the conventional thriller. Herbert had chosen the horror genre as his main theme, and he would dig deep into the heart of the genre, ignoring the oblique and cheap fantastical elements. His apprenticeship to the horror genre was the real-life awfulness of growing up in the East End of London, not necessarily the atrocities he read about in storybooks.

For the first time in *The Survivor* Herbert would speculate on the afterlife, which has continued to be a constant theme throughout his novels. However, this fact is largely ignored today and the book is often overlooked in favour of the bigger 'extravaganza' novels that followed. This could be due to the poor movie version of the book starring Robert Powell and Jenny Agutter, which is a pity if true because *The Survivor* is a good novel that sits somewhere between disaster movie and traditional horror flick.

Herbert was both frustrated and angry with the film because he had no contact with the producer or director. Even more exasperating was that after it had been optioned a major Hollywood studio wanted to buy it, which would have increased the production budget immensely.

> '"First of all, Mr. Keller, I am not a crank," he began, "but you have to take my word for that. I am a practising medium up until a few years ago and, if I may say so, a very successful one…" '
>
> (*The Survivor*)

In some of his most popular novels, the power of mediums is an important tool to Herbert, as seen in *The Dark, Haunted, Portent* and *Others*. 'I'm interested in supernatural,' he says, 'And clairvoyants *could be* the link between man and the supernatural. I'm open to thoughts and ideas. I like to speculate. So they could be on to something.'

However, Herbert tries to avoid cliché giving his scenes a personal, emotional edge. For example, in *Others* when clairvoyant Louise Broomfield falls into a trance-like state, the laughable stock phrase 'Is there anybody there?' is substituted for a credible, thought-provoking line, mainly because private investigator Nick Dismas describes the scene in an off-hand way: 'The clairvoyant closed her own eyes for a moment, either out of pity for me, or to picture the scene, who knows which?' He – Dismas – dismisses the idea of a spirit world, or God, putting the reader on the side of the cynic – a clever trick in itself. If he is sceptical it is because he isn't actually seeking spiritual help; it is Louis Broomfield who approaches Nick Dismas, in order to help one of her clients.

Herbert is not sure if mediums do actually help people, as he admits: 'I don't believe all clairvoyants are charlatans. I would say 70 per cent are charlatans, the other 30 per cent are genuine. But genuine in the respect that they believe in what they are doing. I'm not too sure that they do contact the spirits. I've never seen examples of it that have convinced me. There's always an edge to their pronouncements – in other words, they could have been good guesses.' But Herbert does keep an open mind on the subject, concluding, 'I do think there is something going on but I'm not sure if it's what they (clairvoyants) say it is. The power of the human mind is a lot keener, a lot stronger, than we ourselves know. We can do many things with our own mind that have nothing to do with the dead.'

In *The Survivor*, however, a clairvoyant has everything to do with the dead: Hobbs leads co-pilot David Keller through many personal dangers before leading him quite literally to death's door.

Although spiritualists, mediums, clairvoyants – call them what you will – play a large and important role in Herbert's fiction, they invariably overstretch themselves and come into a very real and personal danger, not necessarily through any physical manifestation of evil but through something more ethereal.

Perhaps one of the most notable examples of this is demonstrated in *Haunted*. Psychic investigator David Ash uncovers a charlatan clairvoyant, Elsa Brotoski. But Brotoski's tricks are uncovered and as her betrayed clients leave her séance, she starts to have a fit. The true spirits – those dead relations of all the people she has lied to – reap their revenge on her, mentally torturing her – haunting her. As David Ash leaves, the final pay-off occurs: his name is called, screamed aloud from Brotoski's exhausted body. Ash knows to whom the cry belongs. It is his dead sister, beckoning to him like she did in his childhood when he lay awake in his bed at night and she lay dead in her open coffin downstairs.

When *The Survivor* was released in America, the book was promoted as, 'The soul-chilling novel of gruesome horror from beyond the grave.' And if that wasn't enough, 'The mind-shattering novel of gruesome horror that takes you beyond *The Rats* and *The Fog* to the blood-curdling chills of the living dead!'

Overblown promotion it may be, but there was an element of truth in it. *The Survivor* did go beyond the boundaries of Herbert's preceding novels; fine-tuning the horror, filtering through the chills. If he had started churning out parodies of *The Rats* and *The Fog*, he wouldn't have lasted very long. Although he did write sequels to *The Rats*, each one was not written directly on the back of its predecessor, and each one became a personal, as well as literary, progression.

If *The Rats* was proof that Herbert could write a novel, *The Fog* was really an exercise in imagination and characterization, as well as being an example of a more sophisticated style. So where does that leave *The Survivor*, his third, smaller, disaster-movie? It shows a refining of style and diversity, expressing Herbert's now-familiar voice. Comparisons between London and the countryside – so prevalent in his latter novels – are consciously made. Keller drives to and from the city, following the branching river Thames, surveying the inviting meadows of the countryside and then returning to his London-based flat. These observations would become the foundations of Herbert's future work, as would the greed of people who capitalised on the air disaster. 'The trouble they'd had since the accident; mobs of 'em flocking to the scene of the crash ... The worst of it was when the vendors had arrived, selling peanuts, ice cream, soft drinks; that had really sickened him. Trouble is, it's so near London. It was a nice day out for the city dwellers.'

It can be argued that a jumbo jet crashing into a rural scene is another example of how the civilised world infects the countryside, as is the government blunder that unleashes the fog, or the rats as depicted in *Lair*: giant mutated vermin, running wild in the city before threatening to infect the countryside.

'We are all concerned about our environment,' Herbert says. 'But I think we're all getting a bit tired of the message. It's becoming boring ... If I can get my message across, and do it in an entertaining way, but still giving pause for thought, then hopefully the message will get through to people who don't normally give it a second thought. Maybe they'll think a little more about it. Maybe they'll regard it as just another piece of entertainment, but that's up to them, they can do what they like. But I do hope the books do some good.'

This isn't a pretentious quip. Most, if not all, novelists believe that they have something to say through their fiction. As time goes by, the moral undertones in Herbert's work have become more prevalent. Essentially, *The Survivor* was the first book to be sedate enough to let the sub-theme come through straight away; and for the first time it would be taken seriously. In his first two novels, Herbert had boggled critics and readers alike with the amount of horror he had harnessed. Any other message became obscured, only being understood with the passage of time.

'*The Survivor* was a departure from the almost science fiction of *The Rats* and *The Fog*,' says Herbert. '*The Survivor* was supernatural, but *Fluke* – the book that came afterwards – was a total departure in style, tone and content... I do vary. I've changed all the way through. I think it's very difficult to categorise me. People do, but they're usually people who haven't read the books. They say, "Oh Herbert, he did *The Rats* and that sort of thing, people go mad." And they put me down because of that, simply because they haven't read the books or, if they have, they've only gone for the early ones, which are really cut-and-thrust.'

So *The Survivor* broke the mode, adopting a more relaxed and intricate style. And its supernatural elements were aspects readers would grow to love in works such as *The Spear*, *The Dark*, *Shrine*, *Sepulchre*, *Haunted* and *The Ghosts of Sleath*. Herbert also believes that the central idea for *The Survivor* was used much later in the film *The Sixth Sense*, just as the theme of *Haunted* was used in the film *The Others*. (Despite the similarity of one of the titles, these films were not adapted from James Herbert novels.)

> '*The first glimpse of understanding touched him; glimpses, but far greater than the sum of all earthly knowledge. This was self-knowledge, the essence of everything.*'
>
> (*The Survivor*)

It is important to analyse Herbert's books in juxtaposition to his life story, because it allows us to understand the man who has become one of Britain's leading horror/thriller writers. Only then can we break down the preconceived ideas that we may have of him, as I explained in my *Author's Note*.

After *The Survivor*, it was clear that Herbert wasn't going to be dictated to by publishers. He worked in the dog-eat-dog world of advertising, he was used to dealing with big money and he wasn't afraid to get his point across. If he was to write his books in his spare time (generally at the expense of his family), they had to be done to his satisfaction. With hindsight, this has paid dividends for Herbert, but not before his publishers tried desperately to shape his future for him, especially with his next book, *Fluke*.

Through *The Survivor*, Herbert was attempting to show that he could write more than unadulterated horror; that he wasn't obsessed with creating terrible acts of violence and was capable of greater subtlety. *The Rats* was a one-off idea, it wasn't preconceived. *The Fog* was an experiment into seeing how far he could push the genre he had naturally fallen into. As both books were written about his East End upbringing and not an unhealthy diet of horror movies and novels, his imagination would then turn to what truly interested him within the genre: the supernatural. Unaware of this, publishers NEL demanded more horror, but Herbert wanted to continue with the supernatural and speculate further on related themes that interested him.

CHAPTER SEVEN

A Fluke, or Sheer Hard Work?

In 1977 James Herbert released his fourth novel, *Fluke*, perhaps his most gentle work to date. Although it may seem inconceivable today, the book was met with a great deal of surprise when received by his publishers, who were expecting something along the lines of his previous novels. Instead *Fluke* was a book about reincarnation. There was no obvious horror, just a dog that believed he was once a man. But why did Herbert decide to write such a different book? 'I've always written what I've wanted to write,' he says. 'I've not been influenced by anything else.' Did he appreciate that *Fluke* was so different it could have been detrimental to his writing career? 'In a way, you could say that after *The Rats*, *The Fog*, and *The Survivor*, *Fluke* was a bad career move,' he confesses. 'But I was still in advertising, I had nothing to lose.'

His publishers were so concerned about the book, they took Herbert out to lunch in a futile bid to make him change the story: 'First of all they wanted to change the book jacket – make it a dog with fangs. I said, "No way." Then they wanted to change the whole story, turning it into a rabid dog story.' The details of his lunchtime meeting clearly show how passionate he felt about his work (and how determined he could be in any type of business meeting): 'It got to the stage where I started to shout the guy down and he went to the toilet. I picked up my manuscript, which he had left on the table, and saw all these red biro corrections throughout. Huge chunks had been taken out. I couldn't believe that they would do this to one of my books.'

Herbert really wanted *Fluke* to be a departure; to go one step further than *The Survivor*; to speculate, give pause for thought: what if there is something called reincarnation? And do we take the thoughts of one life into the next?

Fluke was naturally a more philosophical novel than *The Survivor*, as Herbert qualified to me in a letter: '*Fluke* ... is in its way, my own attempt at *The History of Mr Polly*. It's a special one to me, written after my first three out-and-out, over-the-top horror stories and one nobody wanted me to do. However, its success over the years both in terms of sales and appreciation has vindicated my decision.'

It could be argued that the success of Herbert's earlier novels enhanced both the reputation and selling power of *Fluke*, not dissimilar to the fate of Stephen King's Richard Backman books (when people found out Backman was indeed King). Naturally, the individual success of a writer's work is reflected in the strength of his back catalogue, but this couldn't have affected the sales of *Fluke* too much, being only his fourth novel. However, *Fluke* could have influenced the selling power of Herbert's future novels abroad, not necessarily in a positive way. '*Fluke* probably did me a lot of harm in America,' says Herbert. 'But to this day I never work that way of adapting my work to please a particular publisher or audience... I just want to tell my story the way I want to tell it. It's not arrogance. It's more about being true to myself.' (Ironically, the best movie adaptation of a Herbert novel is the American movie *Fluke*.)

Above: James Herbert in 1961, as a graphic design student at Hornsey College of Art. He is in the front row, fourth from left.

Below left: Taking a break in Southern France in the early '60s.

Below right: Jim's mother and father, Herby and Kitty, at Eileen and Jim's engagement party.

Pictures from the Herbert family album.

Above left: Jim's grandfather.

Above right: Jim's mother.

Below: Kitty serving a customer at their fruit stall on Bethnal Green Road in the early '50s.

Above left: Kitty and Herby's shop in Hackney Road. The flat above was home for a couple of years when Jim was a child. Growing up in post-war East London provided some of the images that would contribute strongly to first his art and, later, Herbert's novels.

Above right: A recent photo of Jim's nursery school on Columbia Road in Hackney.

Below: On the fruit stall with Mum in the early '70s. Dad is in sunglasses, behind the stall.

The sound of wedding bells. *Above left:* Jim with his best man and brother, John, on the happy day.

Above right: Eileen, Jim's bride.

Below: With Eileen on a holiday cruise.

It was Buddy Holly's music that first inspired Jim to learn rhythm guitar whilst at college. In later years, music provided a break from writing.

A world far removed from the terror of his novels…

Above: At home in the library with, (*from left to right*), daughters Emma, Casey and Kerry.

Below left: Kerry aged 5 and Emma aged 2, playing in the garden in South Woodford.

Below right: Jim with Casey in 2000, after she had just gained top marks in her GCSEs.

Out and about with the family.

Above: Jim and Eileen's Silver Wedding Anniversary party in Brighton. *From left to right:* Emma, Casey, Eileen, James and Kerry.

Below: Outside the Forbidden Planet in London. Kerry and Emma looked after the more talkative guests!

Above left: An aerial view of the family ranch – Hunters View.

Above right: Enjoying the garden with man's best friend.

Below: With wife Eileen at a function.

Fluke has its own individual qualities that make it a popular story today, but before we consider these, Herbert explains how he managed to get his version of the novel in print and not the rabid dog story his publishers were expecting. 'I told them if they didn't want to publish it, I'd take it somewhere else. Remember, I was still working in advertising at the time, and if the book didn't come out, I still had a good job to go to. I wasn't relying on them for anything.'

Obviously, the success of Herbert's first three novels gave his arguments in support of *Fluke* a great deal of backing, and NEL didn't want to kill the golden goose. They had put a lot of time and money into Herbert's success and they didn't want another publishers reaping the rewards of all their hard work. Besides, they knew that Herbert had a lot of mileage left in him. He was a good young writer – popular too – and they had to admit, *Fluke* was a well-written novel.

'The warmth from the sun beat against my eyelids, soft persuasion to open them. Noises crept into my ears then burst through to my consciousness, confusing sounds, a gabble broken by strident pitches.'

(*Fluke*)

'I never read my own books,' Herbert says, 'although I sent a copy of *Fluke* to a friend not so long ago, and I opened it up, read through a few lines and thought, that's nice, I like that. I also gave a copy of it to my youngest daughter Casey to read, because it's a gentle novel, but she didn't get on with it at all.'

Before we dismiss this quote, let us consider the person James Herbert was in 1977 – before Casey was born, in 1984.

Herbert had not yet given up his career in advertising. He lived near Epping Forest with Eileen and Kerry and Emma. Although a horror writer, Herbert would make up fairy stories for his children and draw or paint the odd witch or dragon, losing himself as much in his fairytales as his children. 'It's a shame we never recorded those stories he made up for the children,' says Eileen. 'They were so good.'

So, James Herbert – children's writer? Why not. He has always been protective of children, loved the artwork in children's books and films, and the movie version of *Fluke* is a great family film so a children's version of the novel could do extremely well. But why didn't Herbert write children's fiction if it interested him so much? Indeed fellow writer Roald Dahl used to write children's books and poetry while still writing his adult spine-chillers. 'I never had the time to write children's stories, although I wanted to,' he explains. 'My problem was that I wanted to do the illustrations as well and that would have taken a long time and I really wanted to direct all my attention on my novels.'

Even after all these years, *Fluke* remains one of Herbert's personal favourites among his own novels. With its moral undertone, it ranks alongside *Shrine* and *The Magic Cottage*, and it is this versatility which has won Herbert plaudits: 'Over the years *Fluke* has earned me some accolades. It was on the GCSE reading lists for a while, and also a university took it in Norway.' He further justifies his novel by adding, 'I believe *Fluke* made me more rounded as an author, because it showed people that I could do other things as well. That I could write a gentle story.'

The storyline to *Fluke* is quite simple: gradually a dog realises, not only that he was once a man, but one against whom a terrible crime had been committed. The book is divided into two parts. Part One concentrates on Fluke's growth as he learns to understand the intricacies of a dog's life. Part Two centres around Fluke's increasing awareness that he was once a man before piecing together the facts surrounding the death of his former human self: 'The second part – the circumstances of my death – was more difficult, and because I felt familiar places would begin to open memory valves, a visit to my plastic factory might help. First though: when did I die?'

One of the nicest twists in *Fluke* is when a fellow dog, Rumbo, dies and is reincarnated as a squirrel. The event has a further pay-off for Herbert's loyal fans. In *The Magic Cottage* hero Mike befriends a squirrel, which because it inexplicably behaves like a dog, he nicknames Rumbo: 'I think he appreciated the gesture, or maybe he was happy... because he licked my face and hands like a puppy dog.' Herbert explains why he did this: 'It was a little intimate joke between me and the reader. Not everyone will spot that, but the true loyal reader would see it instantly. And it's me saying, "You know me and I know you, and this is our little joke." ' (Rumbo would also make a third appearance in *Once...* – this time as a fox.)

In 1992 Herbert told me, 'When I wrote *Fluke*, a lot of people wrote to me and said, "You believe in reincarnation like we do." I don't really, I just speculate. What I write is not always what I believe.' Five years later, he followed this up with, 'Nobody knows what happens after death. It's all subjective. You know, I hope there isn't reincarnation. Having to go through all this again? Would you want to do it?'

As well as being a departure from the horror genre, *Fluke* became a further escape from central London, using the suburbs of south London and the surrounding countryside. Starting off in the city, the novel quickly moves down to the rural locations of Edenbridge and Marsh Green, a 'one street village'. It is in Marsh Green that Fluke is reunited with his former human family – his wife and children. Only here does Herbert pull at the heartstrings a little, as although Fluke can't communicate with his family, he can still be with them: 'Everything was rosy. I was home; I was with my family. I had food in my belly and hope in my heart.' From here the novel moves towards its satisfying conclusion.

Unfortunately, *Fluke* is too much of a departure for a lot of James Herbert fans. Admittedly Fluke does have one brief skirmish with a rat, but apart from that and Fluke's ability to actually see ghosts, the horror – if any at all – comes from the plight of the central character. A man who is now a dog, his helplessness in trying to understand the manner of his death and coping with it, and then, perhaps more gothic-like, his reintroduction into the bosom of his human family without them appreciating who he really is.

Although *The Magic Cottage* has enjoyed enormous success over the years, the first of Herbert's very gentle novels, *Fluke* doesn't have the crowd-pleasing vignettes of horror its successor would have. This does not vindicate the publishers' original concerns about the book, as *Fluke* remains one of Herbert's greatest personal achievements and one of his greatest departures within the horror genre.

Fluke is often overlooked by die-hard horror fans because they don't consider it a horror novel. Perhaps it would have fared better on the standard fiction bookshelves. Unfortunately writers must have their works categorised by genre – crime, fantasy, horror, sci-fi – so *Fluke* hasn't truly been allowed to reach its wider audience. As Peter James states, 'Most of the best horror writing is done by non-genre specific writers. *Rosemary's Baby* is a horror classic. But Ira Levin could never be called a "horror" writer.'

Some writers do experiment with other genres and it is a shame that publishers do not take this into consideration when marketing a book – it it's a James Herbert novel, it must be horror!

There is one final point concerning *Fluke*. After Herbert argued to have his version into print, the whole of the first print run was pulped because the book was printed in the wrong typeface. Herbert wanted a much softer typeface – to go with his softer story. Needless to say, he got his way. Herbert can be such a demanding author ... for his publishers.

CHAPTER EIGHT

SUPERNATURAL POWER

' ... ONLY TO THE FEW ... COMES THE KNOWLEDGE, NOT TOO WELCOME, THAT THIS GREATER WORLD LIES EVER AT THEIR ELBOW, AND THAT ANY MOMENT A CHANCE COMBINATION OF MOODS AND FORCES MAY INVITE THEM TO CROSS THE SHIFTING FRONTIER.'
(THE INSANITY OF JONES, ALGERNON BLACKWOOD)

People who write about the supernatural, invite the super-natural. As Hamlet's famous quote observes, 'There are more things in heaven and earth than dreamed of in your philosophy, Horatio.'

Indeed, it is people's fascination with the hereafter that makes them read books about ghosts and the supernatural. Sometimes, thrillers are not enough to satiate the hunger in speculative fiction.

Before we concentrate on Herbert's life and career on the release of his fifth book, *The Spear*, let us take a brief look at how he deals with the supernatural in his day-to-day life. Let us call these incidents, coincidences or, maybe, synchronicity: ' "... You know what synchronicity is, don't you? ... It's a meaningful coincidence in time of two or more similar, or even identical, events that aren't necessarily related." '(*Others*)

Everybody has an uncanny story to tell and James Herbert is no exception, but when something strange happens to him, because he is a horror writer, the coincidence takes on extra meaning. Former radio broadcaster and writer of the supernatural Algernon Blackwood believed that he had seen ghosts and felt strange earth powers in remote locations around the world. In fact, Blackwood's life is a fascinating story in itself. In his younger days, he was a member of the Order of the Golden Dawn, which included among its order the soon-to-be wickedest man in the world, Aleister Crowley. Crowley would become an occultist who allegedly sacrificed babies to the anti-Christ, among other things.

Every writer needs to carry out research in order to give their fiction some forethought. But when the writer of the supernatural does their research, they naturally open up their mind to the more bizarre aspects of life; things which when placed together provide a spooky aside. James Herbert has a down-to-earth approach to such things: 'I've never knowingly seen a spirit,' he told me in 1992. 'I'm very disappointed about that. Stephen King is the same. But the more we wish for it, the more unlikely we are to see one.'

However, come 2001, he announced, 'I've seen a ghost. A couple of years ago. I was with a friend of mine (David Moores, Chairman of Liverpool Football Club) who has a fantastic villa in Marbella, and he just asked me over for the weekend along with another friend and our wives. And there we were, about three in the morning, having had a great night. The wives had gone to bed a couple of hours before, and we were just talking about football, films and music. Then my friend Bob Young, he went white.

'Now, we were in this huge lounge, not unlike a film star's palace, and I asked Bob what was wrong, and he said, "Nothing" so we carried on. About 20 minutes later, both Bob and I saw this figure pass the door. I jumped up immediately and went after it. I was at the door in a flash, because if it was a ghost I wanted some evidence, I wanted to confront it. But outside there was only this huge empty marbled floor hallway and staircase. There was nothing there at all. If one of the wives had come down for a glass of water or something, they would have barely been halfway up the stairs at most.

'I went back into the lounge. Bob was still as white as a sheet and I said to him, "Did you see it?" and he said, "Yes", and that was the end of it.'

Herbert still had a clear recollection of what the spirit looked like: 'A small woman. Could have been a monk, because it was wearing what looked like a brown robe. That's how I remember it. I didn't see the features, but the image itself was sharp. It wasn't wispy at all, it was like a person walking past. I don't know what that thing was. I have no explanation at all. All I know is – I saw it.'

Other strange things happen to Herbert as well. 'Two things immediately spring to mind. I remember, years ago, I was in a film office. I was talking about *The Survivor* and I was asked if I wanted a drink. So I said that I would like a beer, and they put a can and a glass on the table in front of me. They were seated at the far end of this table and, as is my want, I was talking about Stephen King. In a way, I get embarrassed talking about myself, so I deflect it, and we were both very new at the time ... So I was talking about Stephen's book, *Carrie*, which was all about telekinesis – making things happen with your mind – and, as I'm talking to these two guys their mouths drop open.

'They looked down, and I looked down. The glass and the can were moving away from me, right down towards them. And I thought, whoops. So I said, "Take no notice, that often happens around me," and they loved that. But what I think really happened was that we were in Piccadilly, on the third floor of an office block, and underneath there're so many railway tunnels, so the wet can and glass on a glass table was susceptible to vibrations.'

Herbert is not troubled by the uncanny. Surprisingly, he takes a very logical view of it; or a humorous view, as he continues to explain: 'The following night, I was going to see some other film people about *The Fog* (not to be confused with John Carpenter's movie) and as I walked into up to the bar, all the panelling collapsed. I couldn't believe it. I thought, what's happening here?'

Coincidence, or synchronicity, does seem to be a thing that

follows Herbert. 'A few years ago, I was sitting in a friend's house in Marble Arch, and we had had lunch and were on to coffees. Now I had my coffee cup in front of me, Eileen was next to me, and everybody else was around the table, all with coffee cups in front of them. There was a tablecloth on the table, it wasn't just wood. And it was *my* cup that started jangling away on the tablecloth, nobody else's, and I said, "Take no notice, it *always* happens." '

It isn't always inanimate objects that give Herbert these little departures from normality. 'I never forgot the day I found a rook in my lounge. I had a huge 28x24 foot lounge with a white carpet and white walls, and I went in one day – now bear in mind that all the doors and windows are locked – and there's this enormous rook sitting on the back of the sofa. A huge thing. There was no way it could have got in. We had a fireplace but it was tiny and there was no way that a bird of that size could get through there. And to this day, I have no idea how it got in. It just sat there watching me. In the end, I opened all the windows and I flew out!'

Herbert often tries to find the logical explanation for an uncanny story – he is not easily taken in. Like the occasion when he bought two chairs that once belonged to Aleister Crowley. Herbert keeps these chairs in his hallway, next to the door leading to his indoor swimming pool.

One day he came downstairs and noticed that the floorboards underneath the chairs had dramatically warped. He told the antique dealer he had bought the chairs from about this, and he was advised to bring in an exorcist. Herbert preferred to look for the logical explanation and unfortunately found it: cold air blowing through the hallway from the front door and warm air blowing through the hallway from the swimming pool resulted in dampness, which caused the floorboards to warp.

All quite normal and scientific really. However, he would later tell me that it happened again ...

CHAPTER NINE

THE SPEAR OF LONGINUS

'I desire to state that I, personally, have never assisted at, or participated in, any ceremony connected with Magic – Black or White.' So wrote Dennis Wheatley in his Author's Note to *The Devil Rides Out*. Why Wheatley had to make such a declaration is quite simple: while conducting his research for the book, he met some of the most powerful practitioners of black and white magic alive. They terrified him so much, the resulting experiences would prompt him to put in his note: 'Should any of my readers ... come into contact with a man or woman of Power ... it is only right to urge them, most strongly, to refrain from being drawn into the practice of the Secret Art in any way.'

In April 1934 Wheatley and his wife, Joan, returned from a tour of South Africa. The result of this would be Wheatley's novel, *The Fabulous Valley*, a typical adventure story. However, it was on completion of the book that he started to write *The Devil Rides Out*. Although the book was a departure from his usual adventure story, it nonetheless concerned a subject that had interested him for almost 20 years: the occult.

Wheatley was genuinely interested in the occult, but not as a practitioner; he would invite Men of Power to dine with him at his London home. He was the perfect host, offering the finest food and wine. But who were the occultists that visited him? And, more importantly, how dangerous were they? Did they attempt to draw him into the Secret Art? And did he witness anything – even as a casual observer – that would give him an absolute conviction of Satanic danger?

Wheatley did his research a little too well. He got too close to dangerous men, such as the Reverend Montague Summers, who cordially invited him and his wife to stay at his country house for a weekend. But after having their room infested with huge spiders, *things* started to happen – the whole visit suddenly became a nightmare. Summers asked Wheatley to accompany him into the library, where he handed Wheatley a small leather-bound book. He went on to tell him that the book was very old and very rare, but he would let him have it for £50.

Wheatley never disclosed what the book was, but it was obviously an instruction on the black mass. Wheatley declined the offer, saying that he couldn't afford it and, even if he could, he didn't want it anyway. He explains what happened next in his book, *The Devil and All His Works*: 'Never have I seen a man's expression change so swiftly. From benevolent calm it suddenly became filled with demonic fury. He threw down the book and flounced out of the room. An hour later I had sent myself a telegram. By Saturday evening my wife and I were home again in London.'

The Devil and All His Works is a fascinating account of Wheatley's dealings with the occult. It clearly shows that although he never took part in a black mass, he was at least offered the opportunity to do so. Because his dealings with Men of Power terrified him so much, he turned down an offer in the mid-1930s to write a non-fiction work about the occult. He would wait until most of the practitioners he knew were dead before writing his book, in the 1970s.

So what connection does this digression have with James Herbert? Well maybe a little more than we initially think.

The Spear (1978) was Herbert's first serious venture into the world of the occult, and it proved to be the most problematic book he would ever write. It concerns the spear of Longinus that pierced the side of Christ two thousand years ago. It also deals with a Nazi religious cult (showing shades of Dennis Wheatley's novel, *They Used Dark Forces*) and an insane passion to resurrect Heinrich Himmler.

The important thing to remember about *The Spear* is the amount of research that went into it (Herbert had given up his day job before publishing the book at the outset of 1978). In fact it was the first of Herbert's books to include an Author's Note listing the books he used in his research, though this only appeared in the first hardback edition of the novel. It also included a very atmospheric two-page prologue called '5th April, 33AD', which again only appeared in the first hardback edition. It was substituted for a five-line piece called '33AD' from John 19:32 (RSV) in later editions, though extensive quotes from Hitler and other prominent Nazis still headed individual chapters.

So why was *The Spear* cut so heavily after its first hardback release? And why was the release of the shortened paperback version delayed until after the release of *Lair* (Herbert's following novel) in paperback, some two years later?

The answer: Herbert came into contact with his own Man of Power while researching *The Spear*. And the experience wasn't very pleasant.

Herbert was taken to court by 'occultist' Trevor Ravenscroft for copyright infringement. Herbert freely admitted in his Author's Note that the idea for his novel came from Ravenscroft's book, *The Spear of Destiny*, which detailed Adolf Hitler's association with the Heilige Lance (Holy Spear), but that wasn't tribute enough. Ravenscroft wanted financial compensation of £25,000, as Herbert explains. '*The Spear* was the last book I wrote as a weekend job. I was in hospital having a small sinus operation, when somebody brought in a magazine, which had an article about *The Spear of Destiny*, a book by Trevor Ravenscroft. And I thought the whole history was incredible. So immediately after I left hospital, I bought the book.'

But what was in the book? 'A lot of it was quite extreme,' says Herbert. 'And what I failed to recognise was what parts were gained by "transcendental meditation", and what were actually historical facts. I was sued for using what I believed were historical facts but were actually gained by transcendental meditation – that is, exclusive to Ravenscroft.' And if they were exclusive to Ravenscroft then Herbert was not permitted to use them without prior permission, so Ravenscroft wanted compensation.

Herbert continues, 'Now if I paid him a certain amount of compensation, I could use those facts. Well, I thought if I give into this it means every English writer that uses research is going to be in difficulty, because we all use other books and articles to gather our research. And of course, in the hardback of *The Spear* I had acknowledged Trevor Ravenscroft, who I thought was a professor of history.'

Ravenscroft was into many things but he was never anything as prestigious as professor of history.

'He wanted £25,000 for using those "transcendental facts" but I said, no way, people have got to be able to use facts for their research, which Ravenscroft had done in *his* book. He had used whole paragraphs from Trevor Roper's book (which also concerned the lance). So Ravenscroft came back to me requesting £20,000, and then after I had again refused, it went down to £12,000. Again, I said no. I said that there was a principle here, and that he had to take me to court.'

Even today, Herbert is still hurt by the whole incident – especially the court case. 'I remember the whole thing very clearly. We had just moved to our new house in Sussex, and if the move wasn't enough, we had just learned that Eileen's brother had been killed falling out of a train and hit by an express going the other way. So we were in a very poor state, but then suddenly this grey envelope arrived. It was from Ravenscroft's solicitor.' (For clarity's sake, the house move and subsequent court case, held at the High Court in London, happened after the release of *Lair* and the research Herbert conducted in Epping Forest.)

Unfortunately the injustice of Ravenscroft's actions didn't filter through to Herbert's publishers, as Herbert describes: 'My publisher wanted to settle with Ravenscroft, but I just refused. I said no, you can't have a situation where you can't use other people's work for research – as Ravenscroft had done, far more than I had.

'The court case was hard for me. Every day I had to sit there and listen to other people's opinions on my book.'

'We dug up a lot about Ravenscroft, and he was a very dodgy character, to the extent where his publisher came to court as our witness. But my QC said that we couldn't make out the man to be a charlatan, because it would provoke the question, "Why did you use him in the first place?" I said that I didn't know he was a charlatan at the time – so it was catch-22.

'We couldn't say that Ravenscroft was a nutter. And you know, he was in the witness box, and my QC said to him, "Why are you saying these things about Mr Herbert? You don't know him." And he replied (Herbert puts on deep resonant voice), "I do. I've met Herbert. I've seen him. *I've seen him naked in the bath*." Which had some kind of supernatural element to it. And it went on from there: "I saw Herbert on the left side of the cross, while I was on the right." And we were being crucified together.

'The one thing this Ravenscroft had going for him was he had been to Sandhurst. He had been a commander during the Second World War. Captured on his first raid. 'In the end Ravenscroft got nothing. I had to take out 13 lines from my book, which were too close to his. He had taken whole paragraphs from other people's books, but it wasn't his book that was on trial, it was mine. And I had lines about Hitler being in the Hoffberg Museum trembling excitedly, which Ravenscroft had put in his book. I thought he had got that from eye witnesses, but that was from his transcendental meditation.

'The whole experience is still painful, but I've come to accept it. I just have no faith in the law anymore.'

The court case cost Herbert £32,000. Ironically he later became a good friend of Trevor Ravenscroft's son, Raf, who told Herbert his father lost £145,000 on the case, so perhaps rough justice was done in the end.

When Herbert discusses the Ravenscroft incident, he still gets distressed about it, even though it took place nearly two decades ago. To deflect his anger, he relates an uncanny incident connected to the case: 'Going back to Sussex after the case had finished, I was so agitated, I couldn't sit still, so I walked up and down the train. And then the train stopped between stations. I walked up to the train door as it swung open. It was like an invitation to jump. I remember saying to myself, you've got to be fucking joking. You know, it was as if Ravenscroft was sending me these vibes, because he was in to all kinds of weird things.'

> '"Maggie, let go of the door. Let me take you in," he pleaded. She tried to speak... as she lost consciousness. This time Steadman tugged a little more firmly, but still she clung to the doorframe... He pushed his head past her shoulder and his eyes widened in horror as he saw the nail protruding from the back of the hand.'
>
> (The Spear)

The Spear proved to be the culmination of the finer points of Herbert's first four novels. A woman crucified to a door evoked some of the more explicit images in The Rats and The Fog, while attention to detail and quality of research emanated Herbert's meticulous efforts in *The Survivor*.

The Spear became Herbert's greatest departure as far as novel structure was concerned. He planned the first six chapters in advance, which he has never done before or since, always letting the story evolve as it goes along. 'I planned only the first six chapters, because I realised that by then I was becoming bored,' Herbert explains. 'I knew what was going to happen. From then on it became page by page. The story unfolding itself to me as it went along.'

A large house in the countryside plays a large part in the novel, and this has been a constant theme in Herbert's subsequent novels – for example, *The Jonah*, *The Magic Cottage*, *Sepulchre*, *Others*, *Once...* and, most obviously, *Haunted*. As Herbert confesses in *Dark Places*, 'Dwelling places have played a large part in many of my novels ... These old buildings, usually decrepit, always sinister, exist in a special reserve in my imagination, a place of eerie, cobwebbed interiors ... their origins a combination of locations I've visited and my own humble childhood abode – as creepy as anything you'll find in my stories.'

The Spear really showed Herbert's confidence as a writer. Not only did he adopt a new style when 'planning' the book, he refrained from using many tricks he had learned through writing his previous novels. *The Spear* blended history and legend with the modern-day thriller. And even though the court case would smear his name ungraciously across the papers, the critics applauded the book, praising it as his greatest achievement yet, which indeed it was.

With hindsight, we can place *The Spear* into the same envelope of Herbert classics as *The Fog*, *Sepulchre* and *Others*, some of the very best horror fiction of the late 20th century. To be brutal, although the horror genre was perhaps at its height during the 1980s, very little by way of classic genre literature was published. There was, of course, Clive Barker's *Cabal* and *Books of Blood Vols 1-VI* and Robert Bloch's *Psycho II* and F Paul Wilson's brilliant chiller *The Keep*, but little else really excited.

If we look at Herbert's body of work over the past 30 years, we see a writer whose passion for different strains of the horror genre has never diminished. He has constantly teased with something new and different, building a strong body of speculative horror/thriller fiction, as fellow horror/thriller writer Peter James says, 'Jim has an immensely inventive mind. I am constantly surprised by his books.'

The Spear, like *Sepulchre*, is the closest Herbert has ever come to international espionage, along with the threat of religion. As a rule, religion – ancient legends – and the sadism of the Nazis fascinate people. When they are successfully blended together, we find classic horror literature such as the aforementioned F Paul Wilson's *The Keep* or Dennis Wheatley's *They Used Dark Forces*.

Although good transcends evil in *The Spear*, there is a lasting horror, which festers even after reading the book. *The Spear* is much the stronger for its persecution of key Nazi war criminals, with Heinrich Himmler himself deservedly becoming a figure of ridicule. But the quotes from Hitler that appear at the top of many chapters clearly show the crazed plans that threatened the world in the mid-20th century and remind the reader of a real-life horror that will never fade. The atrocity inflicted by the Nazis will always be the most graphic and despicable horror ever recorded in recent history, and even fiction.

There is another kind of lasting horror bequeathed by *The Spear*. Intriguingly, one of the characters from the cut prologue of *The Spear* (concerning Christ's crucifixion) would find a namesake in *Others*, as hero Nick Dismas explains: '"I learned about the name years later when I went back to the convent, when trying to trace my origins ... Dismas was one of the two criminals crucified alongside Christ, the Good Thief, the one who repented before he died and was promised paradise because of it." ' Maybe this was what Ravenscroft was talking about in his crucifixion quote – both he and Herbert being crucified either side of Jesus Christ. Dismas goes on to explain how he received the name: 'I was so ugly, you see, those nuns thought I was being punished for some terrible thing I would do later in life. You get that? Not for some past sin in another life, because nuns don't believe in reincarnation, but for some crime yet to be committed. So they prayed for my soul every day I was with them and long after I left.'

There is no question that Herbert was badly bruised over *The Spear* court case and today, as a consequence, we are deprived of its full-length version, unless we are prepared to pay good money on the book-collecting market. However, regardless of the problems, *The Spear* has a place in classic horror literature that cannot be denied.

'One is always wrong to open a conversation with the devil, for, however he goes about it, he always insists on having the last word.'

(Andre Gide)

CHAPTER TEN

A FORMIDABLE LAIR

'THE RAT HAD BEEN TRAPPED IN THE BASEMENT FOR
FIVE DAYS. IT HAD CRAWLED INTO A DARK CORNER BEHIND A
ROW OF SHELVES TO GIVE BIRTH TO ITS LITTER ...'
(LAIR)

'It is a rare thing for a horror writer to produce a worthy sequel to a successful novel. Unlike thriller or crime writers, the horror writer doesn't build a reputation on an ongoing series of novels centred round one character or situation (good examples in the crime genre being Ed McBain's 87th Precinct novels or Ian Rankin's Rebus books). There has been the odd exception, of course, most notably Robert Bloch's *Psycho* novels (though Norman Bates only starred in one of the three books). For the most part, the horror sequel is a truly taboo area, mainly because the movies have already manipulated, and consequently slaughtered, that particular prize – consider *Friday 13th*, *Halloween* and *A Nightmare on Elm Street*.

As a rule, monster-movie sequels are an embarrassment to the genre – such as the sequels to *The Creature from the Black Lagoon* or Christopher Lee's first *Dracula* movie. Again, there are the exceptions, namely Karloff's *The Bride of Frankenstein* and, for the most part, the *Alien* movies.

Herbert wrote *Lair* in Woodford, near Epping Forest in Essex. The comparison between rural and urban life is very strong in the novel, and in fact is essential to the plot. It is therefore the perfect book to analyse Herbert's feelings of both. He told me, 'I still don't like London. I guess if I still lived and worked there, I could kid myself that I liked it. The more you're out of a place, the more you see into it, and see how dirty and overcrowded it is. And how bad the traffic is. It's a disgusting place, really. The more you're on the outside, the more you can observe that.'

If *The Rats* gave warning of mutant vermin polluting the countryside, then *Lair* was really the fruition of that prophecy, as Herbert explains. 'The purpose of *Lair* was to show that anyone, no matter where they lived, could be victim to this terrible scavenger. The countryside as well as the city was vulnerable.' When the rats move back into London at the end of *Lair*, they have become stronger, like bloody warlords full of the experiences of battles won.

The rats books are the most vicious of all Herbert's novels. The idea of detestable vermin feeding on human beings is a repulsive and very visual horror, though rats don't really scare Herbert nowadays. He has researched into their habits so much, he can be compared to the maniac diver who photographs Great White Sharks from inside a tiny cage submerged in the sea: lunatic behaviour to you and me but commonplace to him.

Domain, the third rat novel, would become the apocalyptic finale to the rats saga (ignoring graphic novel *The City*). With every book in the series, more science fiction elements are brought to bear. Indeed, if Herbert took the series much further, he would run the risk of breaking into a *Terminator* or *Planet of the Apes* scenario (mechanical or even talking rats).

So the rats saga stands as the perfect horror trilogy: *The Rats*, the shocking open-ended beginning; *Lair*, the diverse and powerful sequel; and *Domain*, the grand finale, which in itself brings in many other elements typically Herbert, as we shall observe later.

Lair was highly praised on its release in 1979. The idea of a follow-up to the infamous *The Rats* really caught the public's imagination and the book was so much in demand that libraries were falling over each other to acquire copies. Unfortunately the books were rapidly defaced by ravenous borrowers all keen to read the sequel, which is why a first edition of *Lair* is so scarce. A good copy commands hundreds of pounds on the collector's market today.

Herbert's faithful readers weren't disappointed with the novel: human beings believed they had rid themselves of the mutant rats, but deep in its lair the grotesque, two-headed, slug-like creature remembers the taste of human flesh. And a new reign of terror begins. Epping Forest is the staging ground for mankind's second battle with the bloodthirsty vermin, with a conservation centre providing the human base from where hero Lucas Pender fights the rats.

The book is divided into three parts: Signs, Onslaught, and Lair. They show how Herbert was constantly refining the violence in his novels, gently unfolding the story through location and character introductions in the opening part, then unleashing horror of the most graphic kind in the second part, eventually fighting back to an unsettling outcome in the final part. There is no horror for horror's sake.

> 'The vicar reached the corner of the church… It was the plot in which old Mrs Wilkinson has been laid to rest the day before… Rage made him tear down the steps: what animal would burrow into the earth for the flesh of a human corpse? He reached the edge of the hole and cried out at the sight below.'
>
> (*Lair*)

Herbert can find countless ways to make our skin crawl in his novels, dreaming up different, and extremely painful, ways to kill people or, if dead already, terrible ways to mutilate their corpses.

Perhaps one of the most ghastly but memorable scenes in *Lair* is where a young woman, Jan Wimbush, is brutally attacked by a rat: '... He almost retched when he saw the open wound. The top of her spine was exposed but, fortunately, the rat had burrowed beside it and not into it. She would have been permanently paralysed, if not killed, if he had.'

The real horror of this scene doesn't necessarily come from the violence that befalls Jan Wimbush, but from Herbert's introduction to her. The reader's heart goes out to this quiet, inoffensive girl who considers herself: 'Too thin, neck too long, chin a little too firm. No breasts to speak of. Her hair... too straight and always lank two days after washing.' And so it goes on, eventually leading to the awful conclusion: 'Clinging to her back, weighing down her frail body, was a huge, evil-looking black creature. Its head was buried beneath the hair at the back of the neck, its shoulders jerking spasmodically as it drank in her blood.' If she hated her natural features before the attack, what would Jan think of herself now? Horror indeed.

Lair provides retribution for one scene in *The Rats*, the mutilation of a baby, with the heroic rescue of a child: 'A man stood fully clothed on the roof of his house, a small bundle that must have been a baby cradled in his arms, kicking out at the rats as they scurried up the walls in an effort to reach him.' Although the plight of the man and child is uncertain, we are given the impression they could survive. And if they don't survive, Herbert resists the temptation of describing their fate, using a moral code he had acquired since writing *The Rats* and would enforce throughout his future novels: the protection of children.

Lair is a novel that builds up from rural splendour to battlefield horror. The massacre of innocent people conjures up memories of the countless non-stop death scenes in *The Fog*, while its fast-paced action is reminiscent of *The Rats*. *Lair* shows all the power and punch of Herbert's first two books, but with a refining of style.

Lair is often seen to be the third best book in the rats trilogy. But although nothing will ever rival the infamy of the first book, or the incendiary power of the last, *Lair* is a well-crafted and ingenious novel, employing great character development.

Location plays an important part in all of Herbert's novels. When he gets an idea for a story, he ensures that his research is painstakingly accurate, which sometimes means he finds himself in places he shouldn't be. 'When I'm researching locations, people come out and get a bit aggressive. But when I tell them that I'm a writer, they tend to cool down a bit and want to know what I'm doing. They get quite interested. The trick is to go anywhere you want and not be put off by warnings.' Herbert found himself in such a situation while researching Epping Forest. Even though he lived locally the warden didn't like the idea of a horror writer snooping round, as Herbert explains. 'I contacted the warden and told him that I was going to write a book about Epping Forest and he said, "We really don't like this sort of thing." ' Needless to say the warden wasn't very helpful, which probably explains why his counterpart in the novel is also unsympathetic.

Herbert always gets the geographical information he needs from location research. This way, he can keep his stories firmly placed in the real world, and sometimes acquire extra inspiration as well, as he explains in *Dark Places*. 'These real places, and many, many others, each with its own special ambience of loneliness, have inspired my tales of horror and hauntings, of terrible episodes by day, foul deeds by moonlight, and sinister happenings at any time.'

Discussing the location for *Lair* in *Dark Places*, he says, '[I] used the leafy stillness of Epping Forest, where silence is a precursor of terror ...' It is here that Herbert found his Lair. 'Epping Forest ... provided ... a superb battle ground ... and it was a wonderful (and healthy) place to research. On one of my excursions into the forest I came upon the fire-gutted shell of a huge mansion (Copped Hall) ... I assumed I was trespassing, but my attitude on such hunts is what the hell, they can only shoot you... When eventually I arrived at the manor ruins I knew immediately that I'd found my "Lair".'

It is reasonable to assume that the storyline of *Lair* is largely influenced by the locations Herbert sort and found in the green belt of Epping Forest. The book itself would clearly show that the natural splendour of the countryside was no protection from the horror of the rats.

Subsequent to *Lair*, Herbert's books would bring in many other aspects of horror, through different sub-plots, making them deeper and more intricate, moving away from childhood influences. But, *Lair*, like *The Rats*, *The Fog* and *The Spear*, has a strong military presence. The army nearly always get involved in Herbert's books, as he explains. 'Films like *The Day the Earth Stood Still* and *War of the Worlds* were very much an influence. Even more so *Quatermass*. The army always came in. I always remember in *Quatermass I* there was an army officer – I believe he was called Rowley – and he was always the idiot, always obstructive and didn't know what was going on.'

A similar idea was adopted in the mid-1970s BBC TV series *Dr Who*. Jon Pertwee's Doctor was always confronted by Brigadier Lethbridge Stewart's desire to blow things up. It was through this narrow-minded stupidity that Herbert could expose more of the corruption that lay under the veneer of society. 'I was transcending the horror we knew in this country at the time. I was advancing the genre but still had these early movie influences.'

After *Lair*, and more importantly because of it, Herbert would reject his recurring military cliché and use the man in the street to repair the damage inflicted on society by its blundering government agencies. This is typical of a British writer. As a rule, American writers like to expose their government agencies from the inside out – for example, *The X Files*. An exception would be Stephen King's *Firestarter*, as some American editions included an Author's Note that stipulated the book was a work of fiction and not based on any experiments conducted by the American government. In short, the British have a way of going straight for the jugular, allowing the anger of the ordinary citizen to expose government corruption.

CHAPTER ELEVEN

A New Career
in a New Town

Herbert's initial spur to write a novel was simply the fact that he needed to be creative. Once his novels took off and his new career was well underway, he left advertising to concentrate his full attention on writing, in his new semi-detached house in Woodford.

Now Herbert could devote more time to researching and refining his text. But because of his background in advertising, and his skills as an artist, he decided to take a hand in the way his books looked – specifically the design of the covers. This followed the falling out with his publishers over the appalling cover to *Fluke* (Herbert designed the paperback edition because he hated the hardback cover so much). He started by redesigning all the covers on his backlist so they had a more uniform appearance.

This was the simple part of the task. The rows with his publishers started when Herbert wanted to decorate his covers with gold and silver leaf: '"We're going to have gold and silver foil on the covers," I said, and they didn't like that. Mainly because publishers in those days were just beginning to put foil on the covers of books, and they would either put one or the other on – gold or silver – not both. So I had a disagreement there. But the big problem was putting the foil on a white cover. They hated that idea, because to them, if it was a horror novel, it had to have a black cover.

'I also wanted the foil embossed, whether for hardback or paperback, and *deeply* embossed at that. I was pushing the publisher's printers to the limit, as I used to in advertising. The point was, with a little extra effort, the printers could do it and soon it became practical for all publishers to follow.' (Interestingly, the first Herbert hardback to have the gold and silver leaf on a white cover was *The Jonah*, not his next novel, *The Dark*, which had a traditional black cover.) Suffice to say, Herbert got his way in the end, and a new set of paperbacks was soon released.

Before we move on to Herbert's next novel, it is interesting to note the significance Herbert's decision to become a full-time novelist had on his writing.

Lair would be his second book as a full-time writer and *The Dark* his third. The latter would also be the first to be released in his third marital home, near the South Downs in Sussex. Both, in a way, were sequels to his first two novels: *Lair* was a direct follow-up to *The Rats*, while *The Dark* simply used one of the fundamental ideas from *The Fog* – a gas-type substance that seeps into people and changes their personality (see Chapter Twelve). But this wasn't Herbert clutching a financially rewarding security blanket now that he had gone professional; it was simply a way of taking stock and refining his style. He also wanted to use research and ideas he had left over from the first two novels. Both *Lair* and *The Dark* were further explorations of the territories he had already created. Thereafter came *The Jonah* and *Shrine*, which were as much a departure in content and style as *The Survivor* and *Fluke*. In a way, Herbert could be accused of starting all over again.

CHAPTER TWELVE

DEVIL IN
THE DARK

'I TURNED IN SURPRISE AND LOOKED INTO THE ROOM;
THE OTHERS WERE IN THERE, SOME LYING ON THE FLOOR, SOME
SPRAWLED IN ARMCHAIRS, SOME UPRIGHT, STARING, AS THOUGH
WATCHING ME. BUT THEY WERE ALL DEAD.'

(THE DARK)

Macabre fiction has changed dramatically over the years. The gothic story really became a popular medium after the release of a book of short stories entitled *Tales of the Grotesque and Arabesque* in 1839. Each story is an unrelenting nightmare conjured up by the pen of Edgar Allan Poe, including one of the most influential horror stories ever written, *The Fall of the House of Usher*. It would become the seminal haunted-house story, influencing F Marion Crawford's *The Dead Smile* (from *Uncanny Tales*) and H P Lovecraft's *The Shunned House*.

In Lovecraft's story, Edgar Allan Poe is a man who daily walks past a 'particular house on the eastern side of the street' that has a terrible secret, and he doesn't even know. Lovecraft brought the haunted-house story to your neighbourhood, as did Algernon Blackwood in *The Empty House*: 'Certain houses, like certain persons, manage somehow to proclaim at once their character for evil.' This perception would become a big part of the British horror genre, in both fiction and film (Hammer made it a recurring theme).

If both Poe and Lovecraft directly influenced American writers such as Robert Bloch and Stephen King, then Algernon Blackwood and Dennis Wheatley would influence British horror writers such as James Herbert and Simon Clark.

Wheatley wrote a short story entitled *The Case of the Red-Headed Woman* (from the anthology *Gunman, Gallants and Ghosts*). It was partly based on a flat that he visited in South Kensington, London, which no one would live in because of a succession of suicides that had occurred there. Wheatley's great skill was telling the reader that unspeakable deeds of horror and occult were happening, not just in the town but in the street where you lived – such as in *The Devil Rides Out*, one of the most influential horror/occult novels of the 20th century. Although considered a little too stuffy for contemporary audiences, Wheatley and his occult novels left the door open for future horror writers to build on themes of darkness and depravity.

> 'Nor *was the house the kind you might expect to be haunted… It was a nice road, but ordinary, with that mid-morning suburban quietness that areas only minutes away from the high street have.'*
>
> (*The Dark*)

Although James Herbert would go on to write a contemporary haunted-house novel, entitled quite simply *Haunted*, he built up to this novel through much harder fiction in the guise of *The Dark* and *Sepulchre*. In fact it was *The Dark* that really got the ball rolling with its sinister, untitled, two-and-a-half page introduction.

> '"*I had been told that the house would be empty. The windows were opaque from the glare of the sun and for a brief, uneasy moment, it seemed the house itself was staring out at me…*" '
>
> (*The Dark*)

Herbert would later admit that *The Dark* was a much more oppressive novel than his other books because of the court case over *The Spear*, which occurred while he was writing the book. However, if we look at the acts of violence that appear in novels such as *The Spear* and *Lair*, we witness that Herbert was at his hardest between 1978 and 1980. After that period his novels suddenly become more mystical and thought provoking.

The late 1970s were a difficult time for Herbert. Giving up the day job was easy, but the loss of Eileen's brother and the court case over *The Spear* made things difficult to say the least. But even with two very young children, they managed to move house twice, the second time into a home that Herbert redesigned himself: a 15-roomed mansion with an indoor swimming pool and three acres of garden. As the 1980s dawned, Herbert's life became less chaotic. It is often said that the right house creates harmony in the family, and Hunter's View has certainly done that for the Herbert family. Thankfully it is nothing like the house he created in *The Dark*. 'There were stairs leading down to what must have been the cellar. All I could see was the blackness down there, a deep, almost solid darkness. And it was the darkness more than the corpses that made me flee from the house...'

In 1979, when Herbert was completing *The Dark*, a TV series was broadcast by ITC Entertainment (ITV regions) called *Sapphire and Steel*, starring Joanna Lumley and David McCallum. The duo portrayed time detectives from another dimension, and little is ever explained about them or their background. However, in their second adventure they investigate a derelict railway station, and a ghost that causes a severe break in time. They encounter George Tully, a psychic investigator, and together they hunt the ghost of a soldier from the Great War, Sam Pearce. The story becomes more complex – and this is where it becomes relevant to James Herbert – when another, more malevolent, force is unleashed: a whispering darkness that races from the shadows to feed on human resentment. The soldier was only the catalyst for a greater danger – something both evil and tangible.

> *'One by one she began to count the stars... And one by one, as she silently counted, the stars went out, until only blackness filled the window frame.'*
>
> (*The Dark*)

Sapphire and Steel fed George Tully to the darkness in a desperate bid to finally satiate its hunger and its destructive influence on the real world. However, Herbert's dark is not so easily foiled: born from the evil ritualistic deaths in a quiet suburban house, the dark takes on strength and substance, becoming a physical entity that moves into the city, driving millions of people out of their minds and gaining momentum until it dominates everything. Herbert's dark takes Sapphire and Steel's whispering entity to its ultimate conclusion. Herbert was unaware of the comparison since he never saw the show, but the important point is that both Herbert and P J Hammond (writer of *Sapphire and Steel*) were influenced by the same idea at roughly the same time: the Bible: '... *And God saw the light was good; and God separated the light from the darkness...*' (Genesis 1:4, R.S.V)

The Dark is evocative of *The Fog*, not just in its unceasing body count but in its physical entity. Like the fog, the dark seeps into its victim, poisoning their mind, the subtle difference being that the dark brings out their evil, while the fog simply drives them insane. Herbert is prepared to accept the comparison: 'Halfway through *The Dark* I thought, I've done this – this is *The Fog* with a supernatural aspect to it. And the truth was, there was so much left over from *The Fog*. I thought I had got it out of my system, and then found that I hadn't. So *The Dark* really became *The Fog* in another guise.'

The Dark builds on the horror he had created in *The Fog*, just as *Lair* had built on the horror of *The Rats*. Both *Lair* and *The Dark* allowed reader and critic to understand how far Herbert had come as a horror writer in little over five years. Nothing and nobody was safe. Like the Black Death, Herbert's darkness would lay waste the countryside, corrupting, infesting and destroying everything. *The Dark* also expands on other ideas previously explored in *The Survivor*: the oppressive terror of the tormented spirits lost in the dark echoes the image of the dead air-crash victims calling out to co-pilot David Keller as one babbling ethereal entity.

The Dark, like *The Fog*, is widescreen terror. The collective audience of a football match facing mass death from the dark isn't dissimilar to when the people of Bournemouth walk into the sea to drown, as victims of the fog. Their mass death is also given a personal touch – like Mavis Evers on the beach in *The Fog*, or even poor Jan Wimbush in *Lair*.

The football match is an evening kick-off. The floodlights are on. The crowd is enthused with the buzz of a big game. And then the floodlights go out. The dark moves in, settling over the crowd, entering their minds – some more easily than others. Mass hysteria follows, and a man called Animal picks on an innocent girlfriend of a fellow fan...

> *'When the new generations looked at religion they could only see manmade ritual, manmade hypocrisy. Even history told them the pursuit of God had meant the slaughter and suffering of millions.'*
>
> (*The Dark*)

If we look further into *The Dark*, we see the traditional themes of light and darkness, good and evil. Although these themes had been tackled in Herbert's work before, they more prominent in *The Dark*, with Bible entries heading the three parts of the book.

> *'Have regard for thy covenant; for the dark places of the land are full of the habitations of violence.'*
>
> (Psalms 74:20, R.S.V)

Before *The Dark*, it took the inclusion of priests and psychics in the novels to explore religious beliefs and the theme of good against evil. But through the constant malevolence of the dark, an ongoing exploration naturally occurs throughout the novel, which allows Herbert to make connections when desired. Darkness breeds evil, which spreads quickly in *The Dark*. Main characters Bishop, Edith Metlock, Jessica and Jacob Kulek harbour the path of light but know deep down that good doesn't always transcend evil: the two forces are in eternal struggle.

The Dark has a similar (but still satisfying) conclusion to that of *The Survivor*: a conclusion that leads to the possibility of a further state of awareness and progression of the human soul. Herbert explains how this came about: 'The end of *The Dark* is quite profound – similar to the end of *The Survivor*, but that's me. People going on to this higher state of awareness. That's how I feel. It's what I hope for. I just hope that there is something after death that is profound. A better meaning.'

Herbert first began to *seriously* speculate about spirits through *The Dark*'s psychic investigator, Bishop. And because of the inclusion of a psychic investigator he could blatantly discuss the powers of darkness, such as when Jacob Kulek speculates about the powers of darkness coming from man alone: 'Evil, Mr Bishop. They believed in evil as a power in itself, a power derived from man alone.' Later he discusses the evil of the dark itself, drifting through the blackness of the night; something with no substance but '... solid shapes within it ... forms of men and women whose will it did not just govern, but who embodied the material part of it, those who physically enacted the evil that it was, its earthly force.'

Herbert says he 'buried himself in the work' when it came to writing *The Dark*, being more determined than ever to complete a quality product on account of the distracting Ravenscroft court case. The end result is indeed one of Herbert's most striking novels. Strangely, at roughly the same time, the prince of the occult novels, Dennis Wheatley, died. The typically British James Herbert would prove a worthy successor, but unlike Wheatley, Herbert's voice was classless. He didn't deal with dukes and almost exclusively the upper-middle classes; he would pull everybody on to the same plateau and let them either fight together or die.

Like Wheatley, Herbert has never created a Frankenstein monster. Most, if not all, of his villains are human, or at least were once human. Ironically enough, when we look at the terrible creatures that plague Nick Dismas' nightmare in *Others*, we find that these technically human creatures are good, not bad. It is the clean-cut doctor, with no physical handicap, that is the evil influence. This is where Herbert injects a greater credibility to his stories. It's not just children being something other than what they are that fascinates people, it's also adults who hide either national secrets, or their own psychosis, beneath a cool veneer of professionalism.

The Dark was a difficult novel for Herbert to write, and he chooses not to talk about it at length. But for all this, it stands as a fierce and heavy horror novel that clearly exposes the dark side of Herbert's mind and, it could be argued, is all the more personal because of that. *The Dark* is a nightmare that Herbert chooses not to analyse too much.

CHAPTER THIRTEEN

LOVING THE JONAH

The theme of split, or dual, personalities has been a popular gambit in the horror genre ever since Robert Louis Stevenson awoke from a fever dream in 1885 and wrote *Strange Case of Dr Jekyll and Mr Hyde*, allegedly in three days. Perhaps the ultimate conclusion to this strain of horror, in an everyday sense, would be Robert Bloch's *Psycho*. However, to divide a split personality between twins is yet another, and perhaps more gothic, variation. There have been some indifferent interpretations of this theme over the years, especially in the movies – for example, Hammer's *Twins of Evil*.

But when Herbert wrote *The Jonah* in 1980/1 he had not been influenced by the *Twins of Evil* theme. Although movies have had an impact on Herbert's work much more directly than books, he has never made a study of cult horror movies and is certainly never influenced by them. His general interests lie elsewhere, as he explains: 'I love all kinds of movies, particularly action movies where I can let it all roll over me with no concentration on my part... I loved *Die Hard* and *Reservoir Dogs*.'

On the release of *Others*, some critics – myself included – made comparisons between the novel and the 1932 movie *Freaks*, directed by Tod Browning (director of Bela Lugosi's *Dracula*). It is a deeply disturbing movie, which uses genuine disabled people as circus exhibits. However, Herbert was not conscious of the comparison. 'I didn't know about the film *Freaks* until recently,' he told me. 'I would never have called the book *Freaks* anyway. Certain writers would have done. But then again, I don't want to be politically correct, because I'm very anti that. I just thought calling the book *Others* gave the subject a fair amount of dignity, which is what the book is all about.'

The Jonah is a very subtle novel (Herbert states that *all* his novels contain subtleties, some of which are missed by certain critics). The story involves Jim Kelso, a good undercover cop. When a police driver is killed on an important job, it is the last grisly coincidence Kelso's superiors will tolerate and he is consequently moved to the drugs squad. Nobody wants to work with a Jonah, so Kelso is sent to a sleepy coastal town to locate one of the biggest drug barons operating there. But he is not alone in his task – Customs and Excise send Ellie Shepherd to help. This is one of Herbert's most loved themes: a man and a woman who share intimate moments after initially disliking each other. However, in *The Jonah* the climax of Kelso's relationship with Shepherd deteriorates into a paranormal experience:

'His weight bore down on her and she relished it; she stroked his back, fingers running beneath the thick hair that hung over his neck. Ellie was about to speak when the windows of the caravan began to rattle.'

Not that Kelso and Ellie knew it at the time, but Kelso's dead sister – the one who died before birth – has a jealous hold over her twin brother. That is why he is a Jonah. She has made him so.

The Jonah constantly breaks the Herbert mould. The endless stream of horrendous deaths is no longer present; this is a subtle horror story that even lacks the thrill of the chase. But *The Jonah* is by no means a lesser work for this, indeed, to me, it is one of his best books, building up the suspense and horror to its logical and climatic finale.

In Chapter Three, I mentioned the book's sibling rivalry element, but what of its other aspects? *The Jonah* is one of those peculiar novels that fall into that bizarre category 'horror/thriller', which is often associated with Herbert's novels nowadays, and rightly so with regard to *The Jonah*, *Domain*, *Sepulchre* and *'48*.

Horror is almost the sub-theme in *The Jonah*. It rears its head from time to time but it is by no means the driving force: this belongs to drug smuggling and the personal plight of Jim Kelso. When Kelso is taken prisoner by a drugs baron and his entourage, he is injected with a dangerously high level of drugs, and it is in this limbo that he witnesses his birth and that of his dead twin sister.

This is not to say that *The Jonah* is an anti-drugs novel. Although the anti-drugs theme is present in the novel, it could have had a stronger emphasis. Herbert would of course argue that he doesn't like to preach to his audience, but presenting a tougher line on drugs in the book would have appeased some of *The Jonah*'s critics, who stated that the novel is a little too one-dimensional in terms of its characterisations.

The Jonah isn't one of Herbert's personal favourites, as he explains. 'I thought the end of *The Jonah* was particularly weak. Nothing specific, just a general dissatisfaction. I'm always dissatisfied with my books anyway, but for some reason I felt the end of *The Jonah* wasn't good enough.' I totally disagree with this statement. In fact I find the conclusion to *Haunted* much weaker.

On the release of *Sepulchre*, Herbert admitted that he didn't like the characters in the book. 'I didn't like the characters much, they didn't have many redeeming features, but I did like the book. It was very dark.' There are similarities between *The Jonah* and *Sepulchre*, especially in the main characters Jim Kelso and Liam Halloran. Both are crack marksmen – Kelso for the police, Halloran for security agency Achilles Shield. And although both men appear radically different aside from this, they each hide their own individual dark side, which eventually shapes their destinies. Herbert states: 'I've always set out to write quality books. And I've always portrayed myself as a serious writer. I use horror because that is the genre I naturally use. And I defend the genre because of this.'

Horror can take many different forms, and the thriller genre holds its own unique chamber of terror through assassination, torture and cold-blooded murder. However, Herbert blends horror and the supernatural in to this cauldron of everyday murder.

Herbert had a dilemma when writing *The Jonah*. How was he going to smuggle drugs into the country? 'I wanted to find a way of smuggling drugs into the country,' he explains in *Dark Places*. 'Yes, really. A fail-proof, feasible way … I consulted a map and decided the best area for such illegal activities was the coastline along Suffolk, with its deserted beaches and waterways …'

Herbert chose Aldeburgh, a small, quiet fishing town on the east coast, as his setting for *The Jonah*. The terrain was haunting – flat and barren – the perfect setting for a horror/thriller. But there was more, as he continues: '… the low mist that would drift in from the sea and make its spectral way along the channels. Ideal cover for boats making covert journeys.' After just one visit to Aldeburgh, Herbert knew the location was perfect, allowing the story to unfold further in his mind. But is location the most important tool to Herbert? 'Places are the backdrops, the sets, even the first inspiration of my novels,' he explains in *Dark Places*. 'Sometimes a brief sighting can linger and grow into something that won't go away – something you *have* to write about … The imagination can take something real, something tangible, and use it to make new worlds of possibility …'

Unlike *The Dark*, *The Jonah* is a stark and psychological novel, which has its feet planted firmly in reality. In fact, the only fantastic horror in the book comes from the physical manifestation of Kelso's dead sister near the end. The rest could be culled from real-life scenarios, including the giant flood that wipes out the town as the book builds to its climax. Horror fans don't favour *The Jonah*, probably because the horror is played down. But although the book is more thriller-like, it fails to make the grade in that genre because of its large supernatural element, so it would be best to classify it as a maverick horror novel, not unlike *Fluke*.

One of the more personal episodes in the novel is where a judge goes walking along the beach at night. He has been warned not to do so because of flood warnings, but nevertheless, the self-opinionated judge knows best and he decides to go for his walk. Obviously he comes unstuck and is one of the first victims of the flood (after Herbert's brush with the legal system over *The Spear*, he wanted to show that a judge wasn't infallible). 'The judge could have run, but it would have done him no good ... He sank to his knees and rolled himself into a ball. He had never been so terrified in his life ... the water pounded over him and he was swept along with the torrent, he knew that he had been wrong to walk along the beach that night.'

The Jonah deals with an area of science still filled with speculation: that of the pre-birth death of a twin and how the surviving foetus harnesses the dying spirit and encompasses the driving force of two. It is a book that continuously holds back, allowing the reader to look between the lines and do their own speculating. And it is here that the horror becomes complete, if it is desired. For once, Herbert gave us more from less, and he didn't really like it.

CHAPTER FOURTEEN

AN UNHALLOWED SHRINE

When writing *Shrine*, Herbert was happily living in the countryside and the nearby village served as a model for the ficticious village in the novel. Herbert also took the hardcover photograph of a young girl standing in a field beneath an old, twisted and dying oak tree with a church (his local church) and graveyard in the background. He used a friend's seven-year-old daughter, dressed in Communion white, for the shot and his own older daughter as comparison for the child. Halfway through taking the photograph, the wife of the field owner came along and demanded to know what he was doing. Herbert explained and told the woman he had obtained permission to use the field. Still disgruntled, she left. Years later Herbert heard another version of the event, in which he was apparently photographing nude women lying on the gravestones. It made Herbert chuckle but it reveals how incidents can be seriously or mischievously distorted.

Rock star Alice Cooper has confessed that the name of his original band – also called Alice Cooper – didn't come from a Ouija board reading (as he claimed in the 1970s) but from the idea of a sweet little girl with her hands clasped behind her back. She has an innocent little face, a cheeky little smile, and nobody is aware that she holds a hatchet behind her back and is going to take a swing at you when you're not looking.

Shrine concerns a sweet little girl called Alice. She is a deaf mute but manages to say a few words to Brighton-based reporter Gerry Fenn. Nobody believes Fenn, not even the local priest, but it isn't very long before Fenn finds himself part of the biggest scoop since the Resurrection: Alice can speak and hear again. Not only that, but she has become the catalyst for miracles; the sick are cured, the faithless reaffirmed. And when everybody is taken in, another corrupt force takes over – the real instigator of the so-called miracles. The Catholic faith is turned inside out, but it will take more than a priest to exorcise this devil.

Herbert conceived the idea of *Shrine* through location research, as he explains in *Dark Places*. 'In 1982 I found... an ancient church; a cemetery, a dying, gnarled and twisted oak tree. To these I added a fourth component: a young innocent girl.' As he observes in the book, 'There are no such things as ghosts, only good ghost stories.' If *Shrine* must fall within any sub-genre of horror, then it would be possession, ranking alongside novels such as *The Omen* and *The Exorcist*. However, *Shrine* offers much more fertile soil than either of its predecessors. Perhaps some of this would be lost in a movie version, unless directed by somebody like Ken Russell: a girl floating in the air, her once pure white dress now soaked in blood and dripping over the faces of her smiling disciples.

Shrine is a book of images – some subtle, others not. When you feel an image from the movie *Don't Look Now*, you find that Gerry Fenn acknowledges the fact. When you feel an image from a Grimm Brothers fairy tale, Herbert starts the very next chapter with a quote from their story, *The Juniper Tree*. Herbert is constantly ahead of the game. He wanted to show that we were all brought up on dark and gruesome fairy stories, and that the horror writers of today are doing nothing different to the brothers Grimm (et al); it is only the style that has changed (a theme Herbert would extend in *Once...*).

The novel also contains an interesting comparison to *The Survivor*. In *Shrine* ordinary villagers cash in on what appears to be their good fortune of having the immaculate conception on their doorstep – an image not dissimilar to the locals of Eton selling popcorn after the air crash. However, in *Shrine* Herbert makes a more passionate attack on the Catholic faith. When a devine spirit is said to be present at a Catholic church, the miracle is used to bring people to the faith almost like an advertising campaign, so even the Church shows its own corruption (Robert Heinlein did this to great effect in *Stranger in a Strange Land*).

Shrine is openly satirical, but the satire comes from a distorted form of irony: at last a miracle is happening on our own doorstep, and this one is no fake. But greed and corruption from every conceivable source blows the goodness away – if it was ever there in the first place. Maybe it was always the power of the devil, gathering more souls from his hell on earth. Then comes the undiluted red-blooded horror, shattering the Catholic faith and betraying the corruptible. Even the innocent must die in order to enjoy love everlasting.

Shrine breaks down dominions in the modern world – those built on tradition and/or faith. Herbert's faith is echoed strongly in his novels, as he explains in *Dark Places*. 'Churches have played a significant part in my life. I was brought up as a Roman Catholic and it was inside a church that I first learned of the supernatural. I was informed of the world of spirits, of saints, and of the Supreme Being. I learned of the constant struggle between God and the Devil ... Between Good and Evil.' Although he never preaches Catholicism in his books, he does explore it, writing from an informed point of view. If priests constantly lose and regain their faith in his novels, it is not necessarily his fault. The characters must act realistically according to their location, age and circumstances (and the revelations of the story Herbert places them in).

Of all Herbert's books, *Shrine* upsets the most people – mainly practising Catholics – and you get the feeling Herbert did this deliberately. There is an uneasiness that stems from the subtext of *Shrine*, something that works on the subconscious as explicitly as *The Exorcist*. But where *The Exorcist* brings unease by way of a demon entering a young girl, *Shrine* does the reverse. It works through the naivety of the people who are misled and corrupted (some as practising Catholics who should know better) like lambs to the slaughter. The possessed girl is almost forgotten during the frenzy. To take this one step further, it is not just the general public that behave inappropriately, but also the media – both TV and the press. Indeed the novel's hero is a press reporter.

But what of Herbert's female leads?

'At thirty-three ... She still had the trim figure of a girl in her twenties. Her dark hair was long, fluffed away from her face in loose curls, and her deep brown eyes could gain a man's attention across any crowded room on any enchanted evening.'

In *Shrine*, Sue Gates (described above) is intelligent and just a little streetwise. A divorcee with one son she doesn't see enough, she loves (some days more than others) newsman Fenn, but she's also grown to love her own independence.

Many of Herbert's female characters are ordinary, practical people – that's how they survive tricky situations, from scavenger rats to deranged vicars. As men and women are brought together in Herbert's novels, they learn to live with each other, share their lives together. Sometimes, if it wasn't for the extreme situations they find themselves in, the characters wouldn't get on with each other in the first place, but disasters have a way of breaking down barriers.

When Sue Gates has enough of her husband's infidelities she divorces him, breaking a law of the church she loved: '"I'm a Catholic – at least I used to be. I'm not sure if I still am; the Catholic church doesn't actually approve of divorce." ' But her own life and that of her son are more important than a blind following of her faith. However, as the story unfolds, we witness how others – even a Catholic priest – have doubted their own faith, perhaps with less reason than Sue Gates.

Then the miracles begin to happen and people have their faith reaffirmed. When the horror occurs and their faith is betrayed, many gain solace from witnessing the supernatural – the possession of an innocent child. That alone rekindles the flame of faith in their hearts, because if the power of darkness was truly behind the miraculous things they witness, then the opposite must still exist – goodness and light. And good must transcend evil.

Herbert never preaches Catholicism in his books, but he does explore it. He is a Catholic himself and his insights into the faith are written from an informed point a view. If priests constantly lose and regain their faith in his novels, it is not necessarily his fault. The characters must act according to their location, age and circumstances.

Shrine is arguably Herbert's most religious novel, but it could also be said that *Shrine* is a homage to the fairy tale, quoting from classic children's literature such as *The Secret Garden*, *The Little Mermaid*, *The Adventures of Tom Bombadil*, *Rumplestiltsken* and *The Juniper Tree*. The novel's central character, the possessed girl Alice, even has a fairy-tale name (*Alice's Adventures in Wonderland*, *Alice Through the Looking Glass*). But if we look at the inclusion of *Rumplestiltsken* and *The Juniper Tree*, we can clearly see where Herbert's fairy tale lives: in the same world as the Brothers Grimm.

Born in Hanau, Germany, in the late 1700s Jacob and Wilhelm Grimm devoted a life's work of research into the folklore of their country, listening to and writing from legends and stories as they heard them in the cottages of peasants and village inns, as well as uncovering material in medieval manuscripts. Unfortunately some of their work is not widely published today because it is regarded as too cruel for young readers, a good example being *The Juniper Tree*, which concerns a boy who is chopped up by his mother, thrown into a pot and cooked with the stew.

Herbert's exploration of fairy tale in *Shrine* doesn't just form part of the subtext; it's right up front, even heading each individual chapter. Indeed the magic of the fairy tale is common to many of his novels. In his preface to *The Magic Cottage*, he speaks directly to the reader when discussing magic. 'Maybe – probably – you don't believe. Maybe you half believe. Or maybe you want to believe.' Setting the scene with this line, Herbert could have started *The Magic Cottage* with the line 'Once upon a time ...' But even he would challenge this cliché in *Once ...* with 'Once ... upon ... a ... death...'

Herbert sees it as his job to make you believe in the most horrific fairy tales, carrying on in the tradition laid down by the likes of the Brothers Grimm and Lewis Carroll, but is this what people are looking for in his novels? *Shrine* was a best-seller, but many of his more horrific novels have outsold it over the years.

Gerry Fenn and Sue Gates, along with Sue's son Ben, are brought closer together through their own personal fairy tale. Whether they ever become a family at the end of *Shrine* is impossible to tell – for Herbert to go as far as the fairy-tale ending 'And they lived happily ever after' is not his style. Suffice to say, the characters are stronger and more open to each other after the chaos they have been put through, so it is truly up to the reader to decide their fate. However, it is worth noting that Herbert hasn't always opted for the happy ending.

> 'The bedclothes lay loose and rumpled around her ankles, and her thin legs were stretched and trembling. "... aye good Thomas, fill me with thy seed..." Her pelvis jerked spasmodically, her cotton nightdress thrown high upon her chest.'
>
> (Shrine)

When an ancient evil attacks Alice in her sleep, we witness a scene that works in a similar way to Regan's possession in *The Exorcist*. However, Herbert shows a little more restraint than William Peter Blatty in his description of the girl's macabre rape. Indeed, what

Alice says underplays the rape. She is not swearing and spitting, but languishing and inviting her possession (albeit an ancient spirit using her tongue): '"... *disperse thyself into me ... more filling than e'er it was ...*" ' before speaking sacrilege '"... *cursed* Mary... *Cursed* MARY..." ' A nun, Mother Marie-Claire, is outside the bedroom door listening to all this and enters the room to see what is going on. She finds the child asleep and a black cat suckling on Alice's third nipple.

Folklore and fairy tales walk hand in hand, both real and fantastical. Many stories, like those of the Brothers Grimm, have their source in historical legends, such as the ancient belief of witchcraft. The third nipple confirms to any man of God that the person inflicted with the obscenity is a witch, and consequently should be executed as such. Men like Matthew Hopkins, self-proclaimed Witchfinder General of East Anglia during the English civil war, would track down and sentence those with such a mark of Satan. It is legends such as this that clearly show the barbarism and religious mania within history.

Twelve years after writing *Shrine*, Herbert would again explore the dark secrets of Britain's bloodthirsty past in *The Ghosts of Sleath*, where a peaceful village harbours its own corruption. An exploration into the parish records uncovers its brutal history, as it does in *Shrine*. In fact, while investigating the location in *Shrine* Herbert found the last two witches to be burned at the stake in Britain had been hiding in the very church where he was conducting his research.

CHAPTER FIFTEEN

VERMIN'S DOMAIN

TIME: 12:37.
DAY: TUESDAY.
MONTH: JUNE.
YEAR: THE NOT TOO DISTANT FUTURE...
PLACE: LONDON.'
(DOMAIN)

Many people consider Herbert's third rats novel, *Domain*, to be the best. Herbert explains his rationale behind the rats saga. 'This is all *post-rationale*, of course, as most rationalisation tends to be. I've always written by instinct, but the years have given me the objectivity to look back on my earlier novels and the thought process (whether conscious or subconscious) behind them.

'*The Rats* was not only a *critique* of our governing bodies, who have successfully allowed our inner cities to rot, but also a cry against self-seeking authority itself. The ministries and scientists who experiment with nuclear explosions, and endanger the planet and the human race, the leaders and politicians who feather their own nests. Those themes, if you like: protests against faceless bureaucracy and authority, negligence, and environmental damage. For me, *Domain* validated the previous two rats novels because it reinforced all the points already mentioned, and its ending contained two great ironies. The leaders and politicians, the elite of society, had their very own nuclear shelters beneath the city – ordinary members of the public had no access – but they were destroyed by the monsters of their own creation; an indication that the rats were still mutating, now into human-like embryos, suggesting that our evolutionary chain might be linked.

'Naturally, the rats themselves were a great vehicle for horror and the existence of the trilogy itself was because that horror continued – it was never truly beaten. Just as a real-life horror and evil are a continuum.'

The Rats and *Lair* placed the horror of mutant vermin squarely in a world the reader could identify with. However, in order for the rats to continue their evolutionary destiny, they had to become the dominant creatures. City and countryside together must be their domain, with man only a secondary being on the evolutionary scale – hence *Domain*.

So man blows himself up in nuclear holocaust, the final farewell. And the rats begin to move in. What better than bloodthirsty, mutant scavengers?

The idea of a secondary race becoming the dominant species on a planet is similar in theme to the movie based on Pierre Boulle's novel, *La Planete des Singes*, translated into English as *Monkey Planet* (aka *Planet of the Apes*): Man blows himself up and the apes take over. However, Hollywood only showed the final genesis of the apes, while Boulle missed the allegory completely, setting the whole novel on another planet. Herbert wouldn't do either. He takes us through three distinct stages in the rats' development before they achieve dominance on earth (in his graphic novel, *The City*, the end product is part man, part rat).

The sci-fi/horror genre has many examples of potential future societies, books such as H G Wells's *The Sleeper Wakes* and *The Shape of Things to Come* being the forerunners to Aldous Huxley's *Brave New World* and George Orwell's *Nineteen Eighty Four*. Other, more fantastic, conclusions include Wyndham's *Day of the Triffids* and Richard Matheson's vampire world *I Am Legend*.

The images of a world after nuclear holocaust have been prevalent in more films than need to be mentioned here, but very few screenwriters have created breathless chase stories through a holocaust. *Domain* is so exciting, you actually forget you're reading the culmination of the rats trilogy until the creatures come scurrying out of every nook and cranny, making the already unbearable tension more exhausting.

With *Domain*, Herbert was at the height of his storytelling ability. He doesn't just transport you to an apocalypse, he makes you live it and try to escape from it as well. Then, just when you think you have, the rats come charging out at you.

I have already discussed the power of using a fantastic image in juxtaposition to an everyday one. But Herbert's strength in *Domain* comes from something he wasn't allowed to research. 'I remember when I was researching *Domain*, they wouldn't let me go to the underground telecom offices at the back of High Holborn. I wrote to them and said that I knew where it was, behind a brick wall with barbed wire on the top with observation cameras. It's meant to be just a telephone exchange and it has all this security? Anyway, they wrote back to me and said that I couldn't go there because it wasn't being used anymore. So I replied saying that if wasn't being used anymore, I wouldn't be in anybody's way. I'd just take a quick look around. They wrote back with another excuse and I wrote back to them again. Eventually they simply said, "This is a definite NO." '

Herbert has discovered many locked doorways and dark passageways beneath London, as he explains in *Dark Places*. 'Walk along the Embankment some time and take note of the various grilles along the pavement. These are air ventilators that serve the network (tunnels and secret underground railways). On the corner of Westminster Bridge is Queen Boadicea's statue. Look at its base and wonder why there should be a discreet locked door set in the stonework. This is just another entrance to the tunnels below.'

Herbert is very tenacious when researching his novels, approaching official bodies and uncovering whatever information he can. It's a wonder he hasn't been reprimanded for his trouble.

'I've never been threatened by a government department. Not yet. And I find that a bit disappointing,' he says.

The first chapter of *Domain* is typical Herbert, detailing individual deaths after the detonation of five nuclear bombs. As a preface, the rats scurry through their dark, peaceful world, listening to the torment of mankind's self-inflicted annihilation above. Then they wait for their moment.

The prologue and first chapter set the scene. From chapter two we are introduced to the novel's hero, Culver, and a man he has saved from the effects of the explosions, Alex Dealey, who unfortunately looked into the white flash of the first explosion and was consequently blinded. However, Dealey can now save Culver's life. He knows where to find sanctuary – a bunker – but they only have half an hour to get there before the fallout settles. It is now a race against time and they must selfishly pass the hundreds of people walking around London (all of them as good as dead now) in order to get there: *to the underground telephone exchange behind Chancery Lane tube station.*

'"*Don't look* at the man leaning against the wall vomiting black blood. Help one and you had to help another. Help another and you had to help everybody," ' Dealey tells Culver. *Domain* is a book about individual survival, clearly showing the selfishness of the 'powers that be' in times of crisis, as they create a means of survival for themselves and ignore the millions of innocent people also affected. It is animal instinct, as Herbert would mirror in his short story, *Extinct*, where an elephant refuses to help a caged tiger when escaping a zoo. 'I did not stop when a caged tiger pleaded with me to bring him food, for my concern was for my own and the tiger had never been friend to the elephant. To go near would risk those wicked claws.'

Herbert further expands on the idea of self-preservation for the 'elite' in *Dark Places*. 'As well as providing safe havens from nuclear attack, the tunnels are also escape routes out of London. Not for the masses, you understand, not you and me, but for the politicians and the elite (those with the right connections) of our society.'

Herbert *is* anti-establishment, and this is clearly apparent in *Domain*. Culver is allowed to be saved by his chance meeting with Dealey – a man with the right connections – but Culver knows that under any other circumstances he would have been left outside to vomit black blood. 'Resentment for the government but sympathy for the squaddie, that was the important analogy in *Domain*,' says Herbert. 'Because the squaddie is the poor sod who has to do the dirty work. *Domain*, like *The Rats*, was full of anger at the system and that's what most of my books are about, because we can't beat it – it's only there for itself. The whole rats trilogy, the energy of it says a lot about what I think about the system.'

The story doesn't degenerate because of this. There is a conflict of emotions present, as Culver falls victim to the infection of minor radiation sickness and is consequently saved by the privileged few that he resents. However, there is chemistry between Culver and Kate, the girl who nurses him back to health. She tolerates the steely personality of her boss, Dr Clare Reynolds, which leaves her vulnerable, and she confides her resentment to Culver, showing that even among the elite there are tensions.

Toward the end of the first part of *Domain*, Advent, the relationship between Kate and Culver is a relaxed one. But it must grow stronger very quickly ... as soon as the rats strike.

A look at Herbert's work in comparison with other respected works in science fiction, not just horror, reveals some interesting results; small things that may appear insignificant to the plot but that explain more about the writer and the greater appeal and validity of his books. For example, in the bunker in *Domain*, the survivors of the human race talk about rebuilding their society in a similar way to Wyndham's characters in *Day of the Triffids*. Then there's the novel's political discussion among the government officials, which mirrors the frustrations of the US government in Robert Heinlein's *The Puppet Masters*. Both books were released in the same year and were written by writers Herbert admires. The point is, although Herbert didn't intentionally copy the styles of Wyndham and Heinlein, he did emanate them in later life, along with his other childhood influences.

Clearly, in terms of horror, the rats within *Domain* have a lesser influence than in previous novels, almost playing second fiddle to the holocaust. But they are still a trump card up Herbert's sleeve and have made more than one cameo appearance since. They would resurface again in '48. 'I took pleasure in watching the rats burn... their thin screams tore through the darkness, and their sharp, ugly snouts stretched and their jaws yawned, exposing razor teeth and their clawed limbs quivered until they crisped and flamed and became twisted, blackened stumps.' Herbert would also use them briefly in *Creed*, even poking fun at himself and his vermin friends: '... rats could easily get in through the rafters of these old buildings. Didn't he read somewhere that rats were taking over the city? Good idea for a book there. Somebody ought to do it.'

Taking this into consideration, will Herbert ever write another rats novel? In 1994 he told me, 'When I finished *Domain* I thought, it hasn't finished yet, there's more to say. I can't help it.' *The City* is often thought to be Herbert's fourth rats novel, but it isn't, as Herbert went on to explain. 'I would like to write the novel of *The City*, but not yet – maybe in about ten years. The reason being is that after *Domain* there was so much research left over, I could write another rats novel.' However, when I asked Herbert the same question five years later, he replied, 'I don't think I will write another one. I have so many ideas. I don't think that I would want to go back and do it again ... I had intended *Domain* to be the final rats story. I don't want to write any more.'

Quite simply, *Domain* has proved to be the breathless and brutal conclusion to Herbert's rats novels. Any further exploration into the idea would be as ludicrous as the movie *Battle of the Planet of the Apes* (in comparison to the chilling first ape movie). 'The great irony in *Domain*', says Herbert, 'is when the embryonic rats are discovered. They resemble the embryo of man. So what I was saying there was: we could very easily have been like the rats, genetically, but somewhere along the line, we divided.' And there the science fiction takes over from the horror.

Personally, I feel that it would be a mistake for Herbert to return to the rats in any major way. The first novel was essentially the right thing at the right time, and although it has passed in to the horror hall of fame, it is neither one of Herbert's most thought-provoking novels nor well-written works. *Lair* was an interesting concept, as a comparison between urban and rural, but it has been largely forgotten today. It is only *Domain* that has all the ingredients of a lasting horror/thriller, with subtext themes that are taken seriously amid the gore.

Having written horror for 30 years, Herbert has outgrown the rats and moved on. This was clearly obvious shortly after *Domain* with *Sepulchre*, one of his very best novels, and was then further enhanced with *The Ghosts of Sleath*, *Others* and *Once...* According to novelist Peter James, 'The original *Rats* was a triumph, and subsequently he has written on much bigger and broader canvases. I think it is hard for any writer to go "back". Better to let him continue to roll with his imagination.'

Although Herbert was flying high as a horror writer, what was happening in his personal life at this time? After ridding themselves of the Ravenscroft court case, the Herbert family settled down to life in their new country house, and soon, on Halloween 1984, Eileen was in hospital, about to give birth to their third child, Casey. Herbert recalls the event: 'It was about 9 o' clock that I raced back to the hospital at Cuckford to be with Eileen for the birth. There was a low-lying mist everywhere. And as I was racing there, I saw all these children with little lanterns, dressed up as witches in the villages, and that's where I got the idea for my first short story (*Hallowe'en's Child*).'

Herbert has never been one for short stories, and has only written a handful – *They Don't Like Us* being his second and *Extinct* his third. 'I simply don't have the time to do it,' he comments.

Although Casey was born on 31 October, she was no horror story (unlike *Hallowe'en's Child*), and with her the Herbert family was complete. But with contentment comes unrest, and the ever-inspired James Herbert had more plans.

CHAPTER SIXTEEN

MOON
INFLUENCE

All good nightmares come late at night, when a silvery spectral moon rides high in the sky, spilling its intoxicating influence into many a slumbering household, influencing the susceptible.

Although Herbert never relies on clichés, he loves to abuse them, creating his own individual images. The silvery light of a full moon is a time-honoured theme that runs through many gothic/horror novels. Herbert has used the influence of the moon many times, so it is only natural that he should write a whole novel about its power. However, because the moon does have such a commanding presence in some of his stories, he would be dissatisfied with the finished product because the imagery was somehow underplayed and so too were many of his fans. *Moon* is probably his weakest novel.

In *Creed*, Herbert uses the moon to illuminate a Nosferatu-like character, and clearly show the influence early gothic movies have on him: 'The bald dome of a head emerged first, cast by the moonlight as dull ivory … The freak … its hands, with their extraordinary long fingers and nails, were visible; white and skeletal ... nasty-looking things. Its huge eyes were almost luminous, as though moonrays reflected on something behind them ...' Remember, it was the 1931 movie version of *Dracula* that prompted him to write *The Rats*, and his reminiscences about visiting cinemas to see horror films as a child are vivid.

Another reason why Herbert would use the moon in his novels is simply because he is interested in ancient civilisations and their customs and beliefs. For many, the moon has strong religious connotations – such as the Sumerian culture, which Herbert describes in the opening vignette to *Sepulchre*. In Sumerian theocracy the moon was called Sin and, along with the sun (Shamash), gave sanctuary to the evil god Bel. It is this kind of information that gives Herbert pause for thought.

'He could sense only a white, shimmering thing, a taunting spectre. It faded, gradually overwhelmed by the moonlight flooding the room.'

(*Moon*)

I have already explored the comparisons between *Moon* and the folklore of London's East End (see Chapter One) and discussed the importance of children in Herbert's novels. It is now important to look at other another serious theme within *Moon*: the power of location. And building from this, earth power, and how people tune into their own psychic abilities: '"The nearest I can get is to say it's like some eerie, hidden power – maybe that's too strong a word, too definite. It's so insubstantial, so unreal, it could be my imagination. I just sense there's something there that's never been explored. Perhaps that's common to all of us, though." '

Moon is a book about a man called Childes, who has fled to an island to escape from his past: not only a broken marriage but his own psychic abilities. However, he can not escape the power of those 'sightings'.

When Childes settles on the island, he quickly finds himself in another relationship with Amy. Their relationship demands honesty and her perception leads him into a confrontation with his own sixth sense, allowing him to overcome the denial of such a special ability: 'She frowned. "I'm not so sure. There's a corner of you I've never managed to reach." "Amy, without sounding too self-absorbed, I often feel there's a point inside me that even *I* can't reach. There's an element in me – I don't know what the hell it is – that I can't explain, a factor that's tucked away in the shadows … sleeping …'

It is here that we witness the plight of some of Herbert's anti-heroes, like Kelso in *The Jonah,* or David Ash in both *Haunted* and *The Ghosts of Sleath*. There is a personal fight with a darker, more hidden side of the mind and its power. And it is often in the mind that the fight between good and evil begins.

To give further clarity to this point, let us look at *Others.* The main character, Nick Dismas, is disabled and he has a constant battle with the things other people take for granted. He has to endure prejudice because of the way he looks, even though he is an intelligent man. But there is a darker side to him; something from his past, something that persists. Fortunately there is the possibility of redemption, even for Dismas. He can answer the call of the others, those poor wretched beings that cry out to him in his psychic dreams pleading for help. And Dismas can fall in love too; a love that is distanced by his ability to reach out to the others, but that nevertheless exists solely because they do. Were it not for his investigation to find the others, he would never have found future girlfriend Constance Bell.

In *Moon,* Childes feels a similar thing. He finds that his psychic ability distances him in his constantly growing relationship with Amy. And she, like Constance Bell, is a woman of strength and courage. In fact, many of Herbert's female characters find a hidden strength that pulls a story to its natural conclusion, while the men, though important to the outcome, are sometimes slightly clueless, like Mike in *The Magic Cottage*.

Another interesting aspect of *Moon* is the sense of companionship and belief instilled by Amy, a theme that is stronger in *Moon* than a more obvious choice like *The Magic Cottage* (Childes and Amy struggle for love and understanding, whereas Mike and Midge are already there). It is perhaps through this uplifting relationship that the horror in *Moon* is allowed to be a little more graphic, evocative of Herbert's very early work.

Moon displays a fair amount of hideous imagery, but its paranormal theme works in juxtaposition to this, diluting some of the horror and adding a sense of mystery to the overall story. The mutilated bodies and the insertion of moonstones inside the dead are akin to the hallmarks of ritualistic sacrifice. There's also the power that lies dormant in the subtext of the novel: the island itself.

In order to research his location for *Moon*, Herbert moved to the Channel Islands for a couple of years: 'I moved over in 1984, came back in 1986. I spent one year in Guernsey and one year in Jersey. My reason was that I was writing a book about an island – *Moon* – and because I research thoroughly, I moved off to an island. Also, I needed to get away from interruptions.' It is mainly due to Herbert's meticulous research of the islands that many rural images are captured in the novel, even in the briefest moment of text. A number of islands are reputed to hold earth powers, largely because they have great areas of unspoilt terrain. The Isle of Wight is another such place, full of ghostly sightings, strange lights, portents hovering in the night, and mystical voices emanating from still waters – all very Herbert in atmosphere.

Herbert would take all this imagery to its extreme in *Portent*, a book that deals almost exclusively with earth power, but *Moon* only touches on psychic/earth power themes, without taking them too far. Perhaps this explains why Herbert isn't too fond of the book. He has explored all its themes more satisfactorily since: gothic influence in *Haunted* and *The Ghosts of Sleath*; ritualistic influence in *The Magic Cottage* and *Sepulchre*; earth power in *Portent*; and psychic ability in *The Magic Cottage, Sepulchre, Haunted, Portent, The Ghosts of Sleath* and *Others*. Quite simply, *Moon* is a lesser work. It would be the last book Herbert published under NEL, thereafter publishing his work under Hodder & Stoughton.

With *Moon* Herbert anticipated the moods of his next two novels. The backdrop of gentle countryside, with its calming influence, is very similar to the rural splendour captured in *The Magic Cottage*, while the nasty mutilations (influenced by themes of the black mass) are a precursor to the atrocities perpetrated in *Sepulchre*.

After *Moon*, Herbert suddenly became established, in the eyes of the critics and public alike. And although the ride forward wouldn't be any easier than previously, *Moon* gave Herbert a newborn confidence. Cynics may say that this was because Herbert could now afford to be a full-time writer for the rest of his life. That may be so, but having just achieved the milestone of ten best-sellers, out of ten published novels, he was becoming an old hand at the horror-writing game. Obviously the two-year break in the Channel Islands did him a lot of good, allowing him to assess his work thus far.

'And Childes wondered where the newly-accepted power would lead him...'

(*Moon*)

CHAPTER SEVENTEEN

A DREAM HOME?

'... BE WARNED: THIS IS NO FAIRY TALE ...'
(THE MAGIC COTTAGE)

One of Herbert's most popular novels is *The Magic Cottage*, which became one of the top-ten selling paperbacks of the 1980s. (Herbert was originally going to call the novel *The Enchanted Cottage*, but he remembered there was an old black and white film with that name.)

The book is often regarded as one for the incurable romantic female, telling the story of a loving couple who find their dream home, which works as an extension of their love and a springboard for future success in their professional careers. *The Magic Cottage* is enchanting from the outset, inviting the reader's instant rapport with the likeable characters of Mike and Midge, and their frustrations with moving house: '"The ragged state of the garden and the generally poor condition of the cottage itself seemed to be impressing themselves on me in a strong way, and when I looked at Midge I was sure I detected the merest flicker of doubt in her eyes, too." '

In *The Magic Cottage* Herbert challenges one of the horror genre's most famous clichés: a family moving into a new house that has something nasty hiding in the attic. He doesn't disguise the fact, either, openly stating it through his character, Mike: '"You've seen the film, you've read the book. You know the one... the young couple find the home of their dreams... But *we* know there's something sinister about the place, because we've read the blurb and paid our money." '

Herbert's obligation to his fans is slowly unfolded. The horror is there, but many other elements are too. The novel builds gradually, starting with Midge's joy of moving to Gramarye, the magic cottage itself. The night they move in, Midge tells Mike what her mother would have thought of him: ' "... a rascal. That's how she'd put it – a *rascal*. And she would have enjoyed that." ' Her eyes begin to glisten with reminiscence and loss. After the euphoria of moving into her dream house, she is overcome by sadness. She wishes that her dead mother could enjoy her good fortune – her partner and new home. Mike reassures her that he would have got on well with her parents.

The scene exposes a depth of character and a glimpse of real-life horror: the feelings of loss and guilt everyone feels from time to time, even on occasions of great joy. There is a sad but somehow comforting sense to this. Perhaps it's the submission to the fact that everybody must eventually die, but that life goes on. Then Herbert goes deeper: '"That's what hurts. They can't know, they can never know about my work, about you... It would have meant so much to them. And to me, it would have meant so much to have them proud of me." ' Midge is still going through a healing process after the tragic loss of her parents, but Mike shows his strength, says the right things and holds her close, in what is a very tender and heart-warming scene.

Not long after this, however, Mike hears a sound emanating from the attic but is too scared to investigate, having watched too many horror movies in his youth. The general feeling of unease is heightened when the couple stumble on The Grey House, a large old building, not far from Gramarye. With the conclusion of this chapter the cosy, romantic fiction begins to crumble and a more sinister storyline takes over.

The first-ever publicity shot of James Herbert, the author in 1976.

A selection of Herbert's sketches. A designer by trade, he would often have input on the final look of the books.

Above: A signing session for *Portent*.

Below left: Signing copies of *The Dark* for fans.

Below right: Behind the camera for a change at a launch.

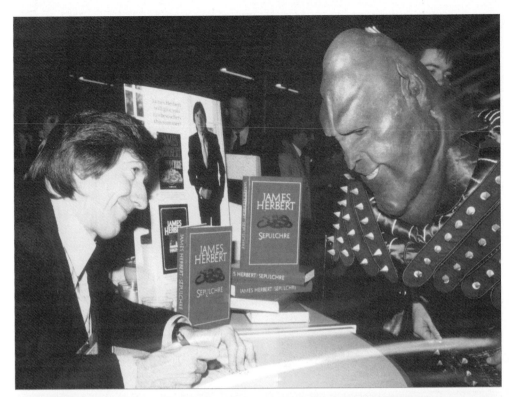

Above: A particularly attractive fan at a signing for *Sepulchre*.

Below: With Lord Archer at the launch of *'48*.

Above: Jim during his advertising days with copywriter Alan Palmer at a TV commercial shoot in the late '70s.

Below: With Barry Norman.

ROYAL CHARITY PREMIERE

AIDAN QUINN
KATE BECKINSALE
ANTHONY ANDREWS
JOHN GIELGUD

Haunted (15)

A SUPERNATURAL TALE OF LOVE AND MYSTERY

LUMIERE PICTURES PRESENTS A DOUBLE "A" PICTURES AND AMERICAN ZOETROPE PRODUCTION
A LEWIS GILBERT FILM
AIDAN QUINN   KATE BECKINSALE   ANTHONY ANDREWS "HAUNTED" JOHN GIELGUD
MUSIC COMPOSED BY DEBBIE WISEMAN EXECUTIVE PRODUCERS FRANCIS FORD COPPOLA FRED FUCHS AND RALPH KAMP
SCREENPLAY BY TIM PRAGER, ROBERT KELLETT AND LEWIS GILBERT
BASED ON THE NOVEL BY JAMES HERBERT PRODUCED BY LEWIS GILBERT AND ANTHONY ANDREWS
AND CO-PRODUCED BY WILLIAM P. CARTLIDGE
DIRECTED BY LEWIS GILBERT

ROYAL CHARITY PREMIERE

of

Haunted

In aid of

British Red Cross
125 years of caring for people in crisis

and the

🦢 European Anorexia Trust

In the presence of

**Her Royal Highness
The Princess of Wales**

at the

on

Thursday 26th October 1995

Doors Open at 6.45pm
Please be seated by 7.45pm
Carriages at 10.20pm

"This Event has been organised by British Red Cross Events Limited,
a company wholly owned by the British Red Cross Society
(charity registration number 220949) in aid of the British Red Cross Society
who will receive 60% of the net proceeds and European Anorexia Trust
(charity registration number 1049177) who will receive 40% of the net proceeds".

SECURITY:
Due to strict security arrangements for the evening, guests are asked to proceed
to their seats in the auditorium immediately on arrival at the cinema.
We also regret that cloakroom facilities will not be available.

  | CIRCLE
GG   021

NO SMOKING

Post Premiere Dinner and Cabaret

Café Nico at the Ballroom
Grosvenor House, Park Lane, London W1

10.30pm Champagne and Canapes
11.00pm Dinner
Midnight Cabaret
1.00am Carriages

Benefiting Charities

 British Red Cross

🦢 European Anorexia Trust

Please use the Ballroom
entrance on Park Lane

Black tie
Please bring this card with you

The promotional flyer and invitation for the Royal charity premiere of *Haunted*.

A good choice in holiday reading for Elton John.

Inset: With Welsh crooner Tom Jones in 1997.

The writer at home in his study.

A DREAM HOME?

"'Yet I found it difficult to shake off the impression of someone standing among the trees. A figure dressed in black, perfectly still and watching. Watching us.'"

(*The Magic Cottage*)

It isn't long before Kinsella and his fellow Synergists are introduced into the story. And what appears to be a harmless bunch of 'kids' turns into a malevolent extremist group. Kinsella himself finds it difficult to step through the front gate of Gramarye, almost like a famous vampire that first must be invited before entering a victim's house.

Kinsella has that ordinary, everyday look that Herbert's most wicked characters seem to posses. Well educated and slightly whimsical, Kinsella is very similar to Felix Kline in Herbert's following novel, *Sepulchre*. Indeed both characters use 'religion' to exercise power; Kline uses the occult and Kinsella uses the science of Synergism, as he explains: "'Just as various chemicals act upon each other... we believe that the thought process of the human mind... can combine with the Divine Spirit, our collective souls, if you like, to produce a unique power.'"

A demonstration of this power occurs when Mike is injured after forgetting to top up his car radiator. He releases the radiator cap and a jet of boiling water explodes, scolding his arm badly. Kinsella and the Synergists come to the rescue, showing that their faith really does work. Mike is cured of his injury, and subsequent pain, but as a consequence is introduced to the most powerful member of the Synergist group – Mycroft: "'You've witnessed our mutual strength, now reflect upon that for a while on your own.'"

It is Mycroft's wish that Mike and Midge join the group. He tries to charm the couple with the proof that Synergism works, but they are not convinced. It is here that things begin to get sinister, and the power that has lain dormant inside Gramarye – and one of the main characters – join forces against the powers of darkness.

Herbert works both ends of the horror genre, from the most gentle to the most graphic, but he doesn't always make horror the main thread of a novel. In both *The Magic Cottage* and *Lair*, more than half the book centres on something important to the story, and has little to do with horror. The horror builds slowly, and in *The Magic Cottage* this unsaid anticipation increases from the moment when Mike fails to check out the attic.

'Magic' is the mantra of the book. If you don't believe in any form of magic, you won't enjoy the book. But what is magic exactly? Something intangible or something that lies in every one of us and is filtered into the real world in large and small ways, depending on your ability to harness its powers – for good or evil motives?

Novelist Peter James believes *The Magic Cottage* is Herbert's finest work: 'I think it has some of the best characters he has written, and for me, novels are ultimately about the characters. *The Magic Cottage* also has huge charm and the book feels incredibly "real" to me.'

James first met Herbert shortly after the release of *The Magic Cottage* in 1987, as he goes on to relate: 'I had just written my novel, *Possession,* and my publishers (Victor Gollancz) asked me to try and get some "puffs" (quotes) from other established authors. The then book reviewer on the *Sussex Evening Argus*, Kathryn Bailey, who had recently interviewed Jim and was a great fan of my earlier novels, offered to contact Jim and asked him if he would read it. Jim kindly agreed and gave me a glowing quotation, which ended up on tube posters all over the London Underground.'

Peter James believes that Herbert is unspoiled by his enormous success. 'He is great company, very interested in people, a generous host (along with his wife, Eileen, who is a brilliant hostess), has a terrific intellect, and is very good fun to get pissed with!' Interesting observations to say the least, which also prove that horror writers don't live their job 24 hours a day. James concludes by saying, 'I think we both share a love of genuinely innovative writing and we are both pretty good at seeing through bullshit. We are both survivors in a tough business, and we both have a huge range of interests. Very importantly, for the terrain we both write in, we are both interested in the supernatural and religion – without in any way being obsessed or our lives being dominated by this.'

In *The Magic Cottage* Herbert showed yet another side to his writing, which has kept the novel as fresh and innovative today as it was on its initial release. By this stage in his writing career, Herbert had certainly dispelled any beliefs that he could write *only* undiluted horror novels. However, the next book would show, quite categorically, that he was able to write the ultimate in horror/thriller; something he couldn't have done when writing his first two novels.

CHAPTER EIGHTEEN

SECRETS OF THE SEPULCHRE

"'... A BLANK MIND, A CLEAN SLATE; A WHITE SHEET,
WAITING TO BE FILLED WITH IMAGES. I CAN MAKE
EVERYTHING BLACK IF YOU PREFER?"'
(SEPULCHRE)

Whenever Herbert's name is mentioned, it's generally followed by the words 'author of *The Rats* and *The Fog*'. Most artists are labelled by their earliest and most commercial work, and publishers enjoy pigeonholing their writers in a specific genre almost from the release of their first novel.

With *Sepulchre*, Herbert delivered his most complex and complete work to date. Essentially the book is a thriller, and good thrillers demand extensive research. Tried-and-tested procedures have to be followed rigorously, and with *Sepulchre* there were certain things Herbert had to meticulously analyse before putting pen to paper.

Liam Halloran is a bodyguard. He is cold and ruthless, but also thorough, as we observe when he checks his client's car over in the cool light of morning: 'Halloran dropped flat to inspect the underneath of the car, searching with a pen-torch for any object that could have been attached during the night. He ... checked ... wheel wells, shock absorbers and brake lines ... he walked around the vehicle looking for grease spots, pieces of wire, hand prints, even disturbances on the gravel near the car doors.'

There are other areas where Herbert had to go out of his way to add extra realism to the story. After understanding the basic principles of being a bodyguard, he had to construct a plausible international company. He came up with Magma.

To name countries, various mineral deposits and detailed specifics of a large company is not something you put into a novel by speculation alone. Although we have explored how Herbert conducts his research, the finer details are another thing. For example, during the promotion for *Portent*, Herbert freely admitted that the book's research was conducted over a seven-year period. He had a noticeboard where he stuck newspaper clippings and other snippets of relevant information appertaining to global warming. For *Others* he consulted medical books for real-life case studies of 'others' that had been born. Sometimes – and especially while researching *Others* – Herbert was shocked and disturbed by his findings, as he writes in his End Note to the book: '... lest I be accused of possessing an inordinately warped imagination, I should point out that most of the "others" described herein are taken from actual medical case histories. I sincerely hope you have been disturbed.'

While researching *Others*, Herbert had to undergo a course in private detection, as well as sit two exams – the second for advanced studies – so he could write about some of the more intricate details of Nick Dismas's profession. A similar thing happened in preparation for *Sepulchre* and the book is all the better for it. Herbert's trick is to fascinate the reader with the details of a profession and then probe deeper into the dark secrets that lie therein. In the case of *Sepulchre*, it is the secret of an international company and a person who is worth millions to it in the cut-throat business of multimillion-pound exports.

There is a moral aspect to *Sepulchre*. An analysis of the book clearly reveals the greed – lust – that huge companies utilise when hunting for rare mineral deposits. But why is Magma so far ahead of its rivals? Simply because it has a mystery man who can regularly find new, untapped supplies of precious minerals.

Sepulchre builds up an international team of ruthless characters before anything of a paranormal nature rears its head. It is a solid and original book, which takes the serious horror novel into the realms of quality thriller (believable backgrounds, well-crafted sub-plots and an intricate set of characters). Herbert reveals some of the study that went into the novel: 'I did a lot of research into minerals, and a lot to do with the type of work Uri Geller does, finding oils and minerals for big companies. In fact, the basic character of Felix Kline in the novel is based on Uri. He found out about it, got in touch, and now we're good friends.' Kline is not totally characteristic of Geller, as Herbert's character is a thoroughly evil and destructive person.

'I also did a great amount of research for the character of Halloran – the hero, or non-hero if you like,' Herbert continues. 'The character is based upon Pierce Brosnan – before he was famous. I saw him in *The Long Good Friday*. He only appeared twice – once in a swimming pool and then at the end of the film, where Bob Hoskins is being driven away. The rough-looking IRA man in that scene is Brosnan, and that image of him appealed to me. Even with long, unkempt hair and heavily stubbled chin he was dangerously handsome, but there was something icy in his eyes. A perfect anti-hero. In fact, I'd rooted for him to be the new James Bond even *before* his Remington Steele days when he was first discovered.'

Of course, Herbert had to do a little more to construct the character of Halloran than just base him on Pierce Brosnan. 'I also had to research private companies in the protection business because Halloran was a bodyguard. The bodyguard industry is one of the fastest growing in the world – some bodyguards charge up to £160,000 a year. A lot of it is personal prestige, particularly for pop stars, because it makes them look good. Take George Michael, when he was in court with Sony Music. I was watching him on television when he went into court one day, and he had the classic position of bodyguards around him. It's called the "V Position". And he had five: one in front, two by the side and two behind – a classic position. And he really didn't need any protection. Believe it or not, I've taken the whole course in being a bodyguard.'

Herbert truly enjoys his research, even gaining certificates after sitting courses for the varied professions his characters follow.

But the groundwork for *Sepulchre* didn't stop there. Herbert found himself researching countries such as Poland and what they were like during the Second World War. 'There was a tremendous amount of research ... very Frederick Forsyth, and I guess I'm influenced by Forsyth's books in that respect. But when you're writing a novel, it's good to have some authority and you're soon spotted if you don't. There are a lot of writers who just skim the surface of research. Some writers employ researchers too. I don't do that because, in its own way, research throws up more useable ideas. It can inspire little episodes. It's very helpful in getting the creative juices going.'

There is always the risk of putting too much research into a novel. Herbert explains how he combats this. 'You have to strike a balance. Out of one hundred per cent of research I do, I only use about 20 per cent. The rest is all discarded. It's not wasted. It still allows me to write with some authority and avoid making very bad mistakes. But you'll always make *some* mistakes, and that's because you don't do the job. You can't claim to know the whole industry. So I just try to get it as right as possible. Now you might let research overshadow the story. In *Others* I had to write about private detection. And in one three-page sequence, I left in all this background research, which was very wearing to write. I knew at the time my editor would want to take it out, but sometimes it seems a shame to lose it.'

In *Sepulchre*, Felix Kline is a short, irritating young man, extremely self-assured and always appearing to be one step ahead of everyone else. And naturally, Liam Halloran wants to give him a good hiding. Halloran is a tough agent, an Irishman by birth. He is useful with guns (and other weapons) and not bad in arm-to-arm combat too. He is cold-hearted and very dangerous. But Kline is constantly teasing him, pitting him against the strongest members of his own personal entourage. He does this to test Halloran.

The only humour in *Sepulchre* is that personal to Felix Kline. No character, or even reader, can totally appreciate it. Kline has his own moral code and his sense of humour emanates from this, enforcing the dark, macabre, undertone of the novel. All of which is a deliberate ploy on Herbert's part, as the motives behind Kline's private jokes become evident as the story unfolds.

Herbert skilfully uses some of his prominent recurring themes in *Sepulchre* – a large house in the countryside, individual scenes concerning the lives and thoughts of certain characters. The central character, Kline, is often quite laid-back, but Halloran is more complex, and shares a very unprofessional relationship with Kline's personal secretary, Cora Redmile.

'She was slender, dark-haired, her eyes a muddy brown flecked with green. Mid or late-twenties, Halloran guessed. Her smile was mischievous as she looked at him.'

Good and evil are not that well defined in *Sepulchre*. The book's particular strength is exposing the many levels of immoral behaviour and the depths to which an individual can stoop. There are no heroes, just characters who, one way or the other, take pleasure out of other people's misfortunes; from the unscrupulousness of Felix Kline to the more tenacious world of global industry.

Perhaps Cora Redmile is the innocent in the story. She is corrupted by a vile, money-grabbing pimp, Felix Kline. She enjoys sex of a perverse nature, and Halloran is one to partake. He is a man of little moral value himself, but he is not as corrupt as the joker he is protecting. Kline calls the shots; he's one step ahead. He knows, straightaway, about Halloran and Cora. This infuriates Halloran because he thought he had been discreet – how did Kline know?

Halloran knows there is something odd about this job,

something he can't quite put his finger on. To begin with, who is he protecting Kline against? And from what source does this threat originate? He approaches Kline on the matter, but the all-seeing Kline doesn't know. He hasn't been physically threatened, he just *knows* that his life is in danger. There are too many secrets and Halloran feels vulnerable. But when he probes further, Kline decides to let Halloran sample some of his power, first making Halloran row him out into the middle of a lake: '"*Touch the water … Feel its coldness …*" Halloran saw the shapes rising towards him, mutations that should only exist in the depths, mouths – were they mouths? … gaping, ready to swallow him in … to *absorb* him …'

There are many writers who can conjure images of malice and decay – for example, Clive Barker did it in the early 1980s with *The Books of Blood, The Damnation Game* and *The Hellbound Heart*, the latter containing just a hint of sadomasochism. Herbert would use a sadomasochistic theme in *Sepulchre*, but the strongest pieces of horror come from pure imagination, as shown in the above quote.

It has nothing to do with horror for horror's sake. In the chapter called Beneath the Lake we see Herbert at his best, slowly building a scene of confrontation, and only when the level of intimidation is at its peak is the total horror unleashed. Creatures from the depths of hell race forward, and Herbert vividly describes them, going one step further than horror guru H P Lovecraft in his hugely influential novella *At the Mountains of Madness*: 'So we glanced back… Unhappy act! Not Orpheus himself, or Lot's wife, paid much more dearly for our backward glance.' What Lovecraft leaves to the imagination, Herbert explains in full technicolour glory. But is it in his blood to do so? To explain the most graphic monstrosities is Herbert reiterating the energy and style that made a best-seller of *The Rats* and somehow alienated him from the 'serious thriller' world.

The important thing is not to go too far – to keep the horror plausible. We see evidence of this time and again in the works of

Robert Bloch, and even in the works of the grandfather of science fiction, H G Wells. For example, in Wells' short story *In the Avu Observatory* the whole action takes place in complete darkness. Avu is in Borneo, a little known and largely uncharted part of the countryside. A dark, malevolent creature flies into the observatory and, because Wells has captured the reader's imagination with the mysteries of uncharted earth, a spellbinding wonder is blended with the horror, which is never overplayed.

H G Wells' short fiction is largely overlooked nowadays. Stories such as *The Treasure in the Forest, The Diamond Maker* and even the much forgotten but largely imitated *The Crystal Egg* deserve higher accolade for their influences on the sci-fi/horror genre (in both novels and movies) over the past 50 years alone.

Sepulchre gradually gives up its secrets. Through a stream of self-contained chapters we are presented with the life stories of Kline's unofficial bodyguards: Monk, Jansz Palusinski, Khayed and Daoud. And we find that all their lives have been a mixture of sickness, squalor and destitution, and Kline has handpicked them all for their depraved skills. But although we see and understand their corruption, we find Cora's story more subtle and intricate. Chapters such as *Cora's Needs* (a chapter cut before publication) and *Cora's Anguish* give the reader an insight into, and a great degree of sympathy for, a very professional women. However, Cora can be saved from total corruption, and this is where she becomes the heroine of the book; not exactly the innocent virgin, but nonetheless a woman worth saving.

Liam Halloran becomes Cora's knight in shining armour, even though no saint himself. Herbert tells us at the outset of the book: 'There are no absolutes…' and *Sepulchre* is an exploration into the many stages an individual must pass through to achieve a state of pure evil. Kline is only a student to a higher order of corruption; he is learning all the time. To him, to be corrupted is to fall deeper into sin and to eventually become a creature of power.

There is more ancient sorcery in *Sepulchre* than religious doctrine. In other words, the Catholic faith is not allowed to give its opinion through priests and devotees – unlike many of Herbert's other books – and again this makes the story much more unredeeming. There is no light, just shades of grey and eventually darkness. From that blackness emerges a horror centuries old, which correlates with the horror in *The Exorcist* (the evil in both *The Exorcist* and *Sepulchre* is formed from a forgotten ancient wisdom, civilisations that had knowledge beyond their remit but somehow quickly lost it). In his preface, The Sumerians, Herbert tells us of the civilisation that harnessed the evil truth that lies deep in the sepulchre and of their scientific achievements: how they constructed democratic governments and time systems that worked, as well as being the first society to introduce the written word. In short, they were an intelligent race but they simply vanished. *Sepulchre* is Herbert's attempt to answer the mystery of their disappearance, if indeed there is an answer.

Herbert had never written about ancient civilisations and lost religions before, which is strange because such exploration presents many opportunities for speculative writing in the darker reaches of fantasy and horror.

> *'In a night of gross horrors, when nightmares were living, Halloran was further repulsed.'*
>
> (*Sepulchre*)

Unlike many of his contemporaries, Herbert chose not to write about the more well-known areas of ancient civilisations, such as Egypt and of course the lost city of Atlantis, which in itself brings more credibility to the story. Once again Herbert disbands the cliché. Instead of presenting another novel about Fourth Dynasty Egypt, he takes a lesser-known, but equally fascinating, culture and shapes his story around that.

Sepulchre remains one of James Herbert's finest achievements, even though it neglects to state what happened to the Magma

Corporation after Kline goes away. Magma was dependent on Kline for keeping ahead of its rivals, so did it crash after Kline left its fold or go on to better things? Perhaps the answer is obvious: it was swallowed up by a rival company – such is the ever-changing world of big-bucks industry.

'"No, I was happy with the task you set me. Evil for evil's sake. Harm for the sake of doing harm. Corruption for you! Entirely for YOU!"'

(*Sepulchre*)

CHAPTER NINETEEN

To Be Haunted

'To be haunted is to glimpse a truth
that might best be hidden.'
(HAUNTED)

The year 1988 proved to be a busy one for Herbert. Not only was one of his most popular novels released – *Haunted* (inspiring his biggest publicity campaign to date) – but also *Sepulchre* would be launched in paperback by Hodder & Stoughton at the London Dungeon as part of a special party to assist ITV's Telethon '88. The *Sepulchre* launch was impressive, with many a shop front packed with copies of the book – as well as Herbert's backlist. However, priority now had to be given to *Haunted*.

Are ghosts melancholy apparitions that enact past tragedies? Or are they something more tangible: a man or a woman who looks normal, who speaks coherently to the living, but is long since dead?

In the 20th century there were millions of well-documented sightings of ghosts, from the famous to the obscure. More often than not, a person doesn't actually need to see anything, just feel, as Sharpe writer Bernard Cornwell says. 'You see, for very old battlefields, time has taken the bad feeling away, while for the more recent ones, the bad feeling is still there. I don't mean ghosts or anything like that, but there's still a very real presence of dread when visiting those places.'

The words 'bad feeling' are the most important here, for anyone blessed with the smallest imagination can muster up the sound of gunfire and spectral screams of terror. But 'bad feeling' is almost tangible, as if the emotions felt by the people who died on that battlefield were so strong they took on a life of their own, and it is that which still haunts the place – the emotions, not the people.

Turning our attention to the more sinister aspect of ghosts, let us look at a case where they actually speak to their victim. One such spooky fireside story was once related to me by Mr West, a south-London building contractor: 'I was walking past Lesness Abbey (Abbey Wood) one night with some friends, and we saw what looked like a small fire burning on the ruined abbey wall. Being brave in numbers, we went to investigate. When we were about a hundred yards away, we could clearly see two people, a man and a woman, dressed in what looked like Victorian clothes, and they were putting books into the fire. As we watched, the man noticed us and walked over. As he came closer, we could see him more clearly. He wore a top hat and black Victorian evening dress and his face was very pale. I asked him what he was doing and he said, "Burning the past". My friends and I exchanged glances, but when we looked back he had disappeared. So had the woman and the fire. In fact, there was no trace of the fire at all.'

When confronted with a story like the one above, Herbert remains open-minded, as he told me several years ago, shortly before he saw a ghost himself. 'People do tell me about ghosts that they have seen. And I'm always ready to listen. Personally I've never seen a ghost, not knowingly anyway.' Perhaps this is why Herbert felt inspired to make up his own ghost story, *Haunted*.

When *Haunted* was released in 1988, it quickly climbed to the number-one spot in the best-seller lists (in both hardback and later paperback). It is a typical English ghost story, with spirits that not only walk around in the daylight, but eat, sleep and converse with the living too.

The plot involves the Mariell family, who play host to psychic investigator David Ash. It isn't the grow-up Mariell children (Robert, Simon and Christina) who summon Ash, but their aged Nanny, Tess (the children's aunt). But where are the ghosts Nanny Tess talks of? And why do the Mariells play such childish games?

There are clues throughout the novel, especially one vignette in which Ash and clairvoyant Edith Phipps attend a séance conducted by charlatan Elsa Brotski. When Ash exposes Brotski for what she is, the real spirits of the assembled bereaved take their revenge on her, but in the confused babble of messages that pour from Brotski's lips can be assembled the following line directed at Ash: '*David... I... will do you harm... one day.*'

The text of *Haunted* is almost over taut, because the book was adapted from an aborted BBC TV mini-series. The script would later be rewritten by many people (including veteran writer Nigel Kneale) before being turned into the slightly confusing, but nicely made, 1994 movie version.

Unlike a lot of Herbert's works, *Haunted* had mass-market appeal. It attracted people who didn't normally read horror novels, simply because it was a softer and more accessible story (not unlike *The Magic Cottage*). Indeed Herbert has incorporated this softer style into many of his latter novels, even those that include some pretty gruesome scenes (such as *The Ghosts of Sleath*).

Although *Haunted* is relatively soft and spooky, like all good ghost stories, it does posses a few lines that are nothing short of horrific, even if the horror exists in the unseen: 'He saw her smile in profile before she had completed the turn towards him. Moonlight illuminated the other side of his face. He screamed.' The horror almost exclusively revolves around the world of the cynical David Ash, cynical because, although he investigates hauntings, he doesn't actually believe in ghosts, as he states: '"Let's call it a thought process from someone now in another place, or an impression they've left behind. It might be that you... are tuned into that particular wavelength." ' Through David Ash, Herbert constantly looks for a scientific explanation – as did Dennis Wheatley and Algernon Blackwood before him.

In truth, David Ash doesn't want to face the reality of the situation. He was responsible for the death of his sister (Juliet) when they were children, and the consequent event of her beckoning him to her open coffin the night before her funeral is one that has haunted him ever since. So Ash becomes a psychic investigator in an attempt to exorcise himself from that experience.

Ash's sister despised him even after death, but did he despise her too? The secrets of Edbrook (the Mariell family home) reveal themselves to Ash in a very personal way, allowing him to unfold his old grief to the beautiful Christina: '"In that one insane moment I wanted her to die. I know I tried to help her, but ... when my father came out of the river, I was relieved, some dark part of me was glad." '

It is the exploration of dark emotions like these that make James Herbert's work intriguing. It is very important to have a believable storyline, but the characters and the way they interact are even more important. The failure to deliver this was one of the main criticisms of the work of Anthony Burgess. Books such as *A Clockwork Orange*, *M-F* , *1985* and *Earthly Powers* stand out as great novels in a body of work comprising over 50 titles.

Haunted doesn't provide an end to David Ash's misery. He can not shake off the presence of his dead sister, as she lives in both the subconscious and a more real place, where she waits for him in *The Ghosts of Sleath*: '... *a young girl, a child whose smile was malicious and whose skin was alabaster. Young yet so old, so degenerate in soul, and Grace knew that this was David's sister, this was Juliet. With that perception she understood David's deepest secret.*' But in *Sleath* somebody else feels Juliet's presence too. A woman called Grace, when she makes love to Ash: '*As if it's a dream, she felt the girl's rage, and she saw her stagger away, she saw her slip, she watched her fall into the pitchy black river.'*

Grace not only witnesses Juliet's hate, through her love-making to Ash, but also Juliet's death scene, allowing her to see the innocence within Ash's actions back on that fatal day. But Grace can not help him exorcise that memory. Like the most self-deprecating remorse, which it is, the cleansing must come from within the bereaved themselves and part of that healing process is accepting the death. However, for David Ash, there would be a further consequence – facing his dead sister's terrible fury.

'"Juliet!" he screamed. He could see her face clearly now, could discern the pretty features that his own mind had always blurred before, unwilling to recognize – determined not to – and thus acknowledge her unnatural existence.'

(Haunted)

Ash's demon is a tenacious foe, and it will take more than *Haunted* and *The Ghosts of Sleath* to exorcise the devil of Juliet. In a way, the ever-nagging presence of Juliet is not dissimilar to the haunting memory of Fox Mulder's missing sister in *X Files* after her extraordinary abduction before her brother when they were children. Mulder has regrets, and feels he could have prevented the act occurring, but of course in truth that would have been impossible. Like the chemist Redlaw in Dickens' *The Haunted Man and the Ghost's Bargain*, certain people have to live with painful memories, for the memories are the basis of a person's compassion even though they may make them more morose.

Haunted is the archetypal haunted house story. It evokes the eeriness of movies such as *The House on Haunted Hill* and *The Innocents,* especially in the latter's scenes of childhood games. But unlike *The Innocents*, childhood games in *Haunted* are played by adults – people who should know better – which in itself adds an extra macabre touch.

Haunted shocks because it succeeds in saying more in the over-stocked haunted-house sub-genre. No one really expected Herbert to come up with that, not after *Sepulchre*, which was a hard contemporary thriller. *Haunted* was a deliberate attack on the haunted-house cliché.

Like *The Magic Cottage*, *Haunted* isn't a horror novel but a chiller, based on classic genre themes. Both novels were serialised in *Woman* magazine, and if we believe Roald Dahl's observation that female writers are better at writing ghost stories than men (as he asserts in his introduction to *Roald Dahl's Book of Ghost Stories*), it should follow that they would be the most tenacious readers of such stories. This theory could explain why both *Haunted* and *The Magic Cottage* are two of Herbert's most successful novels. But having said that, there could be another reason: the publicity for *Haunted* was the most extensive of all of Herbert's work (see the Collector's Guide at the back of this book).

Herbert undertook the obligatory TV and radio promotions, but book-signing sessions were bigger and better than before, with many fans queuing for hours to see their hero novelist. Some of the more collectable variations of *Haunted* are those signed on the opening chapter, A Dream, A Memory, one of Herbert's most praised of opening chapters. When asked what inspired this chapter, Herbert says, 'I wanted to show some of David Ash's history, especially his wicked sister. I needed that opener to lead into the rest of the story.'

Hodder & Stoughton released a limited-edition, cloth-bound version of *Haunted* in slip case. Each copy was numbered and signed by Herbert and rapidly became one of his most sort-after collector's items.

Although *Haunted* proved to be one of Herbert's most lavish of productions, it included one of the most unsatisfactory characterisations, for David Ash deserves, indeed needs, to have a final showdown with his dead sister. It doesn't happen, in neither

Haunted nor *The Ghosts of Sleath*, and the character has been through too much not to warrant his own personal confrontation with his sister (the climax to *Haunted* is total horror for David Ash). However, Herbert disagrees. 'Yes it has happened. The whole thing was exorcised by the fire in the mansion at the end.' This conclusion simply isn't enough, because the 'exorcism' was underplayed, and many Herbert fans feel the same way. But Herbert persists, 'To me, the whole thing was dealt with in the end.' Not so: David Ash deserves a trilogy, just like the rats. But Herbert seems reluctant to let David Ash return, which to me is not only a great shame but the biggest criticism I have of Herbert. Ash needs to finally rid himself of his dear departed sister, because the exorcism in *Haunted* isn't enough – Juliet still haunts him. At present, there is no end to David Ash's nightmare.

I would like to conclude this chapter by mentioning the dedication to Dam Buster George Goodings at the beginning of *Haunted*. Herbert once told me about his old friend, Goodings, and the reasons why he dedicated the novel to him. Having worked as a reporter on the in-house journal of the Ministry of Defence for four years, Goodings' story had particular interest and poignancy for me: 'We met at a party in Knightsbridge and hit it off straight away. We found that we lived fairly close to each other in East Sussex, so we started meeting up for the odd drink and we had such a laugh together.

'Now he didn't tell me until a long time into our friendship that he was a wing commander on the Dam Busters mission. He was very modest that way, but I got it out of him one lunchtime. He told me everything about it.'

Herbert couldn't help but admire the man more, as he explains: 'I was so impressed because I think we owe a huge debt to those people who fought in the Second World War. So, modestly, he told me about how he was shot down twice. And after the second time, he told me how he managed to get back to the Bristol Channel, where a boat came out to pick him up. On board that boat was a nurse, Elizabeth (the sister of Dirk Bogarde), whom he would later marry.

'George was a great character. He was actually a tree surgeon in civilian life. Did a lot of gardening – even helped me with mine. He died of cancer before *Haunted* came out.'

At least Goodings has a number-one best-seller dedicated to him as an epitaph. He will not be forgotten.

CHAPTER TWENTY

IN SEARCH
OF GHOULS

'THE GHOULS ARE "OUTSIDERS"...
THEY REPRESENT THE UNKNOWN WHICH EVERYONE
WILL CONCEDE IS UNTHINKABLE.'
**(VINCENT PRICE, INTRODUCTION TO THE GHOULS,
EDITED BY PETER HAINING)**

In 1989 Herbert started his relationship with Lloyd's of London (something he wrote about in *Once...*) but things didn't go that well for him: 'I was a name at Lloyd's. I didn't have a box. And one time it was very prestigious to be part of that.' Herbert's elder brother, John, was a Lloyd's broker and said it would be a very good idea to be part of the group, as did Herbert's accountant, but Herbert soon got unsettled: 'I kept reading and seeing reports in the media generally that concerned me. I read between the lines and thought, what's going on here? And I resigned just before the crash.'

The Lloyd's crash of the late 1980s came about due to large insurance claims made because of contracting asbestosis, especially in America. A lot of people suing their companies because they were dying of cancer, and one of the biggest firms that was paying out was Lloyd's. Herbert takes up the story: 'Now they were recruiting people to amass money to pay off these debts and I saw this happening, so I resigned. This didn't stop me helping to pay this huge debt, but stopped them from using any more of my money to insure.

'I cut my losses but other people went broke. People had to sell their homes, take their kids out of private school and put them into state school. At least 11 people – possibly more – committed suicide. It totally ruined some people, and I was very lucky because I saw it coming. What I couldn't understand, however, was why other names didn't see it coming?

'They were supposed to be shrewd business people out – why didn't they understand what was going on? Why was I the only one? It cost me quite a bit of money, but by the time I got tax back on that and looked at the good years of dividends, I didn't lose that much at all. But it could have completely wiped me out – very easily.'

Herbert, although relieved he pulled out from Lloyd's in time to stop any major damage to his finances, is still unsettled by the whole incident, as he explains: 'There should have been a huge government enquiry into the Lloyd's crash. Much went on that merited investigation.'

Herbert only signed the final release form from Lloyd's in June 2002, a long time after his resignation.

So at the end of the 1980s, Herbert decided to put on a smile and release his most humorous novel to date.

Creed was a real departure for Herbert because it poked fun at the very genre he had been defending for years – horror. It was the movies that showed Herbert he could get away with this and keep his credibility intact – a good example being *Abbott and Costello Meets Frankenstein*, a truly funny movie that still leaves room for monster-movie stars Bela Lugosi and Lon Chaney Jnr to be their frightening selves. 'Demons today are a shoddy lot,' Herbert teases us at the beginning of *Creed*, and this observation became another reason for writing the book.

Herbert couldn't stand the oblique characters that were appearing in late-1980s horror movies – Jason from *Friday 13th* and Fred Kruger from *A Nightmare on Elm Street*. Where had all the real ghouls gone?

If we look at the minimalist artwork on the dust jacket of *Creed*

– a spectral demon wrapped in a carrion cloak (designed by Herbert himself) – we can see where he is coming from. In the book, Herbert's demon is largely based on the Dracula-like vampire as played by Max Schreck in Frederick Murnau's movie, *Nosferatu*, to show that in order to see a good demon on film, we have to go back to silent movies.

Herbert's satire is informing us that nothing that is genuinely scary nowadays – it's all slash and splatter. But with the old gothic movies, so much more was gleaned from heavy make-up and over-the-top theatricality.

> '... *then there came another blinding flash... blasting and crumbling the marble, as it burst into flame. The dead woman rose for a moment of agony, while she was lapped in flame, and her bitter scream of pain was drowned in the thundercrash.*'
> (*Dracula's Guest* – cut text from *Dracula*, Bram Stoker)

The movie *Nosferatu* was loosely based on Bram Stoker's *Dracula*, and although Stoker's widow successfully sued the German company who made the film, *Nosferatu* remains one of the greatest movie interpretations of *Dracula* because it evokes the underlying menace and eeriness of the original style.

Maybe James Herbert and Stephen King were guilty of bringing explicit violence into the horror genre in the early 1970s but, as they would argue, they did it with style, and as that style matured, novels like *Sepulchre* and *Misery* were born.

It could also be argued that, having set a precedent for the genre in the 1970s, Herbert was now – at the turn of the 1990s – trying to get the cinema to catch up with the literary side of the horror genre. There were some good horror movies, but the most popular mainstream films in the genre were cheap and nasty, as far as characters and plots were concerned.

Creed starred a paparazzi photographer, so Herbert's research took him all over London, accosting such luminaries as Jack Nicholson and Helena Bonham-Carter with real paparazzi photographers. Because of its movie influence, *Creed* opens with the funeral of an actress – a star from Hollywood's silver screen, Lily Neverless. It is a small funeral, but one to be covered by paparazzi photographer Joe Creed. He has set up his equipment in a tomb overlooking the graveside and is ready to snap away at the celebrities who come to pay their final respects.

The job is a little out of the ordinary for Creed, whose sole purpose in life normally is to chase and harass celebrities for the most candid shots, then sell them on to the highest bidder (generally a tabloid newspaper). Creed has a dream: '"... that supreme moment captured on film ... Gimme three big ones ... Prince Charles weeping for his lost friend on the Klosters ski-slope, John Lennon signing an autograph for his assassin-to-be, a burning Buddhist or two. Something *significant*, Lord, something for worldwide syndication, five-figure bids no less, front-page ratings." '

Creed gets such a moment. After everyone leaves the graveside and the diggers had filled in the hole, Creed spies a man standing under the shadow of a tree. The person moves forward to the graveside, then desecrates the fresh grave. Creed is quick to document the moment, but the perpetrator realises he has been caught on film:

'For one brief but infinite second, photographer and crazy watched each other. And in that brief but infinite second, Creed felt that the inside of his skull had been scoured...'

Creed is suddenly out of his depth. Something satanic is afoot, and the innocent party, the person whose privacy was violated by Creed, will stop at nothing to obtain the photographer's film. Somebody breaks into Creed's house, leaving him a note: 'YOU WILL BRING THE FILM TO US. YOU WILL NOT SPEAK OF IT.'

The paparazzi photographer is suddenly the victim of his own success, and a horrific turn of events ensues. Creed is bullied into handing over the film but, being the tough guy he is (or thinks he is), he will not go down without a fight. In a way his antagonists have scared him too much, stripped layers from him, exposed the side of his personality he hates to acknowledge – the coward. But he is ignorant enough to think that no one has the right to invade his privacy that much. And that's the irony – a paparazzi photographer complaining about invasion of privacy.

Although *Creed* is not Herbert's best novel, it is a clever story in so far as the level of intimidation Joe Creed is exposed to reveals the existence of two-facedness. The world is full of double standards, and Creed is the living proof.

The book strikes a good balance between horror and humour – for example, a toilet that develops a mouth with gnashing teeth can be either humorous or scary, depending on how you look at it: 'He was looking down into a porcelain mouth! Creed felt himself go weak at the knees. But he jerked upright in absolute shock and stepped back when that tooth-edged, pissed-on mouth suddenly shot from the bottom of the toilet, glazed sides stretching as though elastic, and gnashed at the air where he had been standing a split-second before.'

Creed is essentially a funny novel. The demons that chase Creed throughout are the fallen angels that have existed since Biblical times and because their powers are waning, Creed finds them in an old people's home.

At the head of each chapter in the book, there is a tiny graphic of a piece of film. This doesn't necessarily symbolise camera film, but Herbert's love of old movies. Not just the ancient gothic films but those sometimes-funny thrillers that don't seem to be made anymore, starring actors like Jack Lemon, Tony Curtis (*Some Like it Hot*) and Cary Grant (*Father Goose*). *Creed* would have made a fine example of such a movie, so it is a shame it may never grace celluloid, but it does highlight Herbert's maverick tendencies: 'It's very difficult to categorise me.' This may explain why the movie *Fluke* couldn't find distribution in the UK on its original release.

'Now who was that one over there? From a different generation to Lily's. Maggie Smith? Looked like her, but then off-stage she looked like anybody. There was Judi Dench, looking nothing like a Dame... Creed began pressing the shutter release, aiming focusing, clicking, moving on. Okay, Sir John, is that a hint of a smile I see?'

(*Creed*)

One person who did pick up on the humour in *Creed* was actor and comedian Lenny Henry, who took Herbert out to lunch to find out what fee Herbert would want to option the book for a movie starring Henry himself. Herbert accepted the lunch and allowed Henry to take the option on the book at nil cost, but sadly the film failed to materialise.

Creed is one of Herbert's largely overlooked novels nowadays, simply because when people buy a James Herbert novel they expect to have their expectations fulfilled – the great extravaganzas of mayhem and disaster. *Creed* and *Fluke* do not fuel those expectations and are somewhat maligned for it.

CHAPTER TWENTY-ONE

PORTENTS OF DOOM

'THE WORLD WILL NEVER BE THE SAME AGAIN ...
THE END IS CLOSER THAN YOU THINK ...
THE BOOK JAMES HERBERT WAS BORN TO WRITE ...'
**(PORTENT PUBLICITY BLURB,
SEPTEMBER 1992)**

August 26 1992 was a special day in the Herbert household, marking the 25th wedding anniversary of Jim and Eileen. A party was organised and Herbert designed a card with two little monsters on it by way of invitation. The anniversary wasn't something Herbert took lightly. Many of his old friends from advertising had married and divorced during the past 25 years, but he had remained happily married. As a practising Catholic family, the celebration meant a great deal to them, but there was work to be done. In just over two months' time, a new novel would be released – *Portent*.

The novel was published on 5 November 1992 and to many people in publishing (and certain reviewers) this was one of Herbert's best novels, a story concerning great disaster, forecasting worldwide doom. It would be the last book Herbert would write for publishers Hodder & Stoughton.

'The book took me seven years to research,' says Herbert. 'I had a noticeboard and I stuck all these clippings and maps on it, each reporting huge disasters all over the world. And when you put all these real-life events together – happening at exactly the same time – you have a very frightening prospect. I haven't exaggerated much.'

Herbert knew he wanted to write a catastrophe novel, but where did the idea of 'portents' prophesying the disasters stem from? 'I was on holiday in Australia, travelling from one city to another, and I saw these beautiful blossom trees. I was told that the trees only blossomed for a short while – around school exam time. So for some students, the blossom was a bad sign of doom – a portent. So that's where the idea came from. And from there I went on to the Great Barrier Reef, dived down and saw its natural beauty first-hand. And the whole story began to grow from there.'

Portent was a commercial novel: not since *Domain* had Herbert written a work on this scale, as he admitted at the time of its release. 'They [the publishers] say that it's the book James Herbert was born to write, because it is the culmination of the skills I have learned as a writer.' However, *Portent* was commercial on another level too: it was the first time Herbert would focus on events in other countries. Whole chapters would be based in countries such as Australia, Canada, India, Mexico, the West Indies and various parts of America. Although being highly relevant to the book, this does give more worldwide commercial appeal, as people outside the UK can identify with the horrific things happening on their own doorstep.

Although Herbert is Britain's leading horror writer, he hasn't made a big global breakthrough (he has sold books in 35 foreign languages, and does make some money in America), probably due to the Englishness of many of his novels. Dennis Wheatley's books were full of upper-middle-class stuffiness and the pride of a forgotten empire, but they sold well overseas because of their exotic locales (researched by his extensive travelling) – *To the Devil a Daughter* and *Gateway to Hell* are good examples. Herbert denies that *Portent* was an attempt to cash in on this commercial stratagem. 'The story was something I wanted to do, it was as simple as that.'

Portent was meticulously researched because the realism of world disasters was a crucial part of the story. Herbert wanted to say, 'This really is going on, you know'. So fantastical horror was played down in favour of 'real-life catastrophe.'

'Rivers opened the Renault's door and flicked the cockroach off the driver's seat and on to the pavement. He crushed the insect with his foot before it could scurry away, an act that even the Animal Liberation Front wouldn't have complained of nowadays.'

There are many such social vignettes in *Portent*. Comments on insect infestation, the use of aerosols poisoning the environment, the over-use of cars in the city – both short-term and long-term environmental damage: '... the end of lunch hour and the streets were busy, diesel taxis everywhere, vans, buses and automobiles crawling along... Like a tarnished monument to self-aggrandisement, the Lloyd's Insurance building rose high ahead, its steel and chrome architecture rendered even more unappealing by blemishes and grime... God only knew what was in the atmosphere to cause such deterioration...'

Portent was the right vehicle for Herbert to show his dislike of London – the dirt, the grime – and not just on a sub-text level. It was blatant criticism, dictating the over-riding message of the book. Despite this, Herbert wasn't sure how he rated the book just prior to its release. Was it one of his favourites? 'It's too soon to tell,' he said. 'I'm still too exhausted from writing it – ask me in a year or so.' Seven years later I asked him again: 'It was a nice thing to do,' came the reply. 'Favourite? No. '48 is one of my favourites because it fulfilled a lot of dreams for me. But then again, I still love it when *The Magic Cottage* and *Shrine* are reissued.'

Although *Portent* was in essence a stereotypical novel for Herbert, in another respect it was a complete departure. Setting the majority of the book on foreign soil distanced some of

Herbert's most loyal fans, who were looking for the usual home-grown entertainment.

Even though *Portent* went to the top of the best-seller lists – and has a very important message – it is not one of the essential James Herbert novels. In a way, like *Moon*, it promised an awful lot, but for some reason fell short.

Herbert's novels tend to end with a huge finale, where all the threads are neatly pulled together, more often than not for a final, sinister conclusion. But not so *Portent*. There is a great deal of optimism at the end of the book, which brings about a new beginning for the earth and every living creature in it. The theme of a higher state of awareness is prevalent again, but this time it's mankind learning by its mistakes, not just individuals. Perhaps it is this pay-off that softens the finale, making it more of an optimistic science-fiction novel than a depraved horror novel, which again distanced some of Herbert's fans. Also it was the first 'fashionable' novel Herbert wrote. Since the late 1980s, a lot of people have been concerned about environmental issues – all Herbert did was put his own slant on it.

Portent has never reached the height of respect its original reviews predicted. Its message is clear and poignant, but for some the ending is too moderate. The children in the book were predictably going to live and not be killed by the extreme evil character (who is in her own way too similar to, and as unpopular as, the evil female in *Moon*).

Portent sold well and Herbert undertook the usual full-blown publicity tour (including several book signing sessions in London, one at The Forbidden Planet with Stephen Jones to coincide with the simultaneous release of *By Horror Haunted*). But despite the novel's success, Herbert grew dissatisfied with Hodder & Stoughton, deciding to leave its fold after an 18-year relationship. 'I'm in the market,' he told me at the time with a wry grin. He wasn't daunted by the prospect; after all, word was being passed along the publishing grapevine that Herbert was in the market – all he had to do was start his next novel and wait for the offers to roll in.

It didn't take long. Soon Eddie Bell (then Managing Director of HarperCollins) made him an offer to join his collection of authors that included Jeffrey Archer and Clive Barker. Herbert accepted the offer, then cut off all communication to concentrate on his next novel.

CHAPTER TWENTY-TWO

DEEP IN THE CHILTERN HILLS

'AH NOW, SO THIS IS THE PLACE. PLEASANT.
NO, MORE THAN PLEASANT: A BEAUTIFUL LITTLE VILLAGE.
SUCH A PITY, SUCH A GREAT SHAME.'
(THE GHOSTS OF SLEATH)

Herbert's first novel with HarperCollins was *The Ghosts of Sleath*, and the release of the book marked his 20th year as a best-selling horror writer. In an odd way, it also became a celebration of his career to date, including major recurring themes such as a rat, fog, comparisons between the countryside and the city, and children being something other than what they are.

HarperCollins Managing Director Eddie Bell announced that he wanted more copies of *The Ghosts of Sleath* sold than any other James Herbert novel. So started an impressive publicity campaign. To begin with, 250 limited-edition signed proofs were sent out to reviewers and Herbert embarked on his usual publicity tour, including the obligatory TV and radio interviews.

Before the book was launched, Herbert was very excited about the relationship with his new publishers. He was contracted to a two-book deal and given a £1.8 million advance. Such a generous advance normally puts immense pressure on an author, but during the latter stages of writing the book, Herbert seemed extremely pleased with it, as he told me in a letter dated May 1994. 'I'm still busy … the book is going well.' Soon after, he delivered the book: 'The Ghosts of Sleath was delivered on deadline. And so far the response from the publishers has been overwhelming.'

The initial reaction in the trade was, 'Herbert has given his novel an unusual title.' Indeed Herbert's titles were normally short and succinct to maximise space on the book jacket – 'The books must look good,' Herbert is often quoted as saying. But the jacket to The Ghosts of Sleath had a striking appearance, embossed with gold leaf, reminiscent of the tooled leather tomes of a previous century. Some reviewers were lucky enough to receive a proof jacket ahead of release, and consequently word soon spread about this special-looking book. But could we judge a book simply by its cover?

> 'The leer of his face had been sickening, and when he'd kicked her for good measure as she lay on the floor, he had sniggered and announced that the boy would get what was coming to him before too long and nobody would do anything about it.'
>
> (The Ghosts of Sleath)

There is a depressing element to The Ghosts of Sleath; something that is mustered in vignettes from Herbert's other books but that normally fails to dominate a whole novel as it does here: death, in its many different guises:

> 'The angel came towards her, gracefully, quietly… Jessie barely heard the words, and it told her it was time to let go, that there was a better place waiting for her, where there was no pain and no sadness, and all she had to do was give up her spirit, discard her life…'
>
> (The Ghosts of Sleath)

The novel contains scenes of extreme and subtle cruelty and it is the credibility of these scenes that evokes that depressing element.

Also, Herbert really gets into the anguish of key characters, such as Ellen Preddle's longing for the return of her son, Simon, who she has just buried: '*Oh Simon, Simon. Why you? Why did the Almighty take you from me? As punishment for the things I did* for *George, those dirty things, things you could never tell another living soul, things to be ashamed of till the day you died, shameful, horrible things. Was this the punishment? Oh Lord, he made me do them. I didn't enjoy it. But I did them for you, don't you see? Oh send my boy back, please God, give him back to me, don't take my precious away I'll do anything dear Lord. Just give Simon back to me. Please. Please.* Please.'

David Ash makes a welcome return in the book, but as Herbert is keen to stress, 'It's a follow-on, not a sequel to *Haunted.*' This statement can also be applied to the book's speculation about the true reasons behind hauntings – the manifestation of ghosts. Herbert digs deep into the scientific explanations, always playing the cynic, thus balancing the supernatural aspects of the story: '"Our task is to validate incidents of the paranormal or supernatural, but it's almost as useful to expose false claims. In fact, it gives the organization more credibility when we do the latter..." '

Herbert's voice is that of the sceptic, which makes the novel more credible. Psychic investigator David Ash is constantly searching for the scientific explanation, but, not unlike the location in *Haunted*, Sleath begins to overpower him and expose his weaknesses, his inner fears. Even in sleep:

'*He tossed and groaned...* and all those wide but little eyes still hold the terror of their own premature deaths. *In sleep, he moaned a long, drawn-out "Noooo..."* And the drowned children moan with him, pleading to be saved, imploring him to help them. But he knows he cannot, that it's too late, they are already dead and nothing can save them anymore. And so they plead with him to join them in their watery crypt...'

There is horror of the most graphic kind in *The Ghosts of Sleath*. Unsettling descriptions and depressing, everyday horrors of domestic violence. Then Herbert digs deeper into the minds of his main characters, returning to his theme of a couple who come together to fight the common evil and find love:

'Odd how close she felt to him though, despite only having met him for the first time that day. Could it be part of this psychic thing he'd mentioned? Could their minds somehow be "in tune", was that what he was getting at? ... then there was this odd feeling between them, this knowing ... somehow there was an awareness of each other that should have come from understanding ... and the peculiar sensation that had struck her twice that day – it had been as though mild lightning had discharged itself into her body and mind just moments before she had met him.'

Herbert puts his sharp reasoning in *The Ghosts of Sleath* down to 'life experience, where you are as a person'. This is what has distanced him from his rats novels.

During the 1990s, Herbert changed publishers twice, moving to Macmillan after fulfilling his two-book deal with HarperCollins. However, he still had business with Hodder & Stoughton while at HarperCollins. The company had control of his back catalogue, and Herbert decided it would be nice to reissue the paperbacks without pictorial dust wrappers, making them single-colour wraps with silver foil titles.

Many saw this as a surprising decision for Herbert, but he had his reasons: 'I wanted to underplay the back catalogue.' But there was more to it than that. He knew the contract with Hodder & Stoughton to publish his back catalogue was coming up for renewal, and he was keen to get his whole catalogue transferred to his new publishers and to work on a series of striking new covers.

'He touched her emotions, her passions, and was overwhelmed by her desire. And Grace welcomed him in, confused but delighted by the invasion and she in turn explored her consciousness, roaming free, absorbing his thoughts and feelings. She plunged deeper...'

Herbert relates, 'A famous television presenter called me up after reading *The Ghosts of Sleath* and she said, "You must be a wonderful lover." And I thought, well, in my head I am (laughs).'

The love scene in *The Ghosts of Sleath* isn't particularly conventional, neither is it extraneous to the storyline. It is important to the plot in that it breaks down emotional boundaries between David Ash and Grace.

'There's a writer who will remain nameless, but he copied that scene from *The Ghosts of Sleath* for his own novel and he got it all wrong,' says Herbert. 'A lot of people do study my books and try and write my way, but this guy failed miserably. Unfortunately, he used all the wrong words, the crude words that diminish the eroticism.'

Herbert is tiresomely labelled 'one of the most widely imitated writers', but the reason why his success has continued, and his imitators have ceased, is because he is always exploring new ideas in his books. And he can be gentle when a storyline demands it.

The Ghosts of Sleath opens on a bright summer's day, with a detailed description of flowers and insects in a peaceful scene. Then the horror seeps in, exposing the way of all flesh: death in the guise of a funeral. A child's funeral. But sometimes death is not the end: 'Ellen Preddle waited and her dead son waited with her.'

During the promotion of *The Ghosts of Sleath*, Herbert was persuaded by Eileen to do an interview at the London Dungeon to promote the book. Tony Mulliken of Midas Public Relations, Herbert's friend and publicist for almost 20 years, organised the television coverage with the BBC. To be interviewed at the London Dungeon was not something Herbert was keen to do, but he acquiesced on this occasion.

In a darkened East End set, Herbert proceeded to talk about his youth, with the giant rats and cats crying out like tortured children … Then a figure in a black cloak stepped up beside him. The spectral, Ripper-like character (with an uncanny resemblance to

Michael Aspel) pulled out a blood-red book and told the horror writer: 'James Herbert, this is your life.'

Herbert was very surprised. 'Have you got the right guy?' he asked. 'Sorry to scare you,' Aspel said, leading Herbert into a cloud of swirling fog with fiendish, exaggerated laughter.

Herbert's *This is Your Life* appearance was broadcast on 12 April 1995, shortly after his 52nd birthday. Family, friends, colleagues, editors and even the obligatory school teacher turned up on the show, and Herbert passed many a comment about the photographs of his younger self with Beatles-style haircut and slick black glasses.

A good time was had by all. 'That should have been it,' says Herbert. 'It was a great accolade. But that should have been the end of my career. How can you top that?'

In truth, Herbert was far from giving up his day job.

CHAPTER TWENTY-THREE

NON-FICTION

'I LIKE A GRAVEYARD ON A SUNNY DAY. I LIKE THE DRONE
OF A BEE, THE TRILL OF A BIRD, PERHAPS EVEN THE DISTANT
SOUND OF CHILDREN AT PLAY, AS I WANDER DOWN THIN
PATHS CUT THROUGH BURIAL MOUNDS.'
(DARK PLACES)

Before we continue, it is appropriate to spend a little time discussing Herbert's two works of non-fiction. The first, *By Horror Haunted*, was released in 1992 to coincide with the publication of *Portent*. Edited by writer/journalist Stephen Jones, the book was a perfect companion to Herbert's backlist, with tributes from such respected genre practitioners as Stephen King, Ramsey Campbell and Clive Barker. The book also included some of Herbert's short fiction and various other pieces he had written, such as newspaper articles and introductions.

By Horror Haunted was lavishly published by NEL, but never made it into paperback, probably because the inclusion of many photographs increased the price above Herbert's latest novel, and sales must have suffered as a consequence. It is a shame as the book was a great tribute, with Herbert celebrating 18 years as a best-selling writer.

Herbert's second non-fiction work was *James Herbert's Dark Places*, published by HarperCollins in 1993. This book was again lavishly illustrated – this time mainly in colour. *Dark Places* was based on locations and legends Herbert had used for research in his novels, and was a book he had been planning (with photographer Paul Berkshire) as far back as mid-1992 (while at Hodder & Stoughton). Herbert wrote his personal essays for the book at weekends so that it didn't interfere with the writing of his novels. This was quite a departure for Herbert, who as a professional writer always kept his weekends free in order to spend time with his family.

Dark Places was an absorbing read and benefited greatly from paperback release. Although never meant for the best-seller lists, it would have easily reached a larger audience if more of Herbert's fans had been made aware of its availability. The book was given little publicity, so even the reviewers who professed to be Herbert fans were unaware of its existence.

Although neither of these books was considered an autobiography, his next book, *'48*, in a strange way was. It could be said that Herbert was a little reflective in the mid-1990s, what with two non-fiction works and a novel that included his childhood home in Tyne Street.

'Let me conjure a figure, perhaps dressed in a black shroud, standing there in the middle-distance. Quiet and still. Watching ...' (Dark Places)

The publicity for *Portent/By Horror Haunted* (and his graphic novel *The City*) was conducted by Midas Public Relations, a company Herbert always worked well with. When it came to *The Ghosts of Sleath*, Herbert would sign stock but little else. This upset many fans, who believed Herbert was locking himself away again, especially after the more accessible years (1986-92). By default, the fans were right. Generally, when a big writer moves publishing houses, the company tends to conduct the first publicity tour in-house (almost as a sign of loyalty). However, Herbert always seems to be more accessible when dealing with promotion from outside (Midas Public Relations). Happier too.

CHAPTER TWENTY-FOUR

A YEAR OF LIVING DANGEROUSLY

'WHAT THE HELL WAS THAT?'

('48)

If Herbert's first novel for HarperCollins was very rural, his second was very urban. '48 fulfilled many dreams for Herbert. It is a chase story set around the London of his youth with his old family home in Tyne Street used as a location. The book is dedicated to his mother, Kitty.

'48 would be the ultimate chase novel through war-ravaged London streets. A distinctive path to '48 can be traced through *The Fog* and *Domain*, and if we observe all three novels in the order they were written, we can clearly see that the horror is substantially toned down, and the pace increased. 'There are times when you have to slow the story down for exposition,' says Herbert. 'But then you build it up and up again.'

Herbert considered '48 a pleasure to write: 'When I write a book I put down one-line ideas, things I can use. Generally I put down about 150 ideas but I had about 250 ideas for this one, eventually only using about 100 of them. It was a great pleasure writing it.' The satisfaction stemmed from Herbert's familiarity with the location: a bombed-out London just after the Second

World War. 'I got several ideas for '48,' says Herbert. 'And they all came together. Firstly, I wanted to do a chase novel. Very fast paced. Also, I read about Adolf Hitler and the experiments he was carrying out toward the end of the war and could have unleashed upon us. So that became the premise of the book. And it all came together.'

The plot describes how in 1945, in one last all-out assault, Hitler unleashes the Blood Death on Britain. Three years later, only a few people are left alive – those with the rare blood group AB Negative, which somehow gives them immunity against the disease. An American pilot, Hoke, and a small group of others fight for survival against a slow-dying group of Fascist Blackshirts, who crave their uninfected blood.

> *'Hubble had never been handsome, but I guess he had the arrogance of features that had some allure for the weak-minded. Pencil thin moustache, beaky nose, he could have been a shorter version of his own hero Sir Oswald Mosley, the leader of England's very own fascist party, a megalo-maniac who'd spent most of the war years locked away in Holloway prison.'*

('48)

In the 1930s the British public became aware of a man named Adolf Hitler. English Fascist leader Sir Oswald Mosley's fanatical Blackshirts were marching through London's East End (Whitechapel, Mile End) terrorising Jews, causing riots in the streets. Mosley was considered a brilliant politician (some say tipped for Prime Minister if he hadn't had been so extreme), but he couldn't persuade the British public to follow Fascism. He was consequently locked away at the beginning of the Second World War. So Mosley and his Blackshirts became the last thread Herbert needed in his hectic year of hell, 1948, or simply '48.

In addition to being a chase story set in deserted London, the novel takes in so many of Herbert's favourite themes: underground tunnels (*Domain*), fascism (*The Spear*), blood disease (*The Rats*), and a pilot as a central character (*The Survivor*).

'48 portrays triumph and tragedy on the same canvas. The inevitability of human self-destruction (a bungling government) together with the power and temerity of the ordinary man and woman on the street.

> '"*So we walked through the nightmare, keeping close together, a tight bunch, the lamplight defining the soft borders of our world, none of us caring to look beyond and none of us focusing on what lay within.*"'
>
> (*'48*)

'48 doesn't present the reader with anything new, incorporating all the characteristics that had made Herbert successful in the first place. It is a self-indulgent novel in that Herbert wanted to prove he 'could still write with pace'. It had been more than ten years since he had produced an undiluted chase novel and he wanted to do it again. Indeed, could he do it again?

'48 is not a philosophical book. Once more, it is cut and thrust and Herbert made no apology for that. However, the book did take its toll on him, as he described to me shortly after its completion: 'I was exhausted when I finished the book. It took so much out of me. I mean, I put so much of myself into it. And I said to Eileen and Eddie Bell that I was going to take a long holiday afterwards. And they looked at each other and smiled. And it didn't take long before I started writing again. I found that I became so unfocused when not writing. I was always busy, and if not busy, I was unwell. I went on holiday (to Mauritius) and I got an idea for a book, and it's a great idea. You see I love it (writing). This is what I do. When I go into the study, I sit down and I get the buzz, and your favourite book must always be the one you're about to write.'

When I pressed him further about his 'great idea' for the next novel, he said, 'I'm not saying anything about it yet. It's too soon. However, I will tell you that I'm taking a course in private detection and the first line of the book is: "My redemption began in hell." '

CHAPTER TWENTY-FIVE

TIME TO MEET THE OTHERS

'I AM IN DARKNESS, BUT I AM NOT ALONE.
I CANNOT SEE THE OTHERS, BUT I CAN HEAR
THEIR TORMENTED CRIES.'

(OTHERS)

Herbert grew dissatisfied with HarperCollins. While on the '48 publicity tour he was informed by shop managers that they were not getting copies of his latest hardback. Unhappy at this, Herbert decided it was time to part from the company and Macmillan became his next port of call. Not only did the publishers offer him a very attractive £2 million deal, they also bought his back catalogue from Hodder & Stoughton, redesigning and reissuing them between April 1999 and July 2000.

'And the mouth. Oh God, the mouth. Its thin lips stretched across her face, each corner almost touching her ear lobes in the wretched, demonic grin, a joker's grin.'

(Others)

Herbert's first book for Macmillan was *Others*, and was released on his birthday, 8 April 1999. Unfortunately, this also happened to be the day his father died. 'I never actually got on with my father,' says Herbert, 'because he was a drinker and a gambler.' Between the ages of 30 and 40 Herbert rarely spoke to his father: 'He never came down to my house in Sussex. Once he had come to my house in Woodford and caused so much trouble we had to carry him out of the door and put him in a taxi. He was a bit of a hard man in his day, and he still imagined that he was.'

He gives an example of this hard-man image: 'Two weeks before he died, he was thrown out of a pub in Bethnal Green Road because he cracked the landlord over the head with his walking stick. And that's my dad at 86 – imagine what he was like in his younger days.' What with his father's death, his birthday and a book launch at London's OXO Tower, 'It was a tough week,' says Herbert. Surely an understatement.

Herbert describes this week, and how he dealt with the death of his father, though I would like to stress that this was not an easy subject for him to discuss with me, even though I had been with him the day before his father's death. Like many things in life, a biographer or reporter can relate the facts but they can rarely expose the mixed emotions that happen within the bereaved.

'My dad had never been out of the East End, so everything else was a foreign land. But when he died, I rushed to the hospital,' Herbert recalls. 'He was in a coma, but I still stood over him and forgave him for everything. Now I had never kissed my father but I kissed his forehead that day.'

Herbert goes on to recount his father's funeral and what happened afterwards: 'It was a big funeral in Bethnal Green. People lined the streets. I wanted my father buried but my two brothers and mother wanted him cremated, so we went to the crematorium and went through the ceremony but I cringed when they played *My Way*. However, virtually everyone in the East End has it played at their funeral, apart from one of my aunts who had *YMCA* by Village People!'

Herbert's humour falls into something close to sentiment again. 'After the ceremony, I asked if I could have his ashes. So I went through the whole formality of that and I got them sent down to me. And they sat on top of a bookcase in my study for three months while I was working away. Then one Sunday morning, Eileen and Casey were going off to mass and it was a beautiful day. I had my gardener dig a hole at the bottom of the garden – just a round hole, quite deep. I took the ashes, two nice tumblers and a beautiful bottle of malt whisky that Uri Geller had given me as a present, and I went down to the bottom of the garden and poured his ashes into the hole. Then I poured him a drink (because whisky was his tipple) and me a drink. I poured his into the hole. I drank mine and then we had another together. Then I had a fruit tree planted there because that was my father's trade – he had a fruit stall. And that was me laying his memory to rest. And I felt better for it and I hope, wherever he is, he feels better for it.'

But life goes on. *Others* was out, and Herbert would be overwhelmed by the response.

'Voices screamed inside my head and wings, huge, powerful things, the wings of unseen unbirdlike behemoths, pounded my flesh. Amidst the cries were plaintive wails of despair and startled shrieks of terror ...'

(*Others*)

The tone of *Others* is set at the opening of the novel, starting with a quote from H G Wells' *The Island of Dr Moreau*, a perfect metaphor for the horror bestowed on the inmates of Perfect Rest – a supposed rest home for the elderly – headed by the evil Dr Wisbeech (for indeed '*his* is the house of pain', quoted from Wells's classic novel).

Others is written in the first person, and being the story of a private investigator, it would be tempting to make a tenuous comparison to Raymond Chandler's novels, but this would not be accurate.

The voice of *Others* is unmistakably Herbert's. That semi-philosophical style of writing was also present, which irritated Herbert's longer serving fans, who preferred the more explicit early novels. But what they overlooked was the fact that in order to survive in an ever-changing world, Herbert had to incorporate other elements in his novels, so a conscious decision was made to brand his novels horror/thriller, as the horror had been toned down and the thriller element enhanced.

Horror was no longer a popular genre in the late 1990s, with crime and thriller novels becoming dominant. Stephen King was quick to observe this and changed to a more mainstream type of fiction. Herbert didn't change *too* much, however. 'I don't conform,' he says, and frankly why should he? As Peter James says of his own writing. 'Everyone's definition of horror is a very subjective thing. I believe that horror literature should explore human kind's fears in all their forms, that it should examine both the grand themes, of what happened before we were born and what happens after we die, the evil in human nature, the dark underbelly of life, and all those things that scare us, which other forms of writing touch on but rarely dwell on.'

This is indeed true of *Others* and plainly shows how the horror novel works today:

> *'So I'm Nick (Nicholas) Dismas and I run the Dismas Investigation agency, a two-room office with leaning walls and crooked doorframes a couple of floors above a charity shop a few doors along from Brighton's Theatre Royal.'*

After 20 years of living in Sussex, Herbert wrote about his local area. *Others* is set in Brighton (close to where he lives) and clearly reveals how much he knew about the area.

'... I began to suspect they had all been on something harder earlier that evening, maybe ice, which was the drug of the moment in Brighton around that time.'

It is a pivotal novel in Herbert's career. Once again he breaks the mould and starts again, just as he had done in *Shrine* (his first book with a Brighton connection).

There is the obligatory psychic in *Others*, but through the 'power' of mediums, Herbert is able to speculate more, just as he had done in *The Survivor, Haunted* and *The Ghosts of Sleath*. *Others* is gruesome, horrific, provocative, unsettling. A book that truly troubles the reader long after it has been placed to one side – like *Sepulchre*.

> '*Often they were returned to the dormitory heavily sedated... what had been done to them?*'
>
> (*Others*)

Herbert was troubled before the book's publication, concerned some of his ideas would be misinterpreted. When *Others* was released, there was a lot of discussion in the media to do with handicapped people paying for the sins of their past lives through their disabilities in this life. This wasn't an observation of Herbert's, as his character, Nick Dismas, is one of a *select few* given a one-off chance to return to this world and have a second shot at getting things right.

The book does not speculate about reincarnation and past sins as an ongoing progression of bettering the soul. Nick Dismas is an exception rather than the rule, and this must be clearly understood in order to appreciate the subtleties of the story.

'Only in this world can there be no perfection,' Herbert stated as a teaser to the novel, and this is the guiding principle of the book. The novel concerns disabled people; not just those with badly twisted limbs, but with badly twisted minds. Those who consider themselves to be professional people, pushing the boundaries of science but at the same time makes others suffer.

Despite its hard edges, however, Others is an optimistic novel, as although there is great tragedy and loss throughout, it does eventually inspire hope.

> '*People do care, you know, even though at times it appears the opposite is true.*'
>
> (*Others*)

Herbert's first book for Macmillan was deeply horrific but at the same time deeply sensitive. The idea of having a disabled person as the hero and making the reader appreciate his everyday horrors endeared Herbert to fans and reviewers alike. As the millennium approached, Herbert had delivered one of his best books: dark and deeply troubling, in spite of its uplifting ending.

'I stiffened when there was movement among the shadows. I could hear something shuffling from the blackness of the far end. Something moving in my direction. I strained my eye, peering into the thick, inky gloom, even more afraid now that the unknown was about to be revealed. I was so scared that I could not even breathe.'

(*Others*)

CHAPTER TWENTY-SIX

ONCE...

'ONCE ... UPON ...A ... DEATH ...'
(ONCE...)

James Herbert's *Once...* was released at the worst of times: the week of 11 September 2001. The events in New York were catastrophic to say the least. Straight out of a Hollywood disaster movie, or indeed the pages of a horror novel. However, *Once...* was not that type of novel. Its promise was 'A scary Tale of Faerefolkis & Evildoers, of Lovers & Erotic Passion, of Horror & Belief. Written only for adults.' It was the book the public needed: escapism on a large scale.

Unfortunately, because of the horrendous events in New York, one of Macmillan's publicity stunts had to be cancelled. It had commissioned the Cunning Stunts agency to place 2,000 gnomes in public places in London, Edinburgh and Manchester, but with the paranoia about the threat of terrorist attack on Britain, it was deemed a bad idea to go ahead with the promotion. (This eventually happened at the beginning of May 2002 to tie in with the paperback release. One thousand gnomes were placed in London, 500 in Edinburgh and 500 in Manchester.)

Herbert spent a long time working with artists and designers on

Once... . Two book jackets were designed – one black, the other white – for the hardback release, and a set of four full-colour plates by artist Bill Gregory were commissioned for inclusion in the book. Smaller line drawings, deliberately influenced by the work of celebrated illustrator Arthur Rackham, adorned the heads of chapters and endpapers, with one of the 'Faerefolkis' drawn by Herbert himself. The overall effect took the beautiful cover design of *The Ghosts of Sleath* one step further, a kind of pastiche of the fairy books of a bygone age.

Herbert was keen for reviewers and the public to see the finished product, consequently only allowing a limited amount of proof copies of the book to be released ahead of publication. The final novel looked stunning, which together with its tone and subject matter, would send it climbing high into the best-seller lists.

> '... *the books he had read as a child were authentic... The folklore, the faerytales, the songs, the poems, passed down from generation to generation, recounted to children whose minds and hearts were open, were based on some ancient truth.*'
>
> (*Once...*)

In *Once...* Herbert blends in aspects of *Shrine* (the use of children's fairy tales and legends), *The Magic Cottage* and *Fluke*, with the return of Rumbo (former dog, then squirrel, now a fox). There is also another connection with *The Magic Cottage* in the use of salves and ointments to cure burns and stings – the ancient arts of natural medicine (something also used by Felix Kline in *Sepulchre*).

Once... is almost an exploration into the things society has lost over the years – on both a conscious and sub-conscious level. For example, the presentation of the book, with its colour plates, line drawings and different types of dust jackets, shows an attention to detail lost since Victorian times. Also, as far as the story is concerned, there are many references to the ways of the countryside, not just in the power of natural remedies but in the beauty of unspoilt woodlands and parks. Herbert himself owns a fair chunk of land nowadays – a lake and open grasslands, sloping upwards to tree-lined hills and a bluebell wood – and the preservation of the countryside is something very close to his heart.

Although *Once...* is an erotic tale, and sometimes quite graphic in its horror, there is a hint of humour too – for example, the episode where the book's hero, Thom, is being chased by a Succubus for a 'goblet' of his semen does have a light-hearted (albeit black-humoured) edge to it: '... let the monster have his semen, even say, "cheers", as it drunk – if that's what it wanted to do.'

The only problem with *Once...* for me is the inclusion of several pages of text to do with the Lloyd's crash of the late 1980s. Although this is personal to one of the characters in the novel, it is evident the whole situation was even more personal to Herbert, as discussed in relation to *Creed* (see Chapter Twenty). The whole style and tone of the book changes for a while as Herbert wraps himself up in his own personal history. But perhaps *Once...* was the perfect book for Herbert to indulge in his own history. The scenes in the cellar of the manor house – some in flashback mode – are very reminiscent of the young Jim Herbert in the cellar at Tyne Street feeding the light meter. Then there are the fairy tales of youth, and the passion to protect the countryside.

Toward the end of *Once...* the novel's occult undertone comes to the fore, with a pentagon drawn on the floor and a messenger of death brought forward – suggestive of Dennis Wheatley's finale in *The Devil Rides Out*. Although *Once...* could be deemed a relatively low-key horror novel for Herbert, it still delivers the big finale, with witches, blazing thunder and lightning, and windows shattering in a *Highlander*-type way.

The hardback version of *Once...* worked well for Herbert, but to him the paperback was released at the wrong time and some of the posters didn't meet with his approval. However, Macmillan had gone to the lengths of commissioning the ultimate James Herbert collectable: a copy of *Once...* in a limited-edition bark cover. Only 100 copies were planned for release, but sadly the project was shelved because of time and costs after only two were produced (both now reside in Herbert's private collection).

Since leaving Hodder & Stoughton in 1992, Herbert had shied away from the big publicity tours. However, he would still do the odd television show, and to coincide with the paperback release of *Once...* he braved the *'V' Graham Norton TV Show*. The trailer to the show depicted Norton and Herbert side by side with Norton saying, 'After the break, horror writer James Herbert will be putting the willies up us.' Typical Norton, but Herbert played along throughout (narrating Norton's werewolf play). Herbert later revealed: 'You're just there as a dupe for Graham's banter (which is outrageously funny). A lot of what I said got cut out.' Nevertheless, Herbert was pleased he did the show.

CHAPTER TWENTY-SEVEN

ONCE... AGAIN

On 18 September 2001, I met up with Herbert during the promotion of *Once...* We didn't have long to talk, but I found him very excited about his latest book, to the extent where he was anticipating my next question and interviewing himself. I have included a short transcript of my interview to provide an understanding of Herbert's train of thought when writing the book:

The book jacket and endpapers has that Arthur Rackham Midsummer Night's Dream feel to them – was that intentional?
'Absolutely. When I decided to do a book on fairies, I thought back to the Rackham books, and to me, the figures of the fairies in his books were always so sensual. And other artists of that period did very sexy fairies as well. So I did a lot of research into Rackham's fairies. The trouble was, trying to get a modern-day artist to emanate that style. Even Bill Gregory, a brilliant artist, who I've worked with for years, drew wide-eyed elves, like Disney elves, which I didn't want at all. The roughs I did ended up being the final artwork.'

Where did the idea for the book come from?

'I've always been interested in both the magic and the darkness in fairy stories. My all-time favourite film is *Snow White and the Seven Dwarves* because it has everything that I require. Romance, humour, dark – *dark* – horror, and fantastic artwork. And I've got two copies of the video – three including the one I bought for my daughter – plus the DVD.

'I thought fairies were a great subject for any horror writer because of the magic and darkness, but I couldn't get a hook into it. I thought, how do I do a modern-day story about fairies? Until I read a very serious tome about the subject, which stated that there are three types of fairy: tiny sprites like Tinker Bell, the taller ones like elves and gnomes, then ones that are almost human-sized – five foot tall. And I thought, that's perfect.

'I thought of a fairy becoming human. She isn't the first to become human, though. I suggest that there are people around the world who are like that. For example, Bijork, the pop star. People think she is a little eccentric, but she's only that way because she hasn't come to terms with what she is yet – half fairy, half human.

'So I had all these ideas, and I sat down to write my fairy tale as an adult story, because it is very erotic.'

I think it is very interesting that you mention Snow White, because I think some of the scariest characters in the movies come from children's films, such as the child catcher in Chitty, Chitty Bang Bang *and the wicked witch in* The Wizard of Oz. *Would you agree?*

'Yes. And a little aside here: at the end of *Once...* a certain person in the book says "Expect me". Now, nobody will get this, but in *The Wizard of Oz* the wicked witch – the actress – when she signed autographs for kids, she always wrote "Expect me" after her name, and I felt that that was very sinister. And that's me enjoying myself – I like to have fun with my own stories.'

The main character, Thom, has been in an accident and is slightly disabled. You also had a disabled character in Others. *We've always had anti-heroes in your books, but is this disabled theme a trend?*

'It's not a trend. I can only answer that by saying, as you read the book it becomes clear what happens to Thom, and it's done to suit the book. It's not a trend, or a sudden fascination.'

So are you going to go back to ghosts and spirits?

'I'm sure I will. I don't know if we're going to see David Ash again – I can't really say – but the next book I'm doing, which I'm just about to start, is very much to do with that. But the important thing is, there has to be a challenge – it's got to keep me interested.'

CHAPTER TWENTY-EIGHT

NOBODY TRUE

'I DON'T MIND DYING. I JUST DON'T WANT
TO BE THERE WHEN IT HAPPENS.'
(WOODY ALLEN)

In early February 2001 Herbert received a letter from Chester Zoo inviting him to the House of Lords for a briefing on a project to protect the endangered Asian elephant. The Development Manager of the project, John Regan, had read Herbert's *Portent* and was impressed by Herbert's awareness of mounting global warming and natural disasters. Regan wrote, '… its subject matter seem to becoming more real every year.'

Herbert was also invited to a special 'behind the scenes' visit to Chester Zoo with family and friends, where he would be allowed to 'go in with the elephants, feed the penguins and giraffes …' This type of invitation was more attractive to Herbert than a presentation at the House of Lords, and inspired him to write his best short story to date, *Extinct*.

Herbert's short stories have been few and far between because he rarely finds time to write them, but *Extinct* came thick and fast and has all the ingredients of his novels. There is horror (biological warfare), sentiment, poignancy and speculation. Indeed the story has something his earlier short stories don't have – that typical

Herbert voice (the full text of *Extinct* can be found in Part Three of this book).

When I discussed his short fiction with him back in 1994, Herbert told me he wasn't very interested in writing such stories, but when we returned to the subject in 2002 he told me he would like to release an anthology of short stories in the future. This in itself shows his greater confidence in the medium; that and maybe the fact that he can now find time to write them – he would write *Extinct* while working on his next novel, *Nobody True*.

Herbert's 21st novel concerns a character called Jim True, and the story is not dissimilar to that of *Fluke*, involving a journey of self-discovery from a detached viewpoint. Everybody would like to be a fly on the wall and hear what friends and relations really think about them, and Jim True – not unlike Dickens's Scrooge – has the ability to do this. He can wander into a room (without the aid of a Christmas ghost) and watch and listen to what people have to say about him.

True has out-of-body experiences (or, as he calls them, OBEs). He's an art director in advertising (so not much research for Herbert there), but on returning to his body after an OBE he finds he has been murdered. And this is where Jim True's journey of discovery begins, and Woody Allen's famous quote is turned around to provide the opening line of the book: 'I wasn't there when I died.'

Herbert wrote the book in first person (not unlike *Others*), which he found a pleasing experience: 'I really loved doing that because I could deformalise the English language.'

Although stories concerning out-of-body experiences are not necessarily new (for example, Dennis Wheatley's *The Ka of Gifford Hillary*), Herbert does bring his own touch of poignancy – redemption – to the story (not unlike Scrooge in *A Christmas Carol* or Herbert's *Fluke*). Herbert explains: 'Now he (Jim True) is not a proper spirit, a soul, he's this other thing. And he walks around and finds that all the people he knows and loves are not true to him – so nobody true (ie nobody is true to him and Mr True has no body).'

The name and occupation of the main character could suggest that *Nobody True* is semi-autobiographical, especially as it is written in the first person – and it wouldn't be the first time Herbert has taken an episode in his own life and used it in his fiction. However, Herbert feels that it isn't that obvious. The story is deliberately taken in other directions after the initial comparison. 'I'm totally unselfconscious about what I do,' he says.

Sitting with Herbert in his study, with the hand-written manuscript of *Nobody True* in front of him, I asked him how he prepares to write a novel. Does he worry about the huge advances? The fans? What his wife, Eileen, will think of the story? 'You can't do that,' he stresses. 'Once you start thinking about the reader, or the fans, you're not writing for you anymore, you're doing it for an audience. And I'm just writing for myself – and one other reader. I don't want to envisage anybody else, because I'm at the sharp end of it. And I don't see or understand what's going on the other end of it. Now I truly appreciate the reader, the fans, but I can't think in those terms. I can't think that the book must be a top-ten best-seller. I can't get it into my head that there is more than one reader.'

But what makes a writer successful? 'There is a particular ingredient certain writers have,' he continues. 'Stephen King has it, Jeffrey Archer has it, Frederick Forsyth has it, and I like to think that I have it. And that's when you open a book, you're there instantly. It's like slipping on an old sock – the familiarity with the writer is there.'

There is no formula to writing best-sellers, just the acquisition of good ideas and good writing, and as long as James Herbert can maintain that formula, he will continue his success on the best-seller stands and his importance within the ever-changing horror genre.

Although not getting any younger, Herbert hasn't lost his enthusiasm for writing. In January 2003 he called me one Sunday evening to tell me he had just completed *Nobody True* and was about to start work immediately on his next novel (originally called *The Hidden* but later settling for a different title). When I went to see Herbert several weeks later, he told me he had woken up the previous night with some ideas for his new book: 'Over four hundred ideas so far. Pieces of dialogue as well.' He did reveal several ideas for future books (titles, characters and basic concepts), but I was sworn to secrecy, so alas I cannot write about them here.

CONCLUSION

'HE TOLD ME THE BAD THING HAD TAKEN BINNY THAT
DAY AND WE SHED THE SMALL WATERS TOGETHER.'
(EXTINCT)

The character of a horror writer is generally assassinated by public perception. The name James Herbert commands both respect and caution: respect because he is a best-selling writer, caution because he is notoriously a writer of the most graphic horror, a reputation earned by his early work.

Throughout this book I have traced Herbert's life and career, illustrating the many differences, and similarities, between the man and his works: James Herbert, the sinister man of the macabre locked away in his study; Jim Herbert, the man who enjoys relaxing with family and friends.

Herbert was an acutely aware youth, drawing, painting and writing, and eventually pursuing his artistic pleasure in advertising. He used some of the skills he had acquired as an art director when he switched careers to novelist, always keen to get the best out of his book jackets, even designing some of them himself.

Herbert has strong ties with his childhood and the things he witnessed during that time: rats, smog, bomb sites, deserted

London. And all of this fuelled his imagination in the 1970s when he became a novelist. But progress there had to be, and books such as *Lair* and *The Dark* created a plateau at the turn of the 1980s, clearly showing how far he had come as a writer.

During the 1980s, Herbert continued to add other strings to his bow, writing pure ghost stories and even trying his hand at more overt humour. But in the 1990s he continued to grow with novels like *Others* (with its moral values) and *The Ghosts of Sleath* (with its speculation on the physical manifestation of ghosts).

For 30 years, James Herbert has crafted his own niche in British fiction. His style has mellowed over time, allowing him to transcend the staid boundaries of an often-abused genre, frequently speculating on the unseen aspects of everyday life, aspects everyone secretly wishes to explore. And as long as Herbert continues to give the reader pause for thought, he will continue his popularity.

> '*I have withdrawn myself from the confusion of cities and multitudes, and spend my days surrounded by wise books, bright windows in this life of ours lit by the shining souls of men. I see few strangers, and have but a small household.*'
> (*The Island of Dr Moreau*, H G Wells)

PART THREE

THE
LEGACY

NOTE TO READER

The last part of this book is a companion work split into self-contained chapters. The first is a light-hearted piece based on an interview with James Herbert in 1994. I wrote it as if we are walking through Herbert's fog. Things loom out at us (quotes from his books) and the piece concludes with its own little pay-off. The second piece is Herbert's own views on the existence of Heaven (an essay written for a charity book), something he has often speculated on in his fiction. Following this is Herbert's little-known short story, *Extinct*. The juxtaposition of these two stand-alone pieces is quite interesting as it clearly showcases two sides to Herbert's fiction so often ignored: speculation and tenderness.

The fourth piece is a previously cut chapter from the number-one best-seller *Sepulchre* and this is followed by a film guide to the movies made from Herbert's books (including additional interview material). Finally, to make this a truly complete companion work, there is a full UK collector's guide of all Herbert's books and associated memorabilia, which clearly shows how much work he puts into jacket designs and promotional material for both first UK editions and their reissues.

A WALK
IN THE FOG WITH
JAMES HERBERT

Insipid, almost translucent, fronds of ice cold beckon, incite, devour, shrouding us, its prey, in an ever-enveloping spume of swirling incandescence. A streetlight looms, its dull yellow glow a sequestered entity within a more grandiose forum of light.

The fog passes through our weathered fingers like a temptress's silk veil, seducing our masculinity, sending a tingling chill into our throats, like a departed maiden's pallid tongue.

Our footfalls are but a muffled echo, as if the weight of the fog has somehow suppressed their telling resonance.

There is a disquieting silence surrounding us, as though the plumes of white that blind us are part of a malevolent womb, enticing – no, teasing – our eager imaginations, as they tumble, twist and twirl like vaporous spirits lost within the fog.

A shallow breath from my companion is quickly snatched into the heart of the nemesis, like the ghost of a herring rapaciously swallowed by a merciless vampire shark. I glance at him, the horror writer; the man whose imagination wanders in such fervent pockets of space and time as this. His skin is pale, yet fresh, alive with character, as boldly we make our way through this avaricious façade.

He glances at me, a slightly mocking smile creasing the right side of his face. There is a mischievous glint in his eyes, as though he knows this sudden silence has been enough to awaken my most ardent, tenacious demons from their troubled slumber. James Herbert speaks: 'People think you live your job. And it is a job.' A thick, yellow-tinged tentacle of fog constricts his throat, then slowly rises and swirls on its way. 'I do get odd looks, and people do want to tell me stories about ghosts and things that have happened to them. And it's because they think you are going to be a bit sinister. But I don't think I am.'

The fog dissipates momentarily, unveiling the complete horror of the ravaged suburbs around us. Maybe... *This tragic event would force people to look outward, to see what was happening in the world around them, to realise just how insignificant their selfish, introverted problems were.*' But we continue on our way, unaltered, unaffected, unresponsive, as the fog pulls in once more to shroud the disaster.

Herbert's words are even conversational: 'You know, life after death fascinates me. We always want to think that we go on to better things, but we'll never find out if we do. That really fascinates me.'

Boldly we step off the kerb, into the road. Herbert continues: 'It's a theme that runs through the books, along with redemption – people who learn something about themselves, something malevolent, and then do something about it.'

My face takes on a thoughtful gaze, as a passage of text drifts through my mind: '*Is it doubt I sense in you, or something more? Maybe a little fear. All I ask is that you let your mind listen, that you forget for a moment your prejudices and beliefs; when I've finished my story you can decide yourself.*'

We continue our trek through the unceasing haze with an almost boundless energy, as if we are rushing, late for some prior engagement. Confusion tempers my brow, but I am soon led in other directions. Herbert speaks: 'It always puzzles me how so many bad things happen to people in this world. If there is a God, how can he allow it all to happen? Especially to children. There seems to be no answer to it all, so why should it happen?

'The insight I have is that we choose life for ourselves. Say there is a spirit world, and we are there before we are born. We may say, "I want to go down to earth in this body – I choose this body for myself. Maybe it'll be a short life, but people are going to learn from that, and eventually it will do some good, so I choose that." What if that is what happens and all these terrible things are what we choose for ourselves? It's your way of doing something for your fellow man, your fellow spirits, whatever. It's all a learning process, and what if you're helping others to learn from that? And at the same time helping yourself. You're experiencing misery, pain, so maybe whatever level you are at, you're going onto something higher.'

A thick bank of fog covers us, obscures us from each other's gaze. As it gently dissipates, a crowd of people appear from the whiteness ahead, their faces alabaster masks lit by the eerie yellow glow... *'But there was a stirring in the crowd and a small boy of fourteen pushed his way through and said in a quavering voice, "Please tell me what's happening, mister?"'*

Neither of us responds. We mount the kerb and continue on our way, captives of the fog once more.

I ask as darkly as I can, 'Are you afraid of dying?' Herbert's eyebrows raise – a faint smile before response. 'Sometimes I'm afraid of dying. Sometimes it doesn't bother me. When I'm ill (laughs) I'm very afraid of dying, but normally it doesn't bother me, because I'm a Catholic. I believe that life does go on. This is just a staging ground for something, I don't know what, but there's a better place you go to after. So in that respect I'm afraid, and then again it's a bit of an adventure. What terrifies me, and I believe terrifies everybody, is the manner in which I die. I don't want to go with cancer, I don't want to go with anything painful. I would just like to fade away, or go instantly, like in a car crash.

It's very normal for people to think that. But I have no fear of death – the end (laughs). I hope there's no reincarnation. You know, when I wrote *Fluke*, a lot of people wrote to me and said, "You believe in reincarnation like we do." I don't really, I just speculate. What I write is not always what I believe. Writing is my mission. I can't get into the image of the horror writer. I'm a bit too down-to-earth for some journalists.'

A young girl's face looms out of the fog, her cheeks as smooth as egg shell and just as fragile. She storms past us, unflinching, tears like silk threads streaking her cheeks. Herbert watches her go: '*She was unresponsive when he quietly spoke her name. How much had the gas, the fog – whatever it was – how much had it affected her? Would she ever be normal again?*'

He looks back, and resumes his train of thought: 'I've become known for a certain type of book. *The Fog, The Dark, Domain.* Big extravaganzas – lots of things happening. Murder and mayhem, disasters. I've built up a bit of a reputation for doing that, but still have small vignettes that show the smaller side of these things, showing what happens to the individual ... I think it's very difficult to categorise me. People do, but it's usually people who haven't read the books. They say, "Oh, Herbert, he wrote *The Rats,*" and that kind of thing. And they put me down because of that. And really it's because they haven't read the books at all. People are always surprised I don't look like Christopher Lee and wear a cape.'

An insidious arm of vaporous moisture drifts through the evening stillness – twisting, turning, peacefully intertwining, like two caring lovers lost in each other's sensual embrace.

Slim, white, almost waxen feminine fingers seductively slip around our warm bodies, a spectral vixen inviting us deeper into her chilling pleasure. Only now do I feel the moisture on my clothes, a direct result of the fog. A voice stops me in my tracks: '*Touch the water... Feel its coldness... Sink your fingers into it... deeper, let it taste you... touch the nether-region.*'

I was pulled onward by my companion. We continued in silence for a moment, but conversation soon returned: 'I remember when I had just become a professional writer, I had this court case over some of the research I used in my novel, *The Spear*. It didn't make me want to give up writing, because I wouldn't let these buggers grind me down. But it did knock me back, because I couldn't believe someone like me would be in court with these bastards, saying all the things they said about me. I've always, always, been straight. And I know the other party, Ravenscroft, wasn't. It really got to me. Here I was, doing a job, a good job, making my own way in the world, then something like this came along. That made me very bitter.

'I've got over it now because Ravenscroft died a very horrible death, a lonely death, so you forgive. I started writing *The Dark* at the time, and that became a very heavy, bleak novel. And that's the great thing about writing – work. It's very therapeutic. When things go bad, you just get on with it. You can't forget about what's going on about you, but at least you can work through it. And doing that with *The Dark* showed me I could still operate, even though all this stuff was hanging over my head. It's probably the bleakest novel I've ever written, but it's nice to look back on it and think, yeah, that was good ...

'You know, there was one thing in *The Jonah*, the book that followed *The Dark*, where I wrote of a judge walking along a beach on the east coast and floodwaters were coming down from the North Sea. And everyone said to the judge, "Don't go out tonight." There were flood warnings and everyone saying, "Stay at home, it's safer." But the judge knew that he was right, he knew they were talking nonsense, because a judge is always right, he is never wrong. And, of course, this great flood comes in and wipes him out.'

The fog eventually cleared, the milky façade dropped, leaving only the full, grotesque horror of our former hometown and its suburbs.

We looked up at the blood red sky, a hardness in our eyes. I gazed across the devastated wreck of east London and saw, in the hinterland, the broken-down silhouettes of the Post Office Tower, Centre Point, St Paul's Cathedral: *'Still that was the City, a great big filthy breeding-place for vermin – animal and human.'*

A finger tapped me on the shoulder. A smile. We continued our walk: *'All that remains after the holocaust ... Hell's metropolis. Where the vermin reign and man is servant to the beast. The stalker stalked. The rats begin to gather ...'*

'Did I ever tell you about the time I met Michael Jackson?' Herbert asked.

'Wasn't that at Uri Geller's wedding?'

'Yes, that's right.'

The rats scurried nearer. Stopped. Studied us with their coal-black eyes for a moment. Then, tentatively, they crept closer ...

Heaven

BY JAMES HERBERT

My idea of Heaven? Broad expanses of green lawns, neat, cultured gardens, lush woodlands in the distance leading to rolling hills, which in turn lead to pale blue, ice-topped mountains, all this beneath an azure, cloudless sky, with the sounds of birds singing and fountains whispering softly filling the air. There are never too many people around but those who do stroll this calm paradise are of beatific nature and gracious disposition; they wear flowing white robes. A feeling of tranquillity and well-being is all-pervading, aches, pains and troubles are gone, thoughts are clear and full of gentle though awesome energy, the ability to visit the universe, and an understanding of all the mysteries is within our providence. Love will be everywhere in the souls you meet, in the very nature of the environment around you, and in yourself; and it will be a love without negative extremes – no passion, no jealousy, no despair – a love that just *is*.

Okay, so that's my idea of Heaven, a fantasy shared, I would guess, by millions of like-minded romanticists. The actuality? Who knows? Who really has the faintest idea? I believe it's a concept beyond all our imaginations, one that is bound to lose credence the moment it *is* conceptualised. The mystery of Faith declares that it should be so, life itself an important but small piece of the jigsaw. To know the answer (the complete picture) would negate the value of that piece, for ultimate knowledge must come with the joining.

My guess – and it's only a guess – is that we take much of ourselves with us when we leave our physical body: memories, learning (or even lack of), and of course, most importantly, our spirit. Death could never be a state of mind, but it could be a state of spirit.

I think our images of Heaven, versions told by those of us who have had near-death experience, or those with visions or dreams of such a place, could well have some truth to them. The journey down a long tunnel at the end of which is a bright light, the feeling of peace and the absence of pain, the welcoming of friends or relations who have gone before us, there to comfort and acclimatize us to our new state; all could be part of the process that allows that which we already know to blend smoothly with that which we are about to learn, a kind of instructional half-way house, if you like, that reassuringly mixes perceived reality with the first of further understanding.

I think that we become part of the whole again (perhaps that jigsaw analogy, as simple as it is, serves its purpose here), a whole that we leave but from which we are never truly disconnected (we're still part of the main picture) when we are born. While remaining individual, eventually we are absorbed into everything that is, ever was, and ever will be. Yes, I believe we are free to explore the universe, and other universes besides, and our quest for ultimate truth continues until we reach the next level (of which there are many) of higher understanding. And where is it all leading? Simply, to the power we know as God.

HEAVEN

So, my thoughts are that Heaven is a glorious and magnificent metaphor for an after existence we all seek either overtly of covertly (and perhaps even unknowingly) and one that probably we are all – or nearly all – destined for despite our faults and misdemeanours in this world. Naturally, I could be wrong; but then, so could everybody else.

This piece was first published in Father Michael Seed's book, *Will I See You In Heaven?*

EXTINCT

BY JAMES HERBERT

They call me Changa. In truth, elephants have no names between themselves, only sounds. Sounds and thoughts. Sounds so low that sometimes the man-people do not hear; and thoughts so deep that man-people cannot understand. My keeper, my friend, is called Jorj. At least, it sounds like Jorj. I think it is Jorj.

Jorj brings me food, the dry grass that I like, the leaves from high trees, the reeds that come from water pools. He bathes me too, with a long stick that has stiff hairs at one end. Sometimes it tickles and I enjoy that. He comes to my small land that is held within a wall of wood and a deep but safe ditch. He comes most times when the sun governs, even though it often can only do so from behind sky mists. Sometimes he comes when the moon rules. I am always pleased to see him.

Jorj talks to me and I like to listen, even though I do not always catch his sounds, because they are too high. I know their meaning though, although I often pretend not to. Just for fun. Jorj likes it when I curl my long trunk around him and squeeze gently. Very gently, otherwise he would easily break. I watch over him when he clears my land of our waste piles or scrubs us with his long stick, for all man-people are frail things. Even the calves could injure Jorj when they become too excited. He loves us and we love Jorj. He cares. He is always there whenever the others draw our life-liquid with sharp things. I have learned that this is not torment but for our good.

You see, Jorj has told me that I am from a faraway place where the winds are hot and dusty and the once-great forests that hold the rain are being destroyed by man-people who do not care that we need its food and its coolness. Many of them covet our fine tusks and cut off our feet – I do not know why – when we are dead. I can still remember the place where once I lived. Jorj said my kind have long memories. He told me that elephants are becoming so few that soon there might be none of us left in my eastern homeland. That is why some, like me, have been brought to this place to live in safety. But I always knew my kind were in peril, for I have always sensed this. A long memory is not all we possess.

I was taken from my home when I was small and brought here after a long and wearying journey over deep waters and across strange lands. I slept for most of the journey otherwise I would have been very afraid.

I am grown now and I live on this small territory – *my* land – with two cows and two calves. My little herd. Although I cannot see far, I can hear the other animals from the many territories outside my land. I hear the chitter-chatter of the monkeys and the different songs of the birds. At night I sometimes hear the roar of the lion or the tiger, and I hear the cackle of the hyena. All are lonely cries.

The man-people and wo-man-people seem pleased when I mate and they celebrate when my young ones are born. We are pleased too. The man-people and wo-man-people come to see us and bring their young, who point and make happy sounds as they watch our calves. It amuses us to watch them. Elephants are easily bored, so distraction is good.

But something changed. Jorj changed. The other man-people and their small herds stopped coming to see us for a while. The odd things that were neither animal nor man-people and had fast round legs and whined as they carried keepers in their bellies ceased passing by our walls. Jorj no longer made the pleasing sounds when he scrubbed us and he did not play with the little ones anymore. Instead, his noises were low and laden with gloom. And also, I think, with fear.

The man-people came back for a short while, bringing with them their young, but there was a sadness like Jorj's about them, as if they were visiting for the very last time, as if they wanted to give the little ones one last chance to see us. Soon only a few came. Then one or two. Finally none at all.

But good Jorj continued to feed us and wash us and take away our wastes. He told me his own wo-man-mate – a sound like Binny was what she was called – was now very sick. I was very sick once and Jorj and a wo-man-people, the one who liked to prick us with those sharp unseen things, or attended Minbu and Jangoli or the calves when they were unhappy with pain, came to help make me better. I liked the wo-man-people for that and I loved Jorj even more than before when he spent the next moon-times with me, stroking my trunk and making nice soft sounds with his mouth. He would not leave me until I had risen to my feet again and set off to nuzzle Jangoli, my favourite mate, and bellowed (more quietly than usual) at the calves, whose playful antics I was not yet ready for. Jorj walked away from me that time with steps that were heavy with tiredness, but I knew he was happy. Now his footsteps had become heavy for another reason. Now it is because of the Great Sadness.

When I lifted my trunk high into the air I could scent this misery as I can scent water vast distances away. This was a malodour. There was a sickness to it. And it came from beyond my small land and the animal territories, perhaps from as faraway as my homeland and even further.

The other animals felt the Great Sadness too, for the air was strong with fear also and animal-kind can always sense fear. Many of them howled as if with their own pain, and many pined, even during the sun-times. The monkeys ceased their chitter-chatter as if they knew more than the rest of us. Was it because these tiresome creatures resembled the man-people in some ways? Was there a mind-connection between them? I can tell you: No. They may have seemed alike, these two kinds, but it is the elephant whose minds are joined with the minds of the man-people, the elephant who feels their moods, understands their sounds, and knows their sorrows. Monkeys secretly despise man-people.

Jorj came to us on one of those last sun-times and his movements were slow, fatigued with the sadness. His eyes were filled with those inner springs that even we ourselves leaked in times of hurt and grief. He did not bring us food now, nor did he scrub us, or clean up our mess. It was as if he had come only for our company, and he petted the little ones when they trotted over to him and nuzzled his hands with their trunks. It was to me he turned though, and the calves knew that this was no time for play or treats. They wandered off, their heads hung low, trunks almost trailing in the dust, and sought their patient mothers.

Jorj leaned his damp face against my flank and stroked my thick but hair-sensitive hide. He made sounds to me and I understood them all. He told me of the Bad Thing – he made a sound that was its name, but I have no thought that can give it meaning, although I knew it was something evil carried by the winds, a great sickness that could not be seen, but which killed every man-people it touched. It had been released by bad man-people who did not value life. Mad man-people.

It was slowly taking the lives of all man-people and their small herds no matter where they hid, destroying the meat that was inside them so that they bled and rotted from within. It was horrible. He told me that only the animals were safe, for the Bad Thing could not enter them.

He told me the Bad Thing had taken Binny that day and we shed the small waters together.

I feared mightily for Jorj, for I was his protector. But after that he came to see us less and less, and was the only man-people who did. Perhaps all the others were by now made dead by the Bad Thing and it sorrowed us that there could be no more visitors and no more little ones to delight us with their happy, wondrous sounds. We knew that they had gone forever and all the animals, even the hyenas and the monkeys, mourned them.

And there followed a great silence.

And our grief turned to fear for ourselves. We grew hungry.

We elephants finished the grass that remained, then stripped the few trees in our territory of bark. I pulled down the highest leaves for the young ones and pulled up the long reeds in our pools. At night the calves and their mothers sheltered against my big body as if afraid to lose my touch.

Soon the food was all gone, the trees bare, the pools empty of reeds. Still we waited. We listened to the hungry moans and wailings of the other animals and began to mourn for ourselves.

The sun and the moon came and went. The little ones ceased their play and stayed by their mothers at all times. My belly felt hollow.

And then, when the sun was only just beginning to sap the wetness from the night air, I sensed, but did not yet see, Jorj's return. I lifted my trunk and called, rousing my wives and their babies. Our keeper came into view and he moved slowly, painfully, and death seemed to follow him like a stalking tiger. He lifted an arm to greet me and I could tell it caused him great effort. He made no sound with his mouth, although it opened and closed. Perhaps he is still too distant, I thought.

Jorj staggered as he drew near, and then fell to his hands and knees. He stayed down for a long time, resembling one of the smaller four-legged animals, and stuff dribbled from his mouth to form a tiny pool beneath him. I called once more and he stirred. His head came up, but was too far away for me to see what lived in its eyes. His body suddenly trembled as though he was gathering his remaining strength and water spoilt my vision even more as I wept for him.

He rose unsteadily, then lurched forward again as I moved towards the big iron part of the wall that could only be opened by the man-people. I warned the calves to stay away, for they were becoming frantic – I did not want Jorj to be pushed or trampled in this weakness that made him slow – and they obediently stood still. Jorj did the usual odd thing with the iron part of the wall, the movement that allowed it to be pushed open. His touch was laboured though, and the task almost too much for him.

My keeper came to me on unsteady legs and his arm trembled as he reached out to me. There were bleeding sores on the thin hide of his face and hands. His sounds were feeble and unclear at first, but gradually I began to sense their meaning. I was afraid for Jorj, for he was not the same man-people as before. The Bad Thing had captured him and I knew he had not long to live.

Even through his pain he tried to soothe me and my love for him was full. My concern and fear were not conquered, but were mastered for a time. He rested his face against the top of my lowered trunk and continued to make the grief and pain sounds. There was a bitter anger in him, a fierce resentment against someone I could not imagine or even sense. I think it might have been against *all* man-people for allowing the Bad Thing to happen, but I could not understand how that was possible.

His sounds were broken, sometimes long distances between each one, but their message soon became very easy to know. They were nearly all gone, the man-people, and he did not just mean those who cared for us in the territories, or those who visited us with their young. He meant all the man-people of the earth itself. This earth would soon be empty. But not of the animals. They would be left to rule.

And Jorj hoped that my kind, the elephant, would rule over them all, because we had the courage, the strength and the intelligence. He also said that only we had the gentleness.

Jorj left shortly afterwards – I felt he did not want to reveal his true pain to us – and before he went he told me he had other places to open in the territories, other cages to be unlocked, birds to be set free. But there could be no freedom for the beasts, the meat-eaters, for they were too dangerous and too cunning and they would feed on the dead. Their way of life had doomed them just as the man-people's way had doomed themselves.

He left the iron wall open and called back. *Take better care than we did*, I think his sounds meant.

I waited. I waited a long time. I watched wonderful birds take to the air. Two proud giraffes and their little one loped past the opening of my land. A rhinoceros tried to nose his way in, but decided otherwise when I bellowed and kicked the dust. He trotted off and joined his companions who had invaded a cave where once man – and wo-man-people had fed their young. Monkeys scattered everywhere, climbing and swinging, filling the air with their excited chitter-chatter once more. I lingered for two moons and two sunrises before the hungry mewls of my calves made me decide what I must do. I gathered my small herd, my tribe, and led them past the open wall.

No barrier halted our journey through the animal territories, but it was difficult to ignore the starved cries of the mean-eaters. I did not stop when a caged tiger pleaded with me to bring him food, for my concern was for my own and the tiger had never been a friend to the elephant. To go near would risk those wicked claws.

As I led the way I realized that my own land was very small compared to the sum of the territories, and I was soon to learn that the land beyond was greater than the sum of *all* animal territories.

At last we left the place that had been our home for almost as long as I could remember (it seemed to me that my life had only began on that first long journey over the big waters). We stood on a strip of clean hard earth that stretched into a distance filled with tall and straight rock towers. There were trees along its edges where monkeys now scampered, and there was much grass, although it was darker and shorter than the kind we were used to. Elephants easily adapt and these tidy plains with their trees and shrubs, would provide for us.

We fed for a while. Then with one last look back at the territories that had been our refuge for so long, I led my little tribe towards the towering rock place.

Towards our new land.

CORA'S NEEDS

BY JAMES HERBERT

W*hen* Sepulchre *was being edited at Hodder & Stoughton prior to proofing, Herbert's editor (Nick Sayers) suggested that one of the chapters,* Cora's Needs, *be cut slightly in order to leave what would turn into a bondage scene to the reader's imagination.*

Herbert had never had paragraphs cut from his books before – they had been suggested but never occurred. However, on this occasion he relented. He would allow Cora'a Needs *to be cut, leaving the final chapter length to two solitary pages in length.*

During the writing of this book, Herbert explained that he rewrote a certain part of Moon *because he thought he was going over the top. He also told me that he left some research in* Others *that he knew his editor would want cut (and she would be right in suggesting this) but Herbert didn't want to make the decision himself.*

So Cora's Needs *is the only time Herbert has allowed an editor to cut a segment from one of his novels without anticipating the cut first.*

Interestingly, when I approached a publisher with the original idea for this book and stated that I intended to print the whole uncut chapter of Cora's Needs *for the first time, I was told that Herbert would not allow it (it was Herbert's editor at the time who told me this), because if Herbert had allowed the cut to happen in the first place then he would not reassess that decision.*

I instantly wrote to Herbert asking if it would be okay to use the uncut chapter and he responded with a postcard that stated simply, 'Cora's Needs fine by me'.

Obviously, when this book was nearing completion, Herbert did query my decision to include it, saying, 'It isn't that much longer and many people don't even know that it was cut.' 'All the more reason to include it,' I replied. What I do find interesting about the uncut Cora's Needs *is the end line, which clearly gives us more of an insight into Liam Halloran's reasons for being Felix Kline's bodyguard in the novel, and his secret desires.*

In short, the chapter is more rounded in its original uncut form and this book provides the perfect forum to release it to the public. To those not so familiar with Herbert's writings, Cora's Needs *is a self-contained chapter showcasing some of the different styles Herbert uses in his novels; to his fans, it is simply an extra treat.*

So here, for the first time, Cora's Needs *uncut...*

'I need company,' she said simply. 'I get ... frightened when I'm alone in this house.'

Halloran had opened the door wider and she'd hurried by him, glancing back over her shoulder as if someone had been stalking her along the corridor. He looked out to make sure there really was no one there.

He turned and she was putting the bottle and glasses she'd brought with her on the bedside cabinet.

'I remembered you liked Scotch,' Cora told him, and there was no confidence in her voice.

He shook his head. 'I'm on watch again in ...' he checked his wristwatch '... a couple of hours. You go ahead if you want.'

She did. Cora poured herself a stiff measure, turning slightly away from him to avoid his eyes, and he wasn't sure if she felt guilty at coming to him in the middle of the night or because she needed a drink. He closed the door.

Cora wore a white bathrobe against the night chill. 'You must think me silly. Or ...' She let the sentence trail away.

Halloran walked towards her, lifting the big automatic from its holster and laying it beside the bottle and empty glass. 'We all have fears,' he had said.

Halloran began to move into her, taking care, even though she dug her fingers into his naked back, urging him on. Her teeth nipped his neck, his shoulder, as she squirmed beneath him, thrusting herself upwards. Cora still wore the bathrobe and he pushed it open so that he could caress her breasts. She moaned and there was a desperation to the sound. He lifted himself so that he could see her flesh, could kiss her breasts. He bent to a raised nipple and softly drew on it with his lips, moistening the tip with his tongue. She caught her breath, then let it escape in an unsteady sigh. He pulled the robe from her and tossed it over a chair, then turned back to her welcoming naked body.

He let his fingertips trail away, touching her side, her hip, his hand moving inwards so that it was between them, his palm smoothing her stomach, fingers reaching down into her hair. Her thighs rose around him and he was inside her, pushing inwards, meeting only slight resistance. Cora's hands were low on his back and they pulled him tight so that he lost control of the movement. He was drawn into her sharply, causing her to give a little cry of pain.

Every part of her seemed stretched, her muscles stiffened as if she had been pierced rather than entered. Halloran's demand now matched hers as he felt the familiar floating sensation, the incredible tensing of his own muscles, the swift rise towards the breaking of that tension. He gasped air and the low moan came from him this time.

But it changed. Her clutching altered in intensity, became

fraught rather than encouraging; her cries became those of frustration rather than passion. Halloran slowed his rhythm, aware that he was losing her.

Cora's legs straightened and her motion subsided, then became still. She turned her face away from him. Perplexed, Halloran raised himself and looked down on her. A tear gathered in the corner of her eye, welling there and finally seeping out.

'What's wrong, Cora?' he asked gently.

She did not respond and he cupped her face, drawing it round so that she had to look at him.

'We can wait,' he said. 'We can talk.'

She shook her head, her expression wretched. 'I want to make love, I want to feel you inside me. I need it so much ...' She forced her face away again as if unwilling to let him see what was in her eyes.

But she sensed the underlying hunger. Motionless though she was, Cora remained rigid with tension. And her hands stayed tight on him, refusing to let him go.

'What is it Cora? What do you need?' He rested on one elbow whilst his other hand stroked her hair. She wouldn't answer at first, but eventually, still staring away from him she said, 'something more...'

He frowned, not understanding.

'In my robe,' she told him.

He glanced across the room at the robe draped over the chair.

'In the pockets...'

He withdrew from her, his erection not softened, and rose from the bed. The sight of her naked form, the lamplight casting tantalising shadows, heightened his desire and it was with reluctance that he left her. He dipped a hand into one of the robe's pockets and brought out two rolled leather thongs. He frowned yet again.

'The other pocket too,' she said.

Halloran reached in and drew out two more thin leather thongs, these also rolled into small coils.

He began to understand.

'Cora...'

'Please, Liam. Help me.'

He returned to the bed and she lifted her arms over her head, stretching them outwards.

He knelt beside her on the bed and her eyes were cold, with only a hint of pleading in them now. He leaned over and kissed her lips. She responded hungrily.

Halloran tied her wrists to separate bedposts and when he'd done, she parted her legs, stretching them towards the end bedposts. He tied her ankles to the posts and she urged him to make the bonds tight, to let them bite into her flesh. He obeyed, feeling dismayed and, despite himself, even more aroused.

Cora's breasts rose and fell with the labour of her breathing and she murmured to him, closing her eyes, whispering for him to come back, not to be gentle but to force himself into her with all the strength he possessed.

Halloran could not help but comply.

JAMES HERBERT
AT THE MOVIES

Many films have been adapted from James Herbert novels, such as *Shrine*. But invariably plans fall to pieces before production starts, or, even worse, they are produced as second-rate movies.

In order to have quality movies made from his stories, writer Clive Barker made the films himself, eventually moving to Hollywood to do so, but even Barker signed a second-rate deal to get his *Hellraiser* movies well made.

This chapter is an exploration into the movies based on James Herbert novels. First, Herbert speaks about them himself, followed by a basic synopsis of each movie to give a clearer picture of each individual film.

JAMES HERBERT ON HIS MOVIES

Herbert hasn't exactly had an easy ride when its come to the movies. *The Rats* (aka *Deadly Eyes*) was a bit of a disaster (rather than a disaster movie), *The Survivor* only marginally better (but lacking most of Herbert's original storyline). *Haunted* was, as Herbert says, 'a nicely made movie', which enjoyed a Royal Premiere with Princess Diana. *Fluke* is, to date, the only film that remains *close* to Herbert's original storyline (even though Americanised).

Here are James Herbert's own opinions on the films adapted from his books:

'The films have done nothing at all. They haven't done any harm and they haven't done any good. You see, horror is just a cheap movie in this country, never big business. And I don't have the clout in America. That's where Stephen King is quite lucky. *Carrie* was great, then he had *The Shining* and *Salem's Lot*. And you need three strikes to make it in the movies, and he got that initial run. But you must be philosophical about it, as my old agent said, "Jim, you write books, anything else is a bonus." '

All the movies based on your work had the potential to be good. Why weren't they?
'It isn't through want of trying on my part. I sold *The Survivor* to one company and they sold it, as part of a package deal, to another studio. I sent the studio a telegram on the day they started shooting, asking them if there were any points they needed clearing up, but I never heard from them.

'Robert Powell (the star of the movie) told me that the blame lies with the producer who took a two-hour film and cut it down to 90 minutes. And one minute you see Joseph Cotton as the priest, and the next he vanishes and doesn't appear in the film again. It was a terrible movie.'

You had more luck with the movie version of Haunted, *a more faithful interpretation of the book, though certain characters were added and the ending changed. Still, it wasn't a bad movie?*
'No, it wasn't a bad film. However, I tried to make them take out the gypsy (who wasn't in Herbert's novel) because she was a

comic type of character. When she turned up on screen at the Royal Premiere, the audience laughed.

'I was taken up to the graveyard where the family tomb was found in the movie. And what I couldn't believe was that the tombstone looked brand new – no lichen on it or anything. Also John Gieldgud was only in it because they wanted a name. His character also wasn't in my original novel.'

Haunted did enjoy a Royal Premiere, which, because Princess Diana attended, has an added poignancy nowadays?

'I was introduced to the princess. I said to her, "You don't mind some horror?" And she replied, "No, I'm used to it." And we laughed, but it became so poignant afterwards.

'But the premiere was a great evening. Leicester Square, the paparazzi, everything. I took my family and the production company had a big party at Grosvnor House and part of it was paid for by *Hello!* magazine, and Antonio Banderaz was there with Melanie Griffiths, and it was just like Hollywood. And I stayed in a suite there, and after the party was over, we went upstairs and carried on drinking. And Anthony Andrews eventually got all the morning papers in and the reviews were so bad. He said, "Well, mixed reviews I think." '

However, the reviews were good for Fluke *when it hit UK television (Channel 5, Sunday 9 June 2002)...*

'Yes, I was pleased by that. The *Radio Times* gave it a good write-up (as did other magazines and newspapers). I was pleased with the way *Fluke* was made.'

When the film was being made, you told me you actually went to America and watched part of the filming. Were you impressed at that stage?

'Oh yes, it was a big film for MGM. The mechanical dogs they had rigged up were terrific. Carlos Carlei directed it and I was very happy with it, so you've got to remain optimistic about potential future projects.'

A BRIEF GUIDE TO THE MOVIES BASED ON JAMES HERBERT'S BOOKS

The Survivor (1980)
Production company: F G Film Production Pty
Running Time: 90 mins
Starring: Robert Powell, Jenny Agutter, Angela Punch-McGregor
& Peter Sumner.
Producer: Anthony I Ginnane
Executive Producer: William Fayman
Director: David Hemmings
Tag Line: 'There was only one survivor – but was he
really alive!'

Critique: A poorly constructed effort and a disappointing film for Robert Powell, who appeared in some good horror movies, such as Robert Bloch's *Asylum*. The movie was ruined in the cutting, which is a pity because some scenes had potential if sense had been made of them. Unfortunately that never happened and apparently Herbert actually fell asleep while watching the film because he couldn't understand it and got bored.

The Rats (*Deadly Eyes*) (1982)
Production company: Golden Harvest Company
Running Time: 88 mins
Starring: Sam Groom and Sara Botsford, Scotman Crothers, Lisa
Langlois, Lesleh Donaldson, James B Douglas, Cec Linder.
Executive Producer: J Gordon Arnold
Co-Producer: Charles Eglee
Music by Anthony Guefen
A Screenplay by Lonon Smith
Screenplay Charles Eglee
Produced by Jeffrey Schechtman & Paul Kahnert
Directed by Robert Clouse
Camera & Lenses by Panavision

Tag Line: 'Tonight, they will rise from the darkness beneath the cities.... To feed!'

Critique: Shown in America under the title *Deadly Eyes*, this is an appalling, low-budget production. Sara Botsford provides a pleasant distraction, but the film really deserves a decent burial. With today's technology in movies, *The Rats* could be turned into a real cinematic masterpiece – especially for the British industry, which is apparently looking for home-grown talent.

Fluke (1994)
Production companies: MGM, Rocket Pictures
Starring: Matthew Modine, Nancy Travis, Eric Stoltz, Jon Polito and Max Pomeranc.
Music by Carlo Siliotto
Film Editor: Mark Conte, ACE
Production Designer: Hilda Stark
Director of Photography: Rafaele Mertes, AIC
Screenplay by Carlo Carlei & James Carrington
Executive Producers: Jon Turtle & Tom Coleman
Produced by Paul Maslansky & Lata Ryan
Director: Carlo Carlei
Camera & Lenses by Technovision
Tag Line: 'I was a man trapped inside an animal's body.
    A dog's body.'

Critique: The important thing to appreciate about this film is that it focuses on the 'family entertainment' value of the story. Heart-warming and well made, it is extremely popular with children. Although Fluke doesn't see any ghosts and the whole location moves from Britain to America, there is a lot to like about it. And the redemption factor is there, so Herbert's message is clear. So far *Fluke* remains the best interpretation of a James Herbert novel to hit celluloid.

Haunted (1995)

Production companies: Lumière Pictures, Double 'A' Pictures,
    American Zoetrope,

Starring: Aidan Quinn, Kate Beckinsale, Anthony Andrews and
    John Gielgud, Anna Massey, Alex Lowe, Geraldine Somerville

Music composed by Debbie Wiseman

Executive Producers: Francis Ford Coppola, Fred Fuchs and Ralph
    Kamp

Screenplay by Tim Pragner, Robert Kellett and Lewis Gilbert

Produced by Lewis Gilbert & Anthony Andrews

Co-Produced by William P Cartlidge

Directed by Lewis Gilbert

Director of Photography: Tony Pierce-Roberts, BSC

Film Editor: John Jympson, ACE

Production Designer: John Fenner & Brian Ackland-Snow

Casting Director: Joyce Nettles

Costumes Designed by Candy Paterson & Jane Robinson

Tag Lines: 'A supernatural tale of love and mystery.' 'From James
    Herbert's number-one best-selling novel.'

Critique: *Haunted* is a nicely made movie, which enjoyed a Royal
Premiere, but the script lacks the grit of the original novel. There
are far too many nude scenes and characters that really don't fit in
(not just because they are not in Herbert's book, but because the
script doesn't benefit from their inclusion). For all its
misdemeanours, the film is watchable (unlike *The Rats* and *The
Survivor*) but it could have been so much better if the producers
had stuck to the original story.

JAMES HERBERT UK COLLECTOR'S GUIDE

James Herbert has sold 50 million copies of his books worldwide. However, there is more to his output than just the novels. Using the skills he learned through his career in advertising, he takes an active part in the many different stages of his books' production, from designing the jackets, marketing flyers, proof copies, point-of-sale dump bins, posters and T-shirts. Because all these other items offer a greater insight into the man's creativity, his loyal fans avidly collect anything bearing his name or book title.

Here I have compiled the most detailed James Herbert UK collector's guide ever published. I have double-checked my research with private collections and original sources in an endeavour to be as accurate as possible. Nonetheless, mistakes and omissions can occur in a guide as large as this, especially as certain items were not available for catalogue (some gaps in descriptions will be observed). I apologise if this is the case. However, if the author and publishers are approached, amendments and updates will be made in any future reissue of this guide.

Key to abbreviations:
hb = hardback
pb = paperback
dw = dust wrapper
b&w = black and white
NEL = New English Library
H&S = Hodder & Stoughton
HC = HarperCollins
Pmac = Pan Macmillan
Mac = Macmillan
unbr = unabridged
BCA = Book Club Associates
GP = Guild Press

Note: quoted prices are the original publisher's price

UK FIRST EDITION HARDBACKS

The Rats (NEL, 1974) hb/dw, £1.95, ISBN 450-01867-9
The Fog (NEL, 1975) hb/dw, £3.95, ISBN 450-02607-8
The Survivor (NEL, 1976) hb/dw, £4.50, ISBN 450-03067-9
Fluke (NEL, 1977) hb/dw, £4.50, ISBN 450-03432-1
The Spear (NEL, 1978) hb/dw (unbr, with Author's Note),
     £4.95, ISBN 450-04040-2
Lair (NEL, 1979) hb/dw, £4.95, ISBN 450-04111-5
The Dark (NEL, 1980) hb/dw, £5.95, ISBN 450-047385
The Jonah (NEL, 1981) hb/dw, £6.50, ISBN 450-04855-1
Shrine (NEL, 1983) hb/dw, £7.95, ISBN 0-450-04894-2
Domain (NEL, 1984) hb/dw, £8.95, ISBN 0-450-06076-4
Moon (NEL, 1985) hb/dw, £9.95, ISBN 0-450-06088-8
The Magic Cottage (H&S, 1986) hb/dw, £9.95,
     ISBN 0-340-39066-2
Sepulchre (H&S, 1987) hb/dw, £10.95, ISBN 0-340-39472-2
Haunted (H&S, 1988) hb/dw, £10.95, ISBN 0-340-41616-5
Creed (H&S, 1990) hb/dw, £12.95, ISBN 0-340-50909-0

Portent (H&S, 1992) hb/dw, £14.99, ISBN 0-340-50910-4

The Ghosts of Sleath (HC, 1994) hb/dw, £14.99,
 ISBN 0-00-224286-6

'48 (HC, 1996) hb/dw, £16.99, ISBN 0-00-224287-7

Others (Mac, 1999) hb/dw, £16.99, ISBN 0-333-76117-0

Once... (Mac, 2001) hb (comes with either white or black
 dustwrapper), £16.99, ISBN 0-333-76140-5

COMPANION WORKS

James Herbert – By Horror Haunted (edited by Stephen Jones)
 (NEL, 1992) hb/dw, £17.99, ISBN 0-450-53810-9

James Herbert's Dark Places (photographs by Paul Berkshire)
 (HC, 1993) hb/dw, £18.99, ISBN 0-00-255496-8

CONTRIBUTIONS

Ghost Movies (Severn House Publishers, 1995)
 hb/dw, £15.99

Will I See You in Heaven? By Father Michael Seed
 (Blake, 1999) hb/dw, £10.00

GRAPHIC NOVELS

The City (illustrated by Ian Miller) (Pmac, 1994) pb, £8.99,
 ISBN 0-330-32471-3

UK FIRST EDITION PAPERBACKS

The Rats (NEL, 1974), 40p, ISBN 450-02127-0

The Fog (NEL, 1975), 65p, ISBN 0-450-02918-2

The Survivor (NEL, 1976), 75p, ISBN 0-450-03241-8

Fluke (NEL, 1977), 80p, ISBN 450-03828-9

Lair (NEL, 1979), 95p, ISBN 0-450-04546-3

The Spear (NEL, 1980), (first edited version) £1.00,
 ISBN 0-45-04300-2

The Dark (NEL, 1980), £1.50, ISBN 0-450-04970-1

The Jonah (NEL, 1981), £1.50, ISBN0-450-05316-4

Shrine (NEL, 1983), £2.25, ISBN 0-450-05659-7
Domain (NEL, 1985), £2.50, ISBN 0-450-05822-0
Moon (NEL, 1986), £2.25, ISBN 0-450-38999-5
The Magic Cottage (NEL, 1987), £2.95, ISBN 0-450-40937-6
Sepulchre (NEL, 1988), £3.50, ISBN 0-450-42668-8
Haunted (NEL, 1989), £3.50, ISBN 0-450-49355-5
Creed (NEL, 1991), £4.50, ISBN 0-450-54743-4
Portent (NEL, 1993), £5.99, ISBN 0-450-58885-8
The Ghosts of Sleath (HC, 1995), £4.99, ISBN 0-00-647597-3
'48 (HC, 1997), £5.99, ISBN 0-00-6476007
Others (Pmac, 2000), £5.99, ISBN 0330376128
Once... (Pmac, 2002), £6.99, ISBN 0330376136

COMPANION WORKS
James Herbert's Dark Places (HC, 1993), £9.99,
    ISBN 0-00-255770-3

REISSUED PAPERBACKS WITH FOREWORD
BY JAMES HERBERT
The Fog (NEL, 1989), £3.50, ISBN 0-450-03045-8

MACMILLAN TRADE PAPERBACKS
Others (Mac, 1999), £9.99, ISBN 0333-76136-7
Once... (Mac, 2000), £9.99, ISBN 0333-76137-5

NEL Limited Edition Hardback Reprints

When NEL reissued James Herbert's hardbacks (1985-88), they
were intended for libraries. However, shops such as Foyles
(London) did buy stock, which duly sold out as late as 1995.
Clean, unstamped copies of the first NEL reissues are difficult to
find nowadays, but they do exist. They are extremely desirable to
collectors because the first editions had different dustwrappers.
They were limited to 2,000 copies each, and in the case of *The Fog*,
3,000 copies (with a special Foreword by Herbert).

The Rats (2,000 copies) (NEL, 1985), £9.95

Lair (2,000 copies) (NEL, 1985), £9.95

Fluke (2,000 copies) (NEL, 1985), £9.95, ISBN 0-450-03432-1

The Jonah (2,000 copies) (NEL, 1988), £10.95,
ISBN 0-450-048551

The Dark (2,000 copies) (NEL, 1988), £10.95,
ISBN 0-450-04738-5

The Survivor (2,000 copies) (NEL, 1988), £10.95,
ISBN 0-450-03067-9

The Fog (3,000 copies) (with special Foreword by the author)
(published to celebrate UK sales of one million copies) (NEL,
1988), £10.95, ISBN 0-450-02607-8

OTHER NEL HARDBACK REPRINTS

For reference purposes, here is a list of other James Herbert
reissued hardbacks published by NEL. Although produced in small
quantities, these books are of no particular value as they are
effectively reissues of the above series and have no original features
of interest.

The Fog, 1978, 1985

The Survivor, 1985

The Dark, 1980 (twice), 1984, 1986

(the latter with mock red leather binding)

HODDER & STOUGHTON UNIFORM EDITIONS

The first hardback Hodder & Stoughton reissues of titles
originally published under NEL all include new dustwrappers
(apart from *The Magic Cottage* and *Sepulchre*, which were added
to the collection at the end because they were originally published
by Hodder & Stoughton, so kept their original in-house covers).
The set was limited to 3,000 copies per title in their first-edition
state. However, copies that claim to be first editions but do not

have prices printed on the inside flap of the dustwrapper were produced for book club purposes only and are not part of the limited-edition run. To complicate matters further, copies that were returned to the publishers from book clubs were given price stickers and offered for sale in that format. There is no record of libraries receiving copies.

Shrine (H&S, 1990) hb/dw, £13.95, ISBN 0-340-52369-7
Fluke (H&S, 1990) hb/dw, £13.95, ISBN 0-340-52367-0
The Rats (H&S, 1991) hb/dw, £14.99, ISBN 0-340-52366-2
Lair (H&S, 1991) hb/dw, £14.99, ISBN 0-340-52365-4
Domain (H&S,1991) hb/dw, £15.99, ISBN 0-340-52364-6
The Dark (H&S, 1991) hb/dw, £15.99, ISBN 0-340-54974-2
The Spear (H&S, 1991) hb/dw, £14.99, ISBN 0-340-53976-3
The Fog (H&S, 1992) (with Foreword) hb/dw, £15.99,
    ISBN 0-340-56876-3
The Jonah (H&S, 1992) hb/dw, £15.99, ISBN 0-340-56877-1
The Survivor (H&S, 1993) hb/dw, £15.99, ISBN 0-340-52368-9
Moon (H&S, 1993) (same cover as original NEL) hb/dw, £15.99,
    ISBN 0-340-59205-2
The Magic Cottage (H&S, 1993)(Pentagon on cover shaded)
    hb/dw, £15.99, ISBN 0-340-39066-2
Sepulchre (H&S, 1994) hb/dw, £11.95, ISBN 0-340-39472-2

NEL Uniform Paperbacks

Paperback issues of the Hodder & Stoughton Uniform editions were later extended to include later Herbert titles issued by Hodder. All titles were released in 1994.
(Please note, I have reprinted the following list in the same order as Hodder & Stoughton presented it to me.)

Creed, £4.99, ISBN 0-450-54743-4 (50,000 copies)
The Dark, £4.99, ISBN 0-450-04970-1 (50,000 copies)
Domain, £4.99, ISBN 0-450-05822-0 (50,000 copies)

Fluke, £4.99, ISBN 0-450-03828-9 (100,000 copies)
The Fog, £4.99, ISBN 0-450-03045-8 (100,000 copies)
Haunted, £4.99, ISBN 0-450-49355-5 (100,000 copies)
The Jonah, £4.99, ISBN 0-450-05316-4 (100,000 copies)
Lair, £4.99, ISBN 0-45-04546-3 (100,000 copies)
The Magic Cottage, £4.99, ISBN 0-450-40937-6 (50,000 copies)
Moon, £4.99, ISBN 0-450-38999-5 (50,000 copies)
Portent, £5.99, ISBN 0-450-58885-8 (40,000 copies)
The Rats, £4.50, ISBN 0-450-02127-0 (100,000 copies)
Sepulchre, £4.99, ISBN 0-450-42668-8 (100,000 copies)
Shrine, £4.99, ISBN 0-450-05659-7 (50,000 copies)
The Spear, £4.50, ISBN 0-450-04300-2 (100,000 copies)
The Survivor, £4.50, ISBN 0-450-03241-8 (80,000 copies)

Note (i) trade could order x2 packs of above paperbacks, as follows:
James Herbert (10) pack 1, £49.90, ISBN 0-450-59745-8
James Herbert (10) pack 2, £47.45, ISBN 0-450-59744-X

Note (ii) in 1996, NEL reissued the above paperbacks again with the same ISBN numbers and cover prices approximately £1.00 more expensive. This new set of paperbacks had one-colour full-bleed covers, with James Herbert's name and badge emblem embossed in silver foil on cover and spine. (The title of the books are printed in white or black lettering.)

PAN UNIFORM PAPERBACKS

When James Herbert moved from HarperCollins to Macmillan, NEL's contract to publish his back catalogue came up for renewal. This was soon purchased by Macmillan, whereupon all of Herbert's books were reissued in paperback in uniform with *Others*. These books included highly attractive dustwrappers, which were later used on the hardback limited editions.

The Rats (Pan, 2000), £5.99, ISBN 0330376144
The Fog (Pan, 2000), £5.99, ISBN 0330376152
The Survivor (Pan, 2000), £5.99, ISBN 0330376160
Fluke (Pan, 2000), £5.99, ISBN 0330376179
The Spear (Pan, 2000), £5.99, ISBN 0330376187
Lair (Pan, 2000), £5.99, ISBN 0330376195
The Dark (Pan, 2000), £5.99, ISBN 0330376209
The Jonah (Pan, 2000), £5.99, ISBN 0330376217
Shrine (Pan, 2000), £5.99, ISBN 0330376225
Domain (Pan, 2000), £5.99, ISBN 0330376233
Moon (Pan, 2000), £5.99, ISBN 0330376292
The Magic Cottage (Pan, 2000), £5.99, ISBN 033037625X
Sepulchre (Pan, 2000), £5.99, ISBN 0330376268
Haunted (Pan, 2000), £5.99, ISBN 0330376284
Creed (Pan, 2000), £5.99, ISBN 0330376276
Portent (Pan, 2000), £5.99, ISBN 0330376241

MACMILLAN HARDBACK UNIFORM EDITIONS

These were intended for libraries only, though some stock was bought by Foyles and branches of Waterstone's. The books included newly commissioned dustwrappers, limited to 3,000 copies each (these editions fall in uniform with Herbert's original novels for Macmillan).

The Fog (Mac, 1999), hb/dw, £17.99, ISBN 0833761197
The Survivor (Mac, 1999) hb/dw, £17.99, ISBN 0333761200
Shrine (Mac, 1999) hb/dw, £17.99, ISBN 03337612X
The Rats (Mac, 2000) hb/dw, £17.99, ISBN 0333781189
Fluke (Mac, 2000) hb/dw, £17.99, ISBN 0333761219
The Spear (Mac, 2000), hb/dw, £17.99, ISBN 0333761227
Lair (Mac, 2000), hb/dw, £17.99, ISBN 0333761235
The Dark (Mac, 2000), hb/dw, £17.99, ISBN 0333761243
The Jonah (Mac, 2000), hb/dw, £17.99, ISBN 0333761251
Domain (Mac, 2000), hb/dw, £17.99, ISBN 0333761278

Portent (Mac, 2000), hb/dw, £17.99, ISBN 0333761286

The Magic Cottage (Mac, 2000), hb/dw, £17.99,
ISBN 0333761294

Sepulchre (Mac, 2000), hb/dw, £17.99, ISBN 0333761308

Creed (Mac, 2000), hb/dw, £17.99, ISBN 0333761316

Haunted (Mac, 2000), hb/dw, £17.99, ISBN 0333761324

Moon (Mac, 2000), hb/dw, £17.99, ISBN 0333761332

OVERSEAS AND AIRPORT EDITIONS

As these paperbacks are not strictly intended for UK issue,
I have only compiled a basic reference list of titles:

Open market editions from NEL as originally issued –
The Survivor, Domain, Sepulchre, Creed.

NEL export copies – *The Fog.*

HarperCollins export copies – *The Ghosts of Sleath,* '48.

Macmillan travellers' editions – *Others, Once….*

PUBLISHERS' IN-HOUSE PROOFS

The following list comprises the rarest and earliest versions of any
James Herbert novels. It is a list of proof copies used by NEL
(with the exception of '48) for in-house proof-reading and
marketing purposes only. They do not constitute official page
proofs (ie the pre-publication copies sent out to journalists and
reviewers). When I approached people who worked at the
publishing house during the 1970s, many people did not see these
in-house proofs, but one or two copies have nevertheless cropped
up on the collector's market. It is believed that there are fewer
than five copies of each book, and some may have hand-written
notes in the text from proof-readers or marketing reps. The books
are easily identified as their text is identical to the first-edition
hardback, they are bound in plain white card and include a
slightly oversized dustwrapper.

The Rats
The Fog
The Survivor
Fluke
The Spear (uncut version)
Lair
The Dark
The Jonah
Shrine
The Magic Cottage (large print edition)
By Horror Haunted
Portent (only proof version of this book to exist, spiral-bound
    A4 copy, printed double page landscape)
Portent paperback (dated 1993)

Note: between 1990 and 1993 Hodder & Stoughton printed its
uniform set of James Herbert hardbacks. All of these books were
proofed with the *Portent* proof above and are extremely scarce
today, with less than five copies in circulation. Additional items
include:

The Fog (dated 1988, lacking a Foreword, which would appear
    in the trade edition).
'48 (spiral-bound A4 copy, printed double page landscape.
    Ref: 8670. Rowland phototypesetting), ISBN 0-00-224287-7

PROOF COPIES

Sent out in advance of finished hardback copies to journalists and
reviewers. All books are paperbacks with, for the most part,
different covers to the final published version.

Domain, ISBN 0-450-06076-4
Moon, ISBN 0-450-06088-8
The Magic Cottage, ISBN 0-340-39066-2

Sepulchre, ISBN 0-340-39472-2 (white cover)

Sepulchre, ISBN 0-340-39472-2 (red cover)

Haunted, ISBN 0-340-41616-5

Creed, ISBN 0-340-50909-0

By Horror Haunted (sample pages only, including piece from Stephen King) (white card plus dustwrapper) (noted as page proofs), ISBN 0-450-53810-9

The Ghosts of Sleath (oversized copy, spiral bound, Fuji paper cover, limited edition, restricted to 500 numbered copies, signed by the author), ISBN not given.

'48, ISBN 0-00-224287-7

Others (in promotional zip-up 'James Herbert the number one chiller' bag), ISBN 0-333-76117-0

Once... (limited to 803 numbered and signed copies), ISBN 0-333-76140 5

Proof Hardback Dustwrappers

Slightly different to final published versions. Limitation unknown (unless otherwise stated). Produced for in-house purposes only.

The Magic Cottage (mis-pressed gold leaf, title printed on slant), ISBN 0-340-39066-2

Portent (identical to final copy, but no price given), ISBN 0-450-53810-9

The Ghosts of Sleath (highly desirable unlaminated copy, sent out to a handful of journalists who requested covers early for publishing in magazine articles to support the main book release, less than five copies believed to exist), ISBN 0-00- 224286-9

Culled Copies

A culled copy is one not intended for publication or distribution for publicity purposes. Subsequently ordered for destruction.

Fluke (NEL, 1977) (Printed in NEL's standard typeface, Times Roman. Herbert requested a softer typeface. All copies deemed to be pulped.)

Portent (H&S, 1992) (Last page 323 stuck to back board, no text printed on page 324 and no endpapers including Testimony.)

Note: a few copies of this version of *Portent* were sent out as part of the very rare *Portent/By Horror Haunted* promotion pack by Midas Public Relations August/September 1992. Less than ten copies are believed to be in existence.)

LARGE PRINT EDITIONS

Hardbacks (unless otherwise stated) with different dustwrappers to standard editions. Released through specialist companies as stated.

The Survivor (Charnwood, 1984), ISBN 0-7089-8165-8
Moon (Chivers Press, 1986) (The Windsor Selection),
    ISBN 0-86220-168-3
Haunted (Magna Print Books, 1989), ISBN 1-85057-652-1
Haunted (Magna Print Books, 1989), pb, ISBN 1-8505-653-X
Fluke (Magna Print Books, 1991), pb
The Survivor (Ulverscroft Large Print Books, 1992)
The Fog (Magna Print Books, 1993), ISBN 0-7505-05869
'48 (ISIS Large Print, 1997).
Others (Ulverscroft Large Print Books, 2000).

OMNIBUS EDITIONS

Moon, Shrine, The Dark, Fluke (Methuen London Ltd, 1988)
    (leatherette with dw), £9.95, ISBN 0-413-60950-2
Moon, Shrine, The Dark, Fluke (Octopus Books, 1988), £9.95,
    ISBN 0-7-64-3808-6
The Rats, The Dark, Fluke (Guild Publishing, 1988), dw,
    ISBN CN2496

Moon, Shrine, The Dark, Fluke (Peerage Books, 1990),
    ISBN 1-85052-001-1
The Fog, The Spear, Sepulchre (Chancellor Press, 1993), dw
The Rats, Lair, Domain (H&S), ISBN 034062336

MISCELLANEOUS EDITIONS

The Rats (Filofiction/Octopus, 1988) (loose-leaf FiloFax version,
    colour pictorial introduction page), £4.95, ISBN 1-871307-03-1
The Magic Cottage (H&S, 19986), (tooled white leather binding
    with gilt inlay on jacket and spine, gold-stained page edging,
    two presentation copies produced *by Reader's Digest* as The
    Special James Herbert Award for the 1988 Young Illustrator's
    Competition, one copy in James Herbert's private collection)
Haunted (H&S, 1988) (limited to 250 copies, signed and
    numbered by author on special inlaid title page, black cloth-
    bound edition with silver foil inlay and slip case, no
    dustwrapper), £40, ISBN 0-340-49367-4
The City (Pmac, 1994) (limited to 1,000 copies signed in silver
    by author and artist at London's Forbidden Planet
    Conservatory, early copies have additional doodle from artist
    Ian Miller, and some have original signing session flyer)

Note: Special leather-bound presentation copies of Herbert's titles
have been released as one-off copies since *The Fog* (1975). These
unique editions are not included in this guide as they were personal
presentations to James Herbert from his publishers. For a guide to
these editions (and overseas editions of Herbert's work), see Stephen
Jones' companion work, *James Herbert – By Horror Haunted.*

FOREWORDS

Swamp Thing by Alan Moore (Titan Books, 1987) (Foreword by
    James Herbert), £5.95, ISBN 0-907610-88-9
Dark Voices: The Best from the Pan Book of Horror Stories (Pan,

1990) (edited by Stephen Jones and Clarence Paget) (Herbert introduces *The Mangler*) hb/dw, £13.95, ISBN 0-330-31565-X

Note: *Dark Voices* also appeared as a paperback, proof copy and a Leisure Circle book club issue.

SERIALISATIONS

The Magic Cottage (*Woman*, four issues – 10, 17, 24, 31 May 1986)
Haunted (*Woman*, four issues – 30 July, 6, 16, 23 August 1988)
    Note: the above are abridged illustrated versions
Creed (*Fear*, issue 20, August 1990) (illustrated excerpt only)

SPECIAL LIBRARY EDITION

Domain (H&S, circa 1990) (dw same as uniform pb edition: rats and St Paul's cathedral)

BOOK CLUB EDITIONS

Large format editions:
The Dark (BCA) ISBN CN6813
The Jonah (BCA) ISBN CN1461
Domain (GP) ISBN 9132
Moon (GP) ISBN CN2660
The Magic Cottage (GP) ISBN CN6519
Sepulchre (gold-leaf cover) (GP) ISBN CN6075
Sepulchre (line-drawing cover) (GP) ISBN CN6075
Haunted (GP) ISBN CN9779

Small-format 'commuter' editions:
Moon, The Magic Cottage, Sepulchre, Haunted, Creed, Portent, The Ghosts of Sleath, *'48, Others, Once...*
Leisure Press: *The Fog* (1988) (with Foreword)

COMPUTER GAMES
The Rats (H&S, 1985), £7.95

AUDIO BOOKS
The Fog (Octopus Books, 1987), read by Christopher Lee
 (abridged x2 tapes)
Moon (Chivers Audio), ISBN CAB 168
Fluke (Chivers Audio, 1996), ISBN CAB 1263
Haunted (Tsi Audio, 1993), read by Sean Barrett
 (unabridged x6 tapes), ISBN 1-85695-708-X
Portent (Tsi Audio, 1993), read by Jonathan Oliver
 (unabridged x8 tapes), ISBN 85695-756-X
The Rats (EMI, 1994), read by Robert Powell
 (abridged x2 tapes), ISBN 1-85548-263-1
The Dark (Talk, 1995) (unabridged x2 tapes),
 ISBN 1-897861-92-3
The Ghosts of Sleath (Talk, 1995), read by Kenneth Haigh,
 ISBN 1-89762-01-6
'48 (ISIS Audio Books, 1987), read by William Dufris.
Sepulchre (ISIS Audio Books, 1998), read by Sean Barrett.
Sepulchre (ISIS Audio CD, 2000), read by Sean Barrett.
Creed (ISIS Audio Books, 1998), read by William Hope (unabridged).
The Fog (ISIS Audio Books, 2000), read by Gareth Armstrong.
Once... (ISIS Audio Books, 2002), read by Robert Powell
 (unabridged).
Others (Mac, 1999), £7.65, ISBN 0333765869
The Fog (Mac, 1999), £7.65, ISBN 0333780094
The Rats (Mac, 1999), £7.65, ISBN 0333780124
The Dark (Mac, 2000), £7.65, ISBN 0333780132
The Survivor (Mac, 2000), £7.65, ISBN 033378250X
Domain (Mac, 2000), £7.65, ISBN 0333782607
The Magic Cottage (Mac, 2001), read by Robert Powell £8.99.
Once... (Mac, 2000), read by Paul McGann, £7.65, ISBN 033378264X
Fluke (Mac, 2001), £8.99,

PROMOTION PACKS

The ultimate items for die-hard Herbert fans, mainly because they include proof/culled copies of the books, as well as photographs, posters, biographical notes and special folders, most of which are designed by Herbert himself. Promotion packs are sent out by publishers and promoters to journalists and reviewers ahead of general release. The James Herbert promotion pack was at its peak throughout the 1980s and 1990s. Towards the end of the 1990s the packs became less sophisticated, mainly because of tight publishing budgets.

Domain: x1 proof copy of book, x1 promotional poster (for shop display), x1 biography letter, x1 b&w author photo.

Moon: x1 proof copy of book, x1 promotional poster (for shop display), x1 biography letter, x1 b&w author photo.

The Magic Cottage: x1 proof copy of book, x1 promotional poster (with biography information), x1 biography, x2 b&w author photos.

Sepulchre: promo folder with full-colour jacket design cut out of serpent, x1 foldout colour author photo featuring finished book artwork, promotional display notes, two-page *Sepulchre* biography notes, x1 b&w author photo, x1 colour photo of proof (red wrap) and promo display, x1 colour teaser poster, and either white wrap or red wrap proof copy of book.

Haunted: spiral-bound colour *Haunted* biography brochure, x1 copy of proof (some with dustwrapper), x1 b&w author photo, x1 biography notes, 'Haunted By Herbert' car sticker. Additional items sent out to journalists and reviewers during *Haunted* promotion: x1 colour shop display poster, *Publishing News* (1 April 1988) James Herbert supplement with interview and news, *Starburst* magazine 'Evening with James Herbert'.

Creed: Oversize full-colour *Creed* brochure (including author biography notes, early copies with pop-up demon centrefold), set of five promotional author photos (large format), x1 copy of *Creed* proof, x1 promo poster.

Additional: *Creed* notepaper, promo video for *Creed* advertisement in attractive packaging and video script.

Portent/By Horror Haunted (simultaneous release): x1 copy of *Portent* official release copy hb/dw (some packs included the culled copy by mistake – officially under ten copies assumed to be in circulation), x1 copy of *By Horror Haunted* hb/dw, x1 promo poster of *By Horror Haunted*, x2 different posters for *Portent* (one of Herbert, one of book jacket), set of five large- format author photos, x1 cover letter and biography, x1 fold- out glossy brochure. Additional: A second brochure was sent out later in promotion, also a very limited set of proof pages for *By Horror Haunted* were sent out by Hodder & Stoughton early in promotion (not Midas Public Relations, which distributed the pack).

The City: x1 copy of graphic novel, three-page biography, x1 promo-only T-shirt (double-sided), x1 double-sided promo poster (same as cover of book), x four small-format publicity photos. Additional: a second poster of a soldier was also printed and sent out to journalists and editors (also a single-sided poster of book jacket).

Note: up to five copies of the two different *The City* posters were signed by Herbert and Miller at The City Signing at London's Forbidden Planet. Sets are now worth a premium. Also a set of five photocopy photos were signed by Herbert and included in a clip folder of artwork from *The City* signing. Variations exist but the copies numbered 1 to 5 are the rare editions (C&K Productions).

The Ghosts of Sleath: x1 copy of finished book with promo review flyer, x1 b&w author photo, biography sheets. Additional: certain journalists and reviewers received the signed limited-edition proof of *The Ghosts of Sleath* ahead of the promotional pack.

'48: x1 copy of proof copy of book, x1 b&w author photo, biographical sheets. (Some packs came with full-colour invitation to book launch.)

Others: proof copy of book, promotional chiller bag, biography notes, x1 b&w author photo (some packs complete with x1 colour photo and/or invitation to book launch).

Once...: proof copy or finished copy of book, publicity note and x1 b&w author photo.

MARKETING/POINT-OF-SALE MATERIAL

Many marketing/point-of-sale items have been released since *The Jonah* hb/*The Spear* pb, much of which Herbert has had a hand in designing. Here is a brief guide to the more collectable items:

The Spear Swastika card pb display dump bin.

The Spear full-colour shop display card (pb cover tie-in).

The Spear colour shop display poster.

Lair pb image, poster for shop display (some with hardboard backing).

The Dark hb cover, single-sheet poster.

The Jonah A5 promo colour flyer for hb promotion.

The Jonah shop display poster.

Domain shop teaser poster.

Moon shop teaser poster.

The Magic Cottage large pictorial in-store promotional poster

Sepulchre/Haunted promotional counter stand featuring Herbert.

Haunted wristwatch ('Haunted by James Herbert')

Haunted giant book poster with hand reaching for words 'Haunted by James Herbert'.

Haunted pen ('Haunted by James Herbert')

Haunted b&w teaser poster ('Could you sleep with a ghost in your house?') (poster depicts a woman in seductive white evening gown pulling the sheet off a naked man in bed)

Portent bookmark.

The City promotional soldier stand (holds 24 copies of the book, 250 made)

The Ghosts of Sleath cardboard point-of-sale milestone with rook ('3 miles to Sleath')

The Ghosts of Sleath cardboard backdrop to milestone cut-out (depicts country roads)

The Ghosts of Sleath large 3D cardboard copy of novel.

'48 blood bag with promotional note inside.

'48 Burnt double-sided sepia-toned poster ('In 1948 London is a Ghost City') from *Publishing News*, 10 May 10 1996 (depicts rows of gas-masked men in suits)

'48 60x40 full-colour promotional poster showing London map licked by flames.

'48 60x40 promotional full-colour poster of book jacket.

Others 60x40 promotional poster (both hardback and paperback).

Others (paperback promotion) set of 34 tube posters (including quotes selected by Herbert, two slightly different posters for 17 sets of quotes exist).

Once... full-colour promotional 60x40 poster for paperback (designed by Herbert).

Once... set of three different witch posters (produced early in promotion but rejected by Herbert and subsequently deleted).

SHORT STORIES

Maurice and Mog – a chapter dropped from American edition of *Domain,* published as a short story in the anthology *Masques Two* (Severn House, 1989). *Masques Two* was also published in paperback (Futura, 1989).

Hallowe'en's Child – James Herbert's first short story. Excerpt published *in Gaslight & Ghosts* (edited by Stephen Jones and Jo Fletcher), (Robinson, 1988). The full text was printed in *Male & Femail* (colour supplement to *Daily Mail*, 29 October 1988). The full text was also published in *By Horror Haunted* (NEL, 1992).

They Don't Like Us – James Herbert's second short story. First published in *By Horror Haunted* (NEL, 1992).

Ghost Hunter – excerpt from *Haunted* (1988).

Breakfast – another chapter from *Domain*, published as a self-contained short story in its own right in Graham Masterton's *Scare Care* (Severn Hose, 1990, hb/dw) (Grafton Books, 1991, pb).

Not Very Psychic (published in *Dancing in the Dark* anthology, 1997)

Others (excerpt published by Stephen Jones in *The Mammoth Book of Best New Horror*, 1999)

Extinct (2001)

FILM TIE-INS

VIDEOS

Creed advertisement. VHS promo video in presentation box.

The Rats (VHS) (Golden Communications Co Ltd) (1982) (running time 1hr 28 mins) (full-colour wrap-around inlay card).

The Survivor (VHS) Video Gems – Authors on Film (1987) (running time 90 mins approx (full-colour illustrated wrap-around sleeve)

The Survivor (original rental video, still depicting Robert Powell and Jenny Agutter on cover)

Haunted (VHS) (Lumière) (Running time 100 mins approx) (full- colour wrap)

Fluke (VHS video release)

PROMOTIONAL ITEMS

The Rats (full colour 60x40 promo poster)

The Survivor (full-colour 60x40 promo film poster)

The Survivor (set of eight front-of-house stills)

Haunted (full-colour 60x40 film poster)

Haunted (set of eight individual front-of-house stills)

Haunted NEL film tie-in paperback (movie poster tie-in cover), £5.99, ISBN: 493555.

Haunted Lumière promotional pack (folder, cast and author

biography notes, set of b&w cast character stills, x3 colour
transparencies from movie, synopsis)

Haunted (oversized full-colour Royal Premiere movie brochure)

Haunted (full colour admission ticket to Royal Premiere of movie)

Haunted (Royal Premiere reception party ticket)

COPYRIGHT NOTICES

FURTHER READING

JAMES HERBERT NON-FICTION

James Herbert – By Horror Haunted, Edited by Stephen Jones
(NEL, 1992)

James Herbert's Dark Places (Photographs by Paul Berkshire)
(HarperCollins, 1993)

Faces of Fear, Edited by Douglas Winter (US paperback) (includes
interview with James Herbert, plus other leading horror writers)

Now We Are Sick (US-only book of horror poetry with
contribution from James Herbert)

RECOMMENDED FURTHER READING IN THE SCI-FI/HORROR GENRE

As I make many comparisons with other writers and novels in the
sci-fi/horror genre throughout this book, I have included a list of
what I consider to be some of the most important and exciting
works in the genre. I have also included what I consider to be
Herbert's best work to bring further perspective to this work.

FICTION

Adams, Douglas: *The Hitchhiker's Guide to the Galaxy,
The Restaurant at the End of the Universe*

Barker, Clive: *Books of Blood I, II, III, IV, V, VI, The
Damnation Game, Cabal, The Hellbound Heart, Weaveworld*

Blackwood, Algernon: *Selected Tales, Tales of the
Uncanny and Supernatural, The Empty House and
Other Stories*

Blatty, William Peter: *The Exorcist*

Bloch, Robert: *Psycho, Psycho II, Psycho House, Lori,
The Skull of the Marquis de Sade and Other Stories, American
Gothic*

Boulle, Pierre: *Planet of the Apes*

Bova, Ben: *Precipice Vols I & II, Mars, Return to Mars,
Moonrise, Moonwar*

Bradbury, Ray: *The Illustrated Man, Fahrenheit 451, The Silver
Locusts (aka The Martian Chronicles)*

Campbell, Ramsey: *The Face That Must Die, Silent Children,
The Count of Eleven*

Clark, Simon: *Blood Crazy, Darker, King Blood*

Clarke, Arthur C: *Childhood's End, A Fall of Moondust, 2001 –
A Space Odyssey*

Crawford, F Marion: *Uncanny Tales*

Dahl, Roald: *Complete Short Stories, Book of Ghost Stories.*

Dickens, Charles: *The Haunted Man and the Ghost's Bargain, A
Christmas Carol, The Signalman*

Doyle, Sir Arthur Conan: *The Hound of the Baskervilles, The
Lost World*

Heinlein, Robert A: *Stranger in a Strange Land (uncut), The
Puppet Masters, Citizen of the Galaxy, Time For the
Stars, Friday, Job, Starship Troopers, The Moon is a Harsh
Mistress, Time Enough For Love, I Will Fear No Evil*

Herbert, James – *The Fog, The Spear (uncut), The Dark,
Domain, Sepulchre, The Ghosts of Sleath, Others, Once...*

James, Henry: *The Turn of the Screw*

FURTHER READING

James, Peter: *Alchemist, Prophecy, Faith*

King, Stephen: *Carrie, The Shining, The Running Man, Pet Sematary, The Stand* (uncut version)

Laws, Stephen: *Macabre, Demonic*

Lovecraft, H P: *At the Mountains of Madness and Other Stories, Dagon and Other Stories*

Machen, Arthur: *Tales of Horror and the Supernatural, The Hill of Dreams*

Matheson, Richard: *I Am Legend*

Orwell, George: *Nineteen Eighty Four*

Poe, Edgar Allen: *The Complete Works*

Rice, Anne: *Interview with a Vampire*

Seltzer, David: *The Omen*

Shelley, Mary: *Frankenstein*

Stevenson, Robert Louis: *The Strange Case of Dr Jekyll and Mr Hyde, The Body Snatchers, Liolla*

Stoker, Bram: *Dracula, The Lady of the Shroud.*

Verne, Jules: *Journey to the Centre of the Earth, 20,000 Leagues Under the Sea.*

Wells, H G: *The Time Machine, The War of the Worlds, The Island of Dr Moreau, The Sleeper Awakes, The Stolen Bacillus, The Shape of Things to Come, The Food of the Gods, In the Days of the Comet*

Wheatley, Dennis: *The Devil Rides Out, The Haunting of Toby Jugg, To the Devil – A Daughter, They Used Dark Forces, Gunman Gallants and Ghosts, Gateway to Hell, The Satanist*

Wilson, Colin: *The Space Vampires*

Wilson, F Paul: *The Keep*

Wydham, John: *The Day of the Triffids*

ANTHOLOGIES:

Haining, Peter (editor): The *Ghouls Books 1 and 2*, The *Ghost Companion, The Dracula Scrapbook*

NON-FICTION:

Barker, Clive and Stephen Jones: *Shadows Over Eden*

Bloch, Robert: *Once Around the Bloch*

Wheatley, Dennis: *The Devil and All His Works*
   (Hutchinson, 1971)

Wilson, Colin: *The Occult*

The work of Harry Price and Edgar Casey.